## ROSE PETALS
## 366 DAYS OF MORNING MUSINGS
*Cultivating Hearts of Love, Faith and Hope!*

## A YEAR AROUND DEVOTIONAL GUIDE

*A Timeless Masterpiece*
PAULINE ROSE EVANS GILLISLEE

# ROSE PETALS -- 366 DAYS OF MORNING MUSINGS

*Rose Petals -- 366 Days of Morning Musings*
Copyright © 2024 by: by Pink Peach Publishing

All rights reserved. No part of this book may be reproduced or transmitted in any form or by any means (electronic, mechanical, photocopying, recording, or otherwise without prior written permission from the author Pauline R. Evans and publisher Pink Peach Publishing.

First Printing: 2024
Printed in the United States of America
Bible Verses-The Holy Bible.
This material may be protected by copyright.

Published by
Pink Peach Publishing Dacula, GA 30019
**Phone: 678 -989-7887**
**Email:** Penotary@gmail.com

Dear Heavenly Father,

I want to express my heartfelt gratitude for the opportunity to write this devotional guide. Thank you for entrusting me with the gift of writing and for using me to create something that will bring others closer to You.

Thank you for the inspiration, guidance, and wisdom that has flowed through me as I wrote each devotion. May Your words be a blessing to all who read them.

I'm grateful that You have allowed me to be a vessel for Your message of love, hope, and encouragement. May this devotional guide be a source of comfort, strength, and inspiration to those who read it.

Thank you for the privilege of serving You and others through this book. May it bring glory to Your name and may it be a blessing to Your people.

In Jesus' name, I pray. Amen.

*Pauline Rose*

# ROSE PETALS -- 366 DAYS OF MORNING MUSINGS

## _DEDICATION_

To all the beautiful people I wake up thinking of each morning, whose faces and names are etched on my heart. May my daily morning musings from the Lord through me to them bring a smile, a sense of calm, and a reminder of God's love and presence in their lives.

- Dedicated to Mrs. Gwendolyn Thompson, my late grandmother, whose love and support inspire me to seek God's peace and hope.

- In memory of Dr. Jennifer Keene Gordon, whose faith and legacy continue to guide me.

-To my husband Robert (hubby), my two beautiful daughters, Nathania and Aaliyah, my beautiful grandbabies, Khalid, Mason, Adrien, Khylan and Suhailah. God blessed me with my little family, the nine of us. You are all mine and I am so grateful to God for each of you. Thank you all for the joy and laughers you all bring to my life and your patients when my face is constantly buried in my laptop and fingers dancing on the keys writing books. I love you all unconditionally.

-To Jennifer Crawford, my dearest friend, you are the sunshine that brightens up my day and the star that light up my night. Your friendship is a gift from above, a treasure I cherish deeply.

Thank you for being my rock, my confidante, and my co-pilgrim in life's escapades. For being there through laughter and tears, for lifting me up when I'm down, and for celebrating with me in times of joy, sorrow and just about every emotion.

I'm grateful for our late-night conversations, our silly jokes, and our deep, meaningful talks. For our adventures together and our quiet moments of understanding.

You make my life richer, fuller, and more meaningful. I'm honored to call you my best friend.

-To the handful of God sent angels in my life, you know yourselves and I want you all to know that I am grateful for the unconditional love you all show me and the respect given to me in our conversations. My heart truly loves you all and more importantly, I like you all a lot which is very important to me. Liking you all, means I like everything about you all. Continue to be graceful and faithful to the Lord.

- To my fellow seekers of truth, may our journeys be filled with God's presence and guidance.

-Dedicated more importantly, to the One who gives me life, hope and peace, Our Lord and savior Jesus Christ. Without you Lord, I would be none existent or just moving through this world aimlessly. I LOVE you beyond words and will remain faithful until my last breath.

I thank you Lord with grateful heart. I am thankful for the growth I have experienced in my life. Your guidance, wisdom, and love have shaped me into who I am today.

*Pauline Rose*

# _PRECIOUS PETAL_

The Beautiful Petal retrieved from a beautiful flower plant.
It was a beautiful Seed an innocent seed.
Seed was buried, oh Seed!
Where is your convent.
I was buried without my consent.

Under the ground I was forced to go.
Down from Heaven came nurturing pouring water.
Seed sprouting, oh what a beautiful flower plant.
You are that beautiful innocent seed.

The Petal of a beautiful flower plant.
Innocent I was as a flower seed buried.
Innocent I grew into a flower plant.
Innocent I became a garden of flowers.
Innocent petal that was not seen.

Garden of innocent Petal now the wind blows,
the petal follows the inspiration of her creator.
Oh, Oh, innocent Petal, rare Petal.
Petal of inspiration, you are that, Petal.
You are that innocent Seed that endured your process.
Yes, you did.

By: Missionary D.S.M. Dawson.

# ROSE PETALS -- 366 DAYS OF MORNING MUSINGS

## _FOREWORD_

Rose Petals: 366 Days of Morning Musings is more than just a devotional guide - it's an invitation to experience the gentle, loving presence of God in your daily lives. With tender vulnerability and insightful wisdom, Pauline Rose guides you on a journey of discovery, hope, and transformation. Each day's reflection is like a delicate rose petal, gently unfolding to reveal the beauty and wonder of God's love.

As you walk through these pages, you'll find comfort in the midst of struggle, strength in times of weakness, and inspiration to live a life that radiates faith, hope, and love. Pauline's words are a reminder that you are seen, heard, and cherished by the Creator of the universe.

This devotional guide is a sacred space where you can breathe in the peace of God's presence and exhale the worries and fears that weigh you down. It's a reminder that God is always with you, always for you, and always speaking hope and life into your soul.

I personally am celebrating with Pauline for her God given talent. She's written over six books and counting, while some of us are here still contemplating how to begin the first page of a book. It literally takes nothing for her to complete an entire book within a day or two. Pauline has a whole library stacked inside of her. I just want to thank her for not being selfish with her talent and for not burying what the Lord has granted to her.

Join Pauline on this 366-day journey, and may the rose petals of wisdom, guidance, and encouragement be a blessing to you. May you find peace, comfort, and inspiration in these words, and may your hearts be forever changed by the love of God.

Missionary Jennifer Crawford

## _PREFACE_

In the depths of my soul, I've discovered a truth that sets me free - that God's love is the anchor of my heart. When the world tries to silence my voice, I find courage in His Word, and I rise up to declare His goodness. Even in the darkest moments, I choose to praise Him, for I know that His presence is my comfort.

As I dance in the rain of His blessings, I'm reminded that every breath is a gift from above. I'm no longer trapped by the chains of my past, but liberated by the power of His grace.

This devotional journal is a collection of my heart's musings, born out of my personal journey with God. Each morning, I seek to share a glimpse of His glory, that others may be encouraged to seek Him more deeply.

May these words be a balm to your soul, a reminder that God's love is your portion, and His peace is your inheritance. May you find solace in His presence, and may your heart be filled with joy, hope, and faith.

With love and blessings, Pauline

# _INTRODUCTION_

## Welcome to Rose Petals: 366 Days of Morning Musings

As we rise with the sun, our hearts and minds are awakened to the beauty and wonder of a new day. In the stillness of the morning, we find the gentle whisper of God's presence, guiding us, comforting us, and inspiring us to live fully and love deeply.

Welcome to this sacred space, where God's love and presence come alive. In the pages of this journal, I invite you to join me on a journey of discovery, hope, and transformation. Each day, we'll explore the depths of God's Word, and the beauty of His character.

Through these morning musings, I pray that you'll find comfort, strength, and inspiration to face whatever challenges come your way. May God's peace be your constant companion, and His joy be your guiding light.

This devotional guide is an invitation to cultivate a heart of faith, hope, and love, one day at a time. Through scripture, reflection, and prayer, we'll explore the themes of gratitude, trust, and joy, and discover the beauty of God's love in our lives.

Use these daily musings as a starting point for your own spiritual journey, a reminder that you are loved,

# ROSE PETALS -- 366 DAYS OF MORNING MUSINGS

valued, and cherished. Take a moment each day to breathe in the beauty of God's presence, and exhale the worries and fears that weigh you down.

May these rose petals of wisdom, guidance, and encouragement be a blessing to you, and may you find peace, comfort, and inspiration in the words that follow.

As we walk this path together, remember that you are loved, you are valued, and you are cherished by the Creator of the universe.

May these words be a reminder that God is always with you, always for you, and always speaking hope and life into your soul.

Let's embark on this adventure together, with open hearts and minds, ready to receive all that God has in store for us.

With love and blessings,

*Pauline Rose*

# ROSE PETALS -- 366 DAYS OF MORNING MUSINGS

## JANUARY 1-31

1. Fresh Start: Embracing the Possibilities
2. Leaving the Past Behind
3. The Power of Hope
4. Renewing Our Minds
5. Letting Go of Fear
6. Stepping into the Unknown
7. Trusting in God's Plan
8. The Beauty of New Beginnings
9. Finding Courage in Uncertainty
10. The Gift of Second Chances
11. The Power of Forgiveness
12. The Joy of Gratitude
13. The Comfort of God's Presence
14. The Strength of God's Love
15. The Peace of God's Presence
16. The Hope of a New Day
17. The Peace of God's Guidance
18. The Hope of God's Promises
19. The Freedom of Surrender
20. The Power of Humility
21. The Joy of Obedience
22. Humility is a virtue
23. The Peace of God's Sovereignty
24. The Comfort of God's Love
25. The Hope of God's Faithfulness
26. God's compassion
27. The Power of Gratitude
28. The Strength of God's Grace
29. The Peace of God's Presence
30. The Hope of God's Promises
31. God's Gentle Guidance

## January 1: Fresh Start: Embracing the Possibilities

_Scripture:_ Isaiah 43:19 - See, I am doing a new thing! Now it springs up; do you not perceive it?

_ Devotion_

As we step into a new year, God invites us to embrace the possibilities of a fresh start. Just as Isaiah declared, God is doing a new thing in our lives. But do we perceive it?

Let us leave the past behind and focus on our purpose and goals. Let us make a conscious effort to seek God above all else, just like David did in Psalm 63:1-8.

Let us be intentional about starting this year on a positive note, living with dignity, joy, and strength. Let us avoid unnecessary stress and remember that we are clothed in God's love and grace.

May this year be a journey of growth, faith, and joy for us all!

Prayer: *Dear God, thank you for the gift of a new year. Please repair, renew and revive our hearts. Help me to perceive the new things you are doing in my life and to partner with you to make my hopes and dreams a reality. Amen.*

## _January 2:_ _Leaving the Past Behind_

_Scripture:_ Philippians 3:13-14 - Forgetting what is behind and straining toward what is ahead, I press on toward the goal to win the prize for which God has called me heavenward in Christ Jesus.

### _Devotion_

As we begin this new year, we may not be tempted to dwell on past regrets or failures. But as the Apostle Paul encourages us to forget what is behind and press on toward the goal ahead.

Let us show gratitude for God's love and grace. He's awakened us to a new day, and we belong to Him. Let us embrace life with courage and faith, seeking His guidance, strength, and wisdom.

May we never give up on His promises, and stay focused on Him. He's our Savior, Rock, and Refuge. Stay faithful and enjoy His beautiful creation!

_Prayer:_ *Dear God, help me to forget what is behind and press on toward the goal ahead. Give me the grace to release the past and move forward in your grace. Amen.*

# January 3: The Power of Hope

## Scripture:
Jeremiah 29:11 says, For I know the plans I have for you," declares the Lord, "plans to prosper you and not to harm you, plans to give you hope and a future.

## Devotion:

Hope is a powerful force in our lives. It's the spark that ignites our dreams, the light that guides us through darkness, and the anchor that holds us steady in turbulent times.

Here are some additional thoughts on the power of hope:
- Inspires us to dream big
- Gives us the strength to carry on
- Helps us navigate uncertain times

Encourages us to persevere:
- Reminds us that a better tomorrow is possible
- Fills our hearts with joy and anticipation-
- Connects us to our purpose and passion

What are some ways that hope has made a difference in your life?

When we place our hope in God, we tap into His limitless power and potential. We begin to see beyond our current circumstances and trust in His promises.

## Prayer:
*Dear God, thank you for the gift of hope. Help me to anchor my hope in you and your promises, and give me the grace to trust in your goodness. Amen.*

## January 4: Renewing Our Minds

_Scripture:_ Romans 12:2 - Do not conform to the pattern of this world, but be transformed by the renewing of your mind. Then you will be able to test and approve what God's will is—His good, pleasing and perfect will.

_Devotion:_

Our minds are constantly being shaped and molded by the world around us. But as followers of Christ, we are called to be transformed by the renewing of our minds.

That's so true! Our minds are constantly being influenced. And shaped with:
- God's Word and truth
- Positive and uplifting content
- Encouraging relationships and community
- Self-reflection and self-care
- Prayer and meditation

Remember, our minds are like gardens – they need nurturing and care to grow and flourish! Let us pray, believe, trust, and thank Him with a grateful heart. Remember, God's word is solid, and He remains faithful. There might be some discomfort as Christ mold us, but difficult roads lead to beautiful destinations. Let us stand firm, and watch God work through us as we embark on this new day knowing we are covered and protected by a great, big wonderful God.

_Prayer_ *Dear God, we come before you with grateful hearts, acknowledging your transformative power in our lives. Thank You for Your faithfulness and unwavering love. We stand firm, trusting Your plans are good, pleasing, and perfect. Amen.*

**January 5:** _ Letting Go of Fear_

_Scripture:_ Psalm 23:4 - Even though I walk through the darkest valley, I will fear no evil, for you are with me; your rod and your staff comfort me.

_Devotion_

Fear can hold us back from fully experiencing God's presence and plan for our lives. But with God by our side, we have nothing to fear.

Fear can be a major obstacle to:
_Intimacy with God
_ Fear can keep us from fully surrendering to God and experiencing His love and presence.
_Fear can cause us to doubt God's goodness and sovereignty, leading to a lack of trust.
_ Fear can hold us back from fully surrendering to God's will and plan for our lives.

But God is bigger than our fears! He wants to help us overcome fear and live in faith and trust. Remember: God has not given us a spirit of fear, but of power and of love and of a sound mind. (2 Timothy 1:7)- "Fear not, for I am with you; be not dismayed, for I am your God." (Isaiah 41:10)

_Prayer:_ *Dear God, help me to fear no evil, for you are with me. Give me the grace to let go of fear and trust in your presence and protection. Amen.*

## January 6: Stepping into the Unknown

_Scripture:_ Joshua 1:9 - Have I not commanded you? Be strong and courageous. Do not be afraid; do not be discouraged, for the Lord your God will be with you wherever you go.

_Devotion:_

As we step into the unknown, we can be tempted to fear and doubt, especially if we feel broken and critical of others. But God encourages us to be strong and courageous, knowing that He is with us wherever we go. Stepping into the unknown can be daunting, but it can also be a thrilling adventure! Here are some thoughts to consider:

_Embracing the unknown requires:

_Trusting that God has a plan and will guide us

_Being willing to take the first step, even when we're afraid

_Believing that God is sovereign and in control

_ Following God's leading, even when we don't understand.

_ Knowing that God has good plans for our future.

_Remember:

_God is always with us

_ He never leaves or forsakes us (Deuteronomy 31:6)

_God has gone before us*: He prepares the way and guides us

(John 10:4)

_God's plans are good*: He desires to prosper us and give us

hope (Jeremiah 29:11).

_Prayer: *Dear God, help me to trust You as I step into the unknown.*

*Give me courage and faith to follow Your leading. May I know*

*Your presence and guidance every step of the way. In Jesus' name,* Amen.

## _January 7_: Trusting in God's Plan

_Scripture:_ Jeremiah 29:11 - For I know the plans I have for you," declares the Lord, "plans to prosper you and not to harm you, plans to give you hope and a future."

_Devotion:_

God has a plan for our lives, and it's a plan to prosper us, not to harm us. But often, we struggle to trust in His plan.

Trusting in God's plan is a powerful act of faith! Here are some reminders to help you trust:
_God's ways are higher_: His thoughts and plans are far greater than ours (Isaiah 55:9).

2. _God is sovereign_: He is in control of all things (Psalm 135:6).

3. _God is good_: His plans are always for our good (Romans 8:28).

4. _God has a purpose_: He has a specific plan for our lives (Jeremiah 29:11).

5. _God is faithful_: He will complete what He starts (Philippians 1:6).

_Prayer:_ _Dear God, help me to trust in Your plan, even when I don't understand. Give me faith to believe that Your ways are higher and Your plans are good. May I rest in Your sovereignty and faithfulness. In Jesus' name,_ Amen.

ROSE PETALS -- 366 DAYS OF MORNING MUSINGS

_January 8:_ The Beauty of New Beginnings_

_Scripture: _ Lamentations 3:22-23 - Because of the Lord's great love we are not consumed, for his compassions never fail. They are new every morning; great is your faithfulness.

_Devotion: _

Each new day brings a new beginning, a chance to start again and
experience God's faithfulness.

What a beautiful truth! Each new day is a gift from God, full of
possibilities and opportunities to:

1. _Start anew_: Leave yesterday's mistakes and regrets behind.
2. _Experience God's faithfulness_: See His love and provision in
fresh ways.
3. _Discover new mercies_: Receive His daily blessings and grace.
4. _Grow in faith_: Trust Him more deeply and walk with Him
more closely.

_Prayer: Dear God, thank You for the gift of a new day.
Help me to leave yesterday behind and embrace the possibilities of today. Show me Your faithfulness and mercy, and help me to grow in my trust of You. In Jesus' name, Amen._

## _January 9_: Finding Courage in Uncertainty_

_Scripture:_ Psalm 27:14 - Wait for the Lord; be strong and take heart and wait for the Lord.

_Devotion:_
Uncertainty can be uncomfortable, but it's in those moments that we can find courage in God's presence.

So true! Uncertainty can be daunting, but it's in those moments that we can:

1. _Seek God's presence_: Draw near to Him and find comfort.
2. _Trust His sovereignty_: Remember He is in control, even when we're not.
3. _Find courage in His promises_: Stand on His Word and its unchanging truth.
4. _Experience His peace_: Receive His calming presence, even in turmoil.
5. _Grow in faith_: Develop a deeper trust in God's goodness and plan.

Remember, uncertainty can be an opportunity to: - Deepen our relationship with God- Develop our faith and trust- Discover new aspects of His character.

_Prayer: Dear God, in moments of uncertainty, help me to seek Your presence and trust Your sovereignty. Give me courage in Your promises and peace in Your presence. May I grow in faith and reliance on You. In Jesus' name,_ Amen.

ROSE PETALS -- 366 DAYS OF MORNING MUSINGS

_January 10_: The Gift of Second Chances_

_Scripture: _ 2 Corinthians 5:17 - Therefore, if anyone is in Christ, the new creation has come: The old has gone, the new is here!
_Devotion: _

God is a God of second chances, offering us new life and new beginnings in Christ.

A beautiful reminder! God's heart is full of love and redemption, offering us:

_New life_: Eternal life in Christ, transforming us from the inside out.
_New beginnings_: Fresh starts, empowering us to move forward with hope.
_Forgiveness_: Cleansing us from sin's stain, restoring our relationship with Him.
_Restoration_: Rebuilding and renewing us, making us whole again.

In Christ, we find: - A new identity, defined by God's love and acceptance- A new purpose, living for His glory and kingdom- A new path, guided by His wisdom and grace

_Prayer: *Dear God, thank You for being a God of second chances. Help me to embrace new life and new beginnings in Christ. May Your forgiveness and restoration be my portion, and may I live for Your glory. In Jesus' name*, Amen.

## _January 11:_ The Power of Forgiveness_

_Scripture:_ Matthew 6:14-15 - For if you forgive other people when they sin against you, your heavenly Father will also forgive you. But if you refuse to forgive others, your Father will not forgive you.

_Devotion:_

Forgiveness is a powerful tool that can free us from the bondage of bitterness and anger.

So true! Forgiveness is a liberating force that can:

_Break chains of bitterness_: Releasing us from the weight of resentment.
_Heal emotional wounds_: Allowing us to move forward from past hurts.
_Restore relationships_: Mending bonds and rebuilding trust.
_Free us from anger's grip_: Calming our hearts and minds.
_Bring peace and closure_: Allowing us to let go and move on.

Remember, forgiveness: - Doesn't mean forgetting or condoning hurtful actions- Isn't always easy, but is always possible with God's help- Can be a process, taking time and effort- Opens the door for God's healing and restoration

_Prayer:_ _Dear God, help me to forgive and let go of bitterness and anger. Break the chains that bind me and bring healing to my emotional wounds. Restore my relationships and bring peace to my heart. In Jesus' name,_ Amen.

# ROSE PETALS -- 366 DAYS OF MORNING MUSINGS

## _January 12_: The Joy of Gratitude_

_Scripture:_ 1 Thessalonians 5:18 - Give thanks in all circumstances; for this is the will of God in Christ Jesus for you.

_Devotion:_

Gratitude is a powerful attitude that can shift our perspective and bring joy to our lives.

Gratitude is a game-changer! Focusing on what we're thankful for can:

1. _Shift our perspective_: From negativity to positivity
2. _Bring joy and happiness_: Filling our hearts with warmth and contentment
3. _Improve relationships_: Strengthening bonds and fostering empathy
4. _Reduce stress and anxiety_: Calming our minds and soothing our souls
5. _Open our eyes to blessings_: Helping us notice and appreciate the good things

Remember, gratitude is a muscle that grows stronger with practice!

_Prayer: Dear God, help me to cultivate a heart of gratitude. Open my eyes to the blessings in my life and fill me with joy and thankfulness. May my gratitude bring glory to You and strengthen my relationships with others. In Jesus' name, Amen._

## _January 13:_ The Comfort of God's Presence_

_Scripture:_ Psalm 34:18 - The Lord is close to the brokenhearted and saves the crushed in spirit.

_Devotion:_

God's presence is our comfort in times of sorrow and pain.

What a beautiful truth! God's presence is our:

1. _Comfort in sorrow_: Wrapping us in His loving arms, soothing our hearts.
2. _Strength in pain_: Sustaining us through trials, giving us courage to persevere.
3. _Peace in turmoil_: Calming our minds, quieting our fears.
4. _Hope in darkness_: Illuminating our path, guiding us forward.

Remember, God's presence is: - Always with us (Matthew 28:20)- Always for us (Romans 8:31)- Always working for our good (Romans 8:28)

_Prayer: Dear God, thank You for being my comfort, strength, peace, hope, and refuge. In times of sorrow and pain, help me to feel Your presence and trust Your goodness. Wrap me in Your loving arms and guide me through the darkness. In Jesus' name,_ Amen.

May we draw near to Him in our times of need, and may His presence be our solace and strength.

# _January 14:_ The Strength of God's Love_

_Scripture:_ Romans 8:37-39 - No, in all these things we are more than conquerors through him who loved us. For I am convinced that neither death nor life, neither angels nor demons, neither the present nor the future, nor any powers, neither height nor depth, nor anything else in all creation, will be able to separate us from the love of God that is in Christ Jesus our Lord.

_Devotion:_

God's love is our strength in times of weakness and uncertainty.

The strength of God's love is:

1. _Unconditional_: Accepting us as we are, without judgment.
2. _Unwavering_: Remaining constant, even when we fail.
3. _Unrelenting_: Pursuing us with kindness, mercy, and grace.
4. _Transformative_: Changing us from the inside out, making us new.
5. _Sacrificial_: Giving everything, even His own life, for our sake.

God's love: - Lifts us up when we're broken- Holds us close when we're hurting- Gives us hope when we're hopeless- Forgives us when we fail- Strengthens us when we're weak

_prayer: Dear God, thank You for Your unwavering love. Help me to experience Your presence and feel Your love surrounding me. May Your love transform me, give me hope, and strengthen me in my weaknesses. In Jesus' name,_ Amen

# ROSE PETALS -- 366 DAYS OF MORNING MUSINGS

### _January 15_: The Peace of God's Presence

_Scripture:_ Psalm 46:10 - Be still, and know that I am God.

_Devotion:_

In a world filled with noise and distractions, God invites us to be still and know His presence.

What a beautiful invitation! In a world filled with:
_Noise_: Constant distractions, vying for our attention.
_Distractions_: Endless tasks, notifications, and stimuli.
_Chaos_: Uncertainty, turmoil, and disorder.

God whispers: _Be still_: _Pause_: Stop the hustle and bustle.
_Listen_: Tune in to His gentle voice. Focus_: Fix your eyes on Him. Breathe_: Rest in His presence. Know_: Experience His peace, love, and guidance.

In stillness, we:
- Find clarity in the midst of confusion
- Discover peace in the midst of turmoil
- Encounter God's loving presence
- Renew our minds and hearts
- Gain strength and wisdom

_Prayer:_ *Dear God, help me to be still and know Your presence. Quiet my heart and mind, and tune my ears to Your gentle voice. May I find peace, clarity, and strength in Your loving presence. In Jesus' name,* Amen.

ROSE PETALS -- 366 DAYS OF MORNING MUSINGS

## _January 16_: The Hope of a New Day_

_Scripture:_ Lamentations 3:22-23 - The steadfast love of the Lord never ceases; his mercies never come to an end; they are new every morning; great is your faithfulness.

_Devotion:_

Each new day brings a new chance to experience God's love and faithfulness.

What a beautiful truth! Each new day:

1. _Brings new mercies_: Fresh starts, clean slates, and second chances.
2. _Unfolds new blessings_: Unexpected joys, surprises, and delights.
3. _Reveals new facets of God's love_: Deeper understanding, greater appreciation, and sweeter intimacy.
4. _Presents new opportunities to trust_: Stepping stones of faith, paths of obedience, and journeys of growth.

Remember, God's love and faithfulness are: - Constant, unwavering, and unshakeable- Personal, tailored to your unique journey- Powerful, transforming, and life-changing.

_Prayer: Dear God, *thank You for the gift of a new day. Help me to experience Your love and faithfulness in fresh ways. May I embrace new mercies, blessings, and opportunities to trust You. Fill my heart with praise and my life with Your presence. In Jesus' name,* Amen.

## _January 17_: The Peace of God's Guidance_

_Scripture:_ Proverbs 3:5-6 - Trust in the Lord with all your heart and lean not on your own understanding; in all your ways submit to him, and he will make your paths straight.

_Devotion:_

God's guidance brings peace to our lives, even in uncertain times.

A wonderful reminder! God's guidance:

_Brings clarity to confusion_: Clearing the fog, revealing His plan.
_Provides wisdom for decisions_: Giving us discernment, insight, and confidence.
_Offers reassurance in uncertainty_: Anchoring us in His sovereignty, love, and care.
_Leads us to peace_: Settling our hearts, calming our minds, and soothing our souls.

Remember, God's guidance is: - Available to all who seek Him
- Tailored to our unique needs and circumstances-
Rooted in His infinite wisdom, love, and knowledge

_Prayer: _Dear *God, thank You for Your guidance. Help me to seek You, trust You, and follow Your lead. Bring peace to my life, even in uncertain times. May Your wisdom, love, and care be my constant companions. In Jesus' name*, Amen.

## January 18: The Hope of God's Promises

_Scripture:_ Romans 15:13 says, May the God of hope fill you with all joy and peace as you trust in him, so that you may overflow with hope by the power of the Holy Spirit.

_Devotion:_

God's promises give us hope for the future and a confidence in His faithfulness.

A beautiful truth! God's promises: _Assure us of His presence_: Always with us, never leaving or forsaking.
_Provide hope in darkness_: Light in the midst of struggles and uncertainty.
_Reveal His character_: Faithful, loving, merciful, and true.
_Guide us forward_: Illuminating the path, directing our steps.
_Strengthen our faith_: Trusting in His goodness, sovereignty, and power.

Remember, God's promises are: - Unshakeable, unbreakable, and unstoppable- Personal, spoken directly to our hearts
- Conditional, dependent on our trust and obedience

Prayer: _ Dear God, thank You for Your promises. Help me to hold onto them, trust in Your faithfulness, and hope in Your goodness. May Your Word be my anchor, my comfort, and my guide. In Jesus' name, Amen._

## _January_ 19: The Freedom of Surrender

_Scripture:_ Matthew 16:24-26 - Then Jesus said to his disciples, 'Whoever wants to be my disciple must deny themselves and take up their cross and follow me. For whoever wants to save their life will lose it, but whoever loses their life for me will find it.'

_Devotion:_

Surrender is the key to freedom in Christ. A profound truth! **Surrender to God**:

_Frees us from bondage

_Releases us from sin's grip, chains of fear, and weights of worry.

_Opens doors to grace

_Allows God's mercy, love, and power to flood our lives. _Brings peace and rest

_ Quiets our souls, calms our minds, and soothes our hearts.

_Unlocks God's strength

_Empowers us to face challenges, overcome obstacles, and walk in victory.

_Transforms our lives

_Renews our minds, renews our hearts, and renews our purpose.

Remember, surrender is: - A daily choice, a moment-by-moment decision- A journey, not a destination- A trust-filled response to God's love and grace.

_Prayer: _Dear God, help me to surrender my life, my will, and my ways to You. Free me from bondage, fill me with Your grace, and empower me with Your strength. May Your peace, rest, and transformation be my portion. In Jesus' name, Amen.

## REFLECTION

_Action Step: _

Take a moment to reflect on an area of your life where you need to surrender. Write it down, and then write "I surrender" next to it. Ask God to help you release control, trust His goodness, and experience freedom in Christ.

What do you need to surrender to God today? Ask Him to help you deny yourself and follow Him.

_Reflection Prompt: _ How can you experience the freedom of surrender today? Write down your thoughts and ask God to give you the grace to surrender.

## January 20: The Power of Humility

_Scripture:_ Mark 10:43-45-As Jesus taught, whoever wants to become great among you must be your servant, and whoever wants to be first must be slave of all. For even the Son of Man did not come to be served, but to serve, and to give his life as a ransom for many.

_Devotion:_

Humility is the pathway to true greatness in God's kingdom.

A powerful truth! Humility:

_Exalts God_: Recognizes His sovereignty, wisdom, and power.
_Lowers self-_: Recognizes our limitations, weaknesses, and dependence on God.
_Opens doors to wisdom_: Allows us to learn, grow, and receive guidance.
_Fosters healthy relationships_: Builds bridges, promotes unity, and encourages servanthood.
_Unlocks God's blessings_: Attracts divine favor, anointing, and empowerment.

Remember, humility is: - A heart attitude, not just a outward behavior- A continuous process, not a one-time achievement- A key to true greatness, not a barrier to success

_Prayer:_ *Dear God, help me to walk in humility, recognizing Your greatness and my limitations. May I exalt You, lower self, and open myself to Your wisdom and guidance. Use me for Your glory and kingdom purposes. In Jesus' name,* Amen.

## _January 21:_ The Joy of Obedience_

_Scripture:_ John 14:21 - Whoever has my commands and keeps them is the one who loves me. The one who loves me will be loved by my Father, and I too will love them and show myself to them.

_Devotion:_

Obedience to God's Word brings joy and intimacy with Him. A wonderful truth! Obedience to God's Word is a powerful way to deepen our relationship with Him and experience joy in our walk with Him. When we choose to obey His commands and live according to His principles, we demonstrate our love and trust in Him. This obedience opens the door to a more intimate and personal relationship with God, filling us with joy, peace, and a sense of purpose.

As we surrender to His will, we experience the joy of knowing and following Him, and our hearts are filled with the fruit of obedience: love, joy, peace, and righteousness.

_Prayer:_ *Dear God, help me to keep your commands and teachings, and show yourself to me. Give me the grace to obey and experience your love and presence.* Amen.

_January 22: Humility is a virtue_

_Scripture:_ Matthew 23:12 - For those who exalt themselves will be humbled, and those who humble themselves will be exalted.

_Devotion:_

Humility is a powerful virtue that opens doors to God's grace and blessing.

Absolutely! Humility is a powerful virtue that unlocks the doors to God's grace, blessing, and favor. When we humble ourselves before God, acknowledging our limitations and dependence on Him, we create a conduit for His grace to flow into our lives.

Humility allows us to receive correction, guidance, and wisdom from God, leading to spiritual growth, wisdom, and a deeper relationship with Him.

By embracing humility, we position ourselves for God's blessings, guidance, and grace, leading to a life of purpose, impact, and spiritual fulfillment.

_Prayer:_ *Dear God, help me to humble myself and exalt you. Give me the grace to walk in humility and experience your blessing and grace.* Amen.

## _January 23:_ The Peace of God's Sovereignty_

_Scripture:_ Romans 8:28 says, "And we know that in all things God works for the good of those who love him, who have been called according to his purpose."

_Devotion:_

God's sovereignty brings peace to our lives, even in uncertain times.

A wonderful truth! God's sovereignty is an anchor of peace in the midst of uncertainty. Knowing that He is in control, that He is all-powerful, all-knowing, and all-loving, brings a deep sense of peace and calm to our lives.

His sovereignty reminds us that nothing happens outside of His plan, and that He is working everything out for our good. Even when we don't understand what's happening, we can trust in His sovereign plan and rest in His peace.

May we find peace in His sovereignty, and trust in His loving plan for our lives.

_Prayer:_ *Dear God, help me to trust your sovereignty and kingdom rule. Give me the grace to see your throne established in the heavens.* Amen.

_January 24:_ The Comfort of God's Love_

_Scripture:_ As Psalm 46:10 says, God is our refuge and strength, an ever-present help in trouble.

_Devotion:_

God's love is our comfort and strength in times of uncertainty.

A beautiful reminder! God's love is indeed our comfort and strength in times of uncertainty. His love is a constant, unwavering, and unshakeable force that surrounds us, sustains us, and uplifts us.

When we feel lost, anxious, or uncertain, His love envelops us, reminding us that we are not alone, that we are cherished, and that we are held in His mighty hands.

God's love is our refuge, our solace, and our hope. It comforts us, strengthens us, and empowers us to face whatever challenges come our way. May we bask in the warmth of His love and find comfort in His embrace.

_Prayer:_ *Dear God, thank you for your unfailing love. Comfort me with your presence and give me the grace to trust in your love.* Amen.

### January 25: The Hope of God's Faithfulness

_Scripture:_ Hebrews 13:5 God has said, 'Never will I leave you; never will I forsake you.

_Devotion:_

God's faithfulness is our hope and assurance in times of uncertainty.

A wonderful truth! God's faithfulness is indeed our hope and assurance in times of uncertainty. His faithfulness is a rock-solid foundation that we can rely on, a promise that He will never leave us nor forsake us.

When everything around us seems uncertain, His faithfulness remains unwavering, a beacon of hope that guides us through the darkness. His faithfulness reminds us that He is always true to His word, always faithful to His promises, and always present in our lives.

May we anchor our hope in His faithfulness and trust in His unwavering love.

_Prayer:_ *Dear God, thank you for your compassions that never fail. Show me your faithfulness and give me the grace to trust in your goodness.* Amen.

## _January 26:_ God's compassion_

_Scripture:_ As Psalm 103:13 says, as a father has compassion on his children, so the Lord has compassion on those who fear him.

_Devotion:_

God's compassion brings mercies and hope to our lives.

A beautiful truth! God's compassion:

1. _Sees our struggles_: Understands our pain, our fears, and our weaknesses.
2. _Meets our needs_: Provides comfort, guidance, and strength in times of trouble.
3. _Brings mercies_: New every morning, fresh and abundant (Lamentations 3:22-23).
4. _Offers hope_: Anchors our souls, revives our hearts, and renews our minds.
5. _Transforms our lives_: From ashes to beauty, from darkness to light (Isaiah 61:3).

Remember, God's compassion is: - Unconditional, loving us as we are- Unending, always available, always near- Unfailing, never leaving or forsaking us

_Prayer:_ Dear God, *thank You for Your compassion. Help me to receive Your mercies and hope. Meet me in my struggles, comfort me in my pain, and transform my life with Your love. In Jesus' name,* Amen.

## January 27: The Power of Gratitude

_Scripture:_ 1 Thessalonians 5:18 - Give thanks in all circumstances; for this is the will of God in Christ Jesus for you.

_Devotion:_

Gratitude is a powerful weapon that can change our perspective and bring joy to our lives.

A wonderful insight! Gratitude is indeed a powerful weapon that can transform our perspective, shift our focus, and bring joy to our lives. By intentionally focusing on the good things, no matter how small they may seem, we can break free from the chains of negativity, worry, and discontentment.

Gratitude opens our eyes to the beauty, blessings, and love that surround us, and fills our hearts with appreciation, peace, and happiness.

As we cultivate gratitude, we begin to see the world in a new light, and our lives are filled with joy, hope, and thankfulness. Let us wield the weapon of gratitude to overcome adversity, uplift others, and honor God.

_Prayer:_ *Dear God, help me to give thanks in all circumstances. Give me the grace to see your goodness and love in every situation. Amen.*

## _January 28: The Strength of God's Grace

_Scripture: _ 2 Corinthians 12:9 - But he said to me, 'My grace is sufficient for you, for my power is made perfect in weakness.

### _Devotion: _

God's grace is our strength in times of weakness and vulnerability.

A beautiful truth! God's grace is indeed our strength in times of weakness and vulnerability. His grace is a powerful force that sustains us, uplifts us, and empowers us to face our struggles and challenges.

When we feel weak, vulnerable, and helpless, His grace pours in, reminding us that we are not alone and that He is our rock, our refuge, and our Savior.

May we embrace our weaknesses and vulnerabilities, knowing that they create a space for God's grace to shine through and work in and through us

_Prayer: _ *Dear God, thank you for your sufficient grace. Show me your power in my weakness and give me the grace to trust in your strength.* Amen.

**_January 29_**: The Peace of God's Presence

_Scripture:_ Joshua 1:5 says, I will never leave you nor forsake you," He promises.

_Devotion:_

God's presence is our peace and joy in times of uncertainty.

A beautiful truth! God's presence is our constant comfort, our steady anchor, and our unshakeable hope. In His presence, we find peace that surpasses understanding, joy that overflows, and love that endures. When uncertainty and doubt assail us, His presence reminds us that He is our rock, our refuge, and our Savior.

As we abide in Him, we experience the peace and joy that come from knowing Him, and we are empowered to face whatever challenges come our way. May we cultivate a deep awareness of His presence in our lives, and may His peace and joy be our constant companions.

_Prayer:_ *Dear God I come to You seeking the peace that only Your presence can bring. In the midst of chaos and uncertainty, I need Your calming presence to soothe my soul.*

*As I rest in Your presence, may I experience the fullness of Your peace, which brings joy, hope, and strength to my life.* Amen.

## _January 30_: Our Hope in God's Promises_

_Scripture:_ 2 Corinthians 1:20- For all the promises of God find their Yes in Him. That is why it is through Him that we utter our Amen to God for his glory

_Devotion:_

God's promises give us hope and encouragement to persevere in our walk with Him.

A wonderful truth! God's promises are a treasure trove of hope and encouragement, empowering us to persevere in our walk with Him. His promises remind us that He is faithful, loving, and sovereign, and that He is working everything out for our good.

They give us the strength to keep going, even when the journey gets tough, and the confidence to trust in His plans, even when we can't see the way ahead.

God's promises are a lifeline of hope, a reminder that He is always with us, always for us, and always working to bring us closer to Himself. As we cling to His promises, we find the courage to persevere, the joy to persevere, and the peace to persevere.

_Prayer:_ *Dear God, thank you for your promises and faithfulness. Help me to persevere and receive what you have promised.* Amen.

## January: 31 God's Gentle Guidance

_Scripture:_ Psalm 23:2-3 - He makes me lie down in green pastures. He leads me beside still waters. He restores my soul. He leads me in paths of righteousness for his name's sake.

_Devotion:_

God guides us with gentleness and love, leading us to places of peace and restoration.

What a beautiful sentiment! Indeed, many people find comfort and guidance in their faith, and the idea of a loving and gentle guide can be a source of strength and inspiration.

The Lord is gentle and compassionate, slow to anger and rich in love." - Psalm 103:8

This verse reminds us that God's guidance is not about forcing us onto a certain path, but rather about lovingly directing us towards our highest good.

May you continue to find peace and guidance on your journey.

_Prayer:_ *Dear God, thank you for your gentle guidance. Help me trust in your leading and follow your paths of righteousness.* Amen.

# ROSE PETALS -- 366 DAYS OF MORNING MUSINGS

As January comes to a close, we reflect on the first chapter of the year. We've set intentions, made resolutions, and taken initial steps towards our goals.

January has taught us to:
- Embrace new beginnings and fresh starts
- Cultivate self-reflection and introspection
- Prioritize self-care and wellness
- Stay committed to our aspirations

As we turn the page to February, we carry forward the momentum of January. May the progress we've made continue to inspire and motivate us. May we build upon the foundations laid, stay focused, and keep moving forward with purpose and determination.

January's lessons will continue to guide us throughout the year, reminding us to stay true to ourselves, our values, and our vision. Farewell, January – hello to a brighter, bolder, and more resilient us!

ROSE PETALS -- 366 DAYS OF MORNING MUSINGS

## FEBRUARY 1-29

1. The Guidance of God's Word_
2. We have peace in knowing God.
3. The Joy of Worship
4. The Strength of God's Peace
5. The Power of God's Word
6. The joy of God's Presence
7. The Joy of God's Love
8. The Faithfulness of God
9. The Hope of God's Mercy
10. The Peace of God's Love
11. The Hope of God's Grace
12. The Faithfulness of God's Promises
13. The Hope of God's Redemption
14. The Love of God's Sacrifice
15. The Comfort of God's Care
16. Rejoice in today
17. The Power of God's Grace
18. Today ask God to remove the mask/masks
19. Today submit to God
20. God's Renewal- Restoration and Transformation
21. The Hope of God's Salvation
22. The Strength of God's Power
23. The Hope of God's Guidance
24. Faith and Perseverance
25. Gratitude is Powerful
26. God's Faithfulness
27. The Joy of Forgiveness
28. The Guidance of God's Wisdom
29. The Power of Prayer in Uncertain Times

## _February 1_: The Guidance of God's Word_

_Scripture:_ Psalm 119:105 - Your word is a lamp for my feet, a light on my path.

_Devotion:_

God's Word is our guide and light in times of uncertainty.

A beautiful truth! God's Word is indeed our guide and light in times of uncertainty. It is a lamp to our feet, illuminating the path ahead, and a light to our darkness, shining bright in the midst of uncertainty. God's Word is a steady anchor that holds us firm, a trustworthy compass that points us in the right direction, and a precious treasure that fills our hearts with hope and wisdom.

As we seek guidance and direction in uncertain times, God's Word whispers truth, comfort, and wisdom, reminding us that He is always with us, always for us, and always working everything out for our good.

May we cherish and cling to God's Word, our precious guide and light in times of uncertainty.

_Prayer:_ *Dear God, thank you for your Word that guides me. Give me the grace to seek your wisdom and follow your path.* Amen.

_February 2:_ We have peace in knowing God.

_Scripture:_ Isaiah 26:3 - You will keep in perfect peace those whose minds are steadfast, because they trust in you.

_Devotion:_

We have peace in knowing God will comfort us in times of turmoil.

What a comforting truth! Knowing that God is our comfort in times of turmoil brings us peace and reassurance. His presence is a calm in the storm, a refuge from the chaos, and a soothing balm to our souls. He promises to be with us in the midst of trouble, to comfort us, and to give us peace that surpasses understanding.

As we anchor ourselves in His love and faithfulness, we can face the turmoil with courage and hope, knowing that He is our rock, our shelter, and our Savior.

May we rest in His comfort and peace, even in the midst of turmoil.

_Prayer:_ *Dear God, thank you for your presence that gives me peace. Keep me in perfect peace and give me the grace to trust in you. Amen.*

## _February 3:_ The Joy of Worship_

_Scripture:_ Psalm 100:2 - Worship the Lord with gladness; come before him with joyful songs.

_Devotion:_

Worship is a powerful way to connect with God and experience His joy.

A beautiful truth! Worship is indeed a powerful way to connect with God and experience His joy. When we worship, we lift our eyes off our circumstances and fix them on Him, our Creator, Savior, and King. We acknowledge His greatness, His love, and His faithfulness, and we humble ourselves before Him. In worship, we enter into His presence, where joy, peace, and love overflow.

Worship aligns our hearts with His, and we become one with Him in spirit and truth.

As we worship, His joy fills us, and we become a vessel for His presence, spreading joy and hope to those around us.

May we worship Him with all our heart, soul, mind, and strength, and experience the fullness of His joy!

_Prayer:_ *Dear God, help me to worship you with gladness and come before you with joyful songs. Fill my heart with joy and gratitude.* Amen.

## _February 4:_ The Strength of God's Peace

_Scripture:_ Philippians 4:7 - And the peace of God, which transcends all understanding, will guard your hearts and your minds in Christ Jesus.

_Devotion:_

God's peace is our strength and refuge in times of uncertainty.

A wonderful reminder! God's peace is indeed our strength and refuge in times of uncertainty. His peace is a steady anchor that holds us firm, a calm in the midst of storms, and a soothing balm to our souls.

It's a peace that surpasses understanding, a peace that guards our hearts and minds, and a peace that fills us with hope and confidence.

When uncertainty and doubt creep in, God's peace whispers reassurance, reminding us that He is always in control, always faithful, and always with us.

May we seek His peace, rest in His peace, and trust in His goodness, even in the midst of uncertainty.

_Prayer:_ *Dear God, thank you for your peace that transcends all understanding. Guard my heart and mind with your peace and give me the grace to trust in you. Amen.*

## _February 5:_ The Power of God's Word_

_Scripture:_ Hebrews 4:12 - For the word of God is alive and active, sharper than any two-edged sword, penetrating even to dividing soul and spirit, joints and marrow; it judges the thoughts and attitudes of the heart.

_Devotion:_

God's Word is our sword and our guide giving us wisdom and discernment. in times of need.

A powerful truth! God's Word is indeed our sword and our guide in times of need. As our sword, it equips us to fight against spiritual darkness, falsehood, and temptation, helping us to stand firm in our faith.

As our guide, it illuminates our path, providing wisdom, direction, and comfort in times of uncertainty. God's Word is a mighty weapon and a trustworthy companion, empowering us to face life's challenges with courage and confidence.

May we wield God's Word with faith and boldness, and follow its guidance with trust and obedience.

_Prayer:_ *Dear God, thank you for your living and active Word. Give me the grace to trust in your truth and apply it to my life.* Amen.

## **February 6**: The joy of God's Presence

_Scripture:_ Psalm 16:11 says, may we continually seek and savor the joy of God's Presence in our lives!

_Devotion:_

The joy of God's Presence peace brings us settle peace.

The joy of God's Presence" is a beautiful phrase! It captures the exquisite delight and happiness that comes from experiencing God's nearness and connection. Being in God's Presence is like basking in the warmth of His love, feeling the gentle touch of His grace, and reveling in the joy that only He can give.

It's a joy that's unspeakable, full of glory, and overflowing with peace!

In Your presence is fullness of joy; at Your right hand are pleasures forevermore"

_Prayer:_ *Dear God, I come to You seeking the joy that only Your presence can bring. Fill me with Your joy, which is my strength, my comfort, and my delight. Help me to experience the fullness of Your joy, which surpasses all understanding and overflows from Your presence. May Your joy be my constant companion, my guiding light, and my heart's delight. Amen.*

May Your joy be the foundation of my life, the source of my happiness, and the essence of my being.

## _February 7: The Joy of God's Love_

_Scripture:_ Psalm 46:1 says may we bask in the warmth of His love and rely on His strength in times of need!

_Devotion:_
God's love is our joy and strength in times of need.

A wonderful truth! God's love is indeed our joy and strength in times of need. His love is a rock that anchors our souls, a refuge that shelters us, and a fountain that refreshes us. It's a love that's unwavering, unshakeable, and unending, filling us with joy and strength to face any challenge.

In God's love, we find comfort, hope, and peace, knowing that we are never alone and always cared for.

Let us remember that God is our strength and our refuge, an ever-present help in trouble.
Here's a prayer for The Joy of God's Love:

_Prayer:_ *Dear God, I come to You seeking the joy that only Your love can bring. Pour out Your love upon me, and fill me with the joy that comes from knowing You. Help me to experience the depth and breadth of Your love, forgives my sins and cleanses my heart, accepts me just as I am, with all my flaws and imperfections, strengthens me in times of weakness and encourages me in times of fear. Amen.*

May Your love be the foundation of my life, the source of
   my happiness, and the essence of my being.

### _February 8:_ The Faithfulness of God_

_Scripture:_ Psalm 119:90 says your faithfulness endures to all generations; you have established the earth, and it stands fast.

_Devotion:_

God's faithfulness is our hope and our comfort, reminding us of His steadfast love and mercy.

A beautiful reminder! God's faithfulness is indeed our hope and comfort, a steadfast anchor that holds us secure in the midst of life's storms. His faithfulness is a reminder that His love and mercy are unwavering, unending, and unshakeable.

It's a comfort that He is always with us, always for us, and always working everything out for our good. God's faithfulness is a beacon of hope, shining bright in the darkness, and a reminder that His steadfast love and mercy are our constant companions.

May we cling to His faithfulness as our hope and comfort!

_Prayer:_ Dear God, I come to You, trusting in Your faithfulness. You are the Rock of Ages, the One who remains steadfast and true. Thank You for Your unwavering commitment to me, for Your promises that never fail, and for Your presence that never leaves. Amen.

May Your faithfulness be my anchor, my comfort, and my strength. Remind me of Your track record of faithfulness in my life and in the lives of those who have gone before me.

## REFLECTION

_Action Step:_

Reflect on a time when God showed Himself faithful in your life. Write it down and thank Him for His faithfulness. Then, ask God to help you trust in His faithfulness for a current situation or need. Share your story with someone else, and ask them to share theirs, encouraging each other in God's faithfulness!

How can you trust in God's faithfulness today? Ask Him to help you see His love and mercy in your life.

_Reflection Prompt:_ Write down ways you can trust in God's faithfulness today

## _February 9:_ _ The Hope of God's Mercy_

_Scripture:_ Psalm 103:8-10 - The Lord is compassionate and gracious, slow to anger and abounding in love. He will not always accuse, nor will he harbor his anger forever; he does not treat us as our sins deserve or repay us according to our iniquities.

_Devotion:_

God's mercy is our hope and comfort in times of need.

A wonderful truth! God's mercy is indeed our hope and comfort in times of need. His mercy is a boundless ocean that washes over us, a gentle balm that soothes our souls, and a loving embrace that envelops us in His grace.

It's a mercy that's freely given, abundantly poured out, and endlessly available, reminding us that we are never beyond His reach or beyond His love.

May we seek His mercy with humble hearts and receive His comfort with grateful souls!

_Prayer:_ *Dear God, I come to You, seeking the hope that only Your mercy can bring. You are the God of second chances, the One who forgives and restores. Thank You for Your mercy covers my sins and failures, heals my wounds and brokenness, gives me hope for a better tomorrow. Amen.*

# _February 10:_ The Peace of God's Love_

_Scripture:_ 1 John 4:16 - And so we know and rely on the love God has for us. God is love. Whoever lives in love lives in God, and God in them.

## _Devotion:_

God's love is our peace and our refuge, where we can find comfort and rest.

A beautiful truth! God's love is indeed our peace and refuge, where we can find:
- Comfort in times of sorrow and pain- Rest from the storms of life- Strength in our weaknesses
- Hope in the midst of uncertainty
- Guidance in our confusion.

God's love is:
- Unconditional, accepting us just as we are
- Unending, always available, always near
- Unfailing, never leaving or forsaking us.

As we rest in God's love, we can:
- Let go of our fears and worries
- Trust in His goodness and sovereignty
- Find peace that surpasses understanding

_Prayer:_ *Dear God Thank You for Your love that is my peace and refuge. In Your presence, I find comfort, rest, and strength. Help me to trust in Your goodness and sovereignty, and to let go of my fears and worries. I rest in Your love, dear God, and trust that You will keep me safe and secure. Amen.*

## February 11: The Hope of God's Grace

_Scripture:_ Ephesians 2:8 says by grace you have been saved through faith, and that not of yourselves, it is the gift of God.

_Devotion:_

God's grace is our hope and our strength, giving us access to His presence and glory.

A beautiful truth! God's grace is indeed our hope and strength, giving us:
- Access to His presence, where we find comfort, guidance, and peace
- A way to experience His glory, which transforms and empowers us
- The ability to live a life that honors Him, despite our weaknesses and failures
- The power to overcome sin and its consequences
- The assurance of eternal life and fellowship with Him.

God's grace is:
- Unmerited, given to us despite our unworthiness
- Unconditional, not based on our performance or achievements
- Unending, always available, always sufficient.

As we receive God's grace, we can:
- Trust in His goodness and sovereignty
- Find hope in the midst of uncertainty and darkness
- Live a life that reflects His love and glory.

_Prayer:_ Dear God, thank You for Your grace that gives me access to Your presence and glory. Help me to trust in Your goodness and sovereignty, and to live a life that honors You. Amen.

## February 12: The Faithfulness of God's Promises

_Scripture:_ 1 Corinthians 1:9 says God is faithful, by whom you were called into the fellowship of his Son, Jesus Christ our Lord.

_Devotion:_

God's promises are our hope and our confidence, knowing that He is faithful to fulfill them.

A wonderful truth! God's promises are indeed our hope and confidence, reminding us that:
- He is faithful and true to His word
- He will fulfill His promises in His perfect timing
- His promises give us hope in the midst of uncertainty and darkness
- His promises are a source of confidence and trust in Him.

Some of God's precious promises include:
- "I will never leave you nor forsake you" (Hebrews 13:5)
- "I will give you hope and a future" (Jeremiah 29:11)
- "I will strengthen and help you" (Isaiah 41:10)
- "I will guide you and watch over you" (Psalm 32:8)
- "I will forgive you and cleanse you" (1 John 1:9).

May God's promises be our hope and confidence today and always!

_Prayer:_ *Dear God, thank You for Your precious promises that give me hope and confidence. Help me to trust in Your faithfulness and goodness. May Your promises be my rock and my refuge in times of uncertainty.* Amen.

## REFLECTION

_Action Step:_

Write down one of God's promises that resonates with you. Reflect on it throughout the day, trusting in His faithfulness to fulfill it. Share it with someone else, and encourage them with God's promise.

How can you trust God's promises today? Ask Him to show you His faithfulness and goodness.

_Reflection Prompt:_ Write down ways you can trust in God's promises today.

## _February 13_: The Hope of God's Redemption

_Scripture:_ Ruth 4:14 - Then the women said to Naomi, 'Blessed be the Lord, who has not left you this day without a redeemer.

_Devotion:_

God's redemption is our hope and our salvation, where we can find new life and purpose.

A powerful truth! God's redemption is indeed our hope and salvation, offering us:
- A new purpose, living for Him and His glory
- Forgiveness, cleansing, and restoration
- Freedom from guilt, shame, and condemnation
- Adoption into His family, as beloved children

Through Jesus Christ, God's redemption:
- Paid the penalty for our sins
- Broke the power of sin and death
- Opened the way to a personal relationship with God
- Gives us eternal life and fellowship with Him

_Prayer:_ *Dear God, thank You for Your redemption, our hope and salvation. Help me to live in the freedom and new life You offer. May Your redemption be my guiding force, giving me purpose and direction. Amen.*

May God's redemption be our hope and salvation today and always!

### February 14: The Love of God's Sacrifice

_Scripture:_ John 3:16 - For God so loved the world that He gave His one and only Son, that whoever believes in Him shall not perish but have eternal life.

_Devotion:_

God's sacrifice is our love and our salvation, giving us eternal life and purpose.

A beautiful truth! God's sacrifice is indeed our love and salvation, offering us:

- Eternal life, free from the fear of death and separation from Him
- Purpose, living for Him and His glory, with meaning and direction
- Unconditional love, demonstrated through Jesus' sacrifice on the cross
- Forgiveness, cleansing, and restoration, through His shed blood
- Adoption into His family, as beloved children, with inheritance and belonging

God's sacrifice: - Paid the ultimate price for our sins, reconciling us to Himself- Demonstrated the depth of His love, willing to give His only Son for us- Opened the way to a personal relationship with Him, through faith in Jesus- Gives us access to His presence, guidance, and empowerment

May God's sacrifice be our love and salvation today and always!

_Prayer:_ *Dear God, thank You for Your sacrifice, our love and salvation. Help me to live in the reality of Your love and purpose. May Your sacrifice be my guiding force, giving me direction and meaning. Amen.*

## REFLECTION

_Action Step:_

Reflect on the depth of God's love, demonstrated through His sacrifice. Write down ways you can respond to His love.

Take a step of obedience, living out your purpose and love for God, empowered by His sacrifice.

_Reflection Prompt:_ Write down ways you can thank God for His sacrifice today

# _February 15_: The Comfort of God's Care_

_Scripture:_ 1 Peter 5:7 - Cast all your anxiety on him because he cares for you.

_Devotion:_

God's care is our comfort and our refuge, giving us peace and hope.

A wonderful truth! God's care is indeed our comfort and refuge, providing us with: - Peace that surpasses understanding, calming our fears and worries- Hope that anchors our souls, giving us confidence in His goodness- Comfort that soothes our hurts, healing our emotional and spiritual wounds- Refuge from life's storms, shielding us from harm and danger- Strength to face challenges, empowering us to persevere

God's care: - Envelops us in His loving presence, surrounding us with His goodness- Listens to our cries, hearing our prayers and concerns- Understands our struggles, empathizing with our weaknesses- Provides for our needs, meeting us in our moments of desperation

May God's care be our comfort and refuge today and always!

_Prayer:_ *Dear God, thank You for Your care, our comfort and refuge. Help me to trust in Your goodness and love. May Your care be my peace and hope in times of uncertainty. Amen.*

## _February 16_: Rejoice in today_

_Scripture:_ Philippians 4:4-Rejoice in the Lord always. I will say it again: Rejoice!

_Devotion:_

I choose to rejoice in God's presence today.

A beautiful choice! Rejoicing in God's presence brings:
- Joy that overflows from His goodness and love
- Peace that calms our fears and worries
- Gratitude for His blessings and faithfulness
- Strength to face challenges with confidence
- Connection with Him, deepening our relationship

As you rejoice in God's presence, remember: - He is always with you, never leaving or forsaking- He delights in your praise and worship- He speaks to you through His Word and Spirit- He guides and directs you in His perfect plan- He loves you unconditionally, without measure

_Prayer:_ *Dear God, choose to rejoice in Your presence today. Fill me with Your joy and peace. Help me to focus on Your goodness and love, grateful for Your blessings.* Men.

# _February 17_: The Power of God's Grace_

_Scripture: _ Ephesians 2:8-9 - For by grace you have been saved through faith. And this is not your own doing; it is the gift of God.

_Devotion: _

God's grace is our power and our salvation, giving us the gift of faith and new life.

A wonderful truth! God's grace is indeed our power and salvation, offering us:
- The gift of faith, trusting in His goodness and love
- New life, transformed by His Spirit and presence
- Forgiveness, cleansing us from sin and its consequences-
Strength, empowering us to live for Him and His glory
- Hope, confident in His promises and plans.

God's grace:
- Saves us from sin and its dominion
- Redeems us, making us His beloved children-
Transforms us, renewing our minds and hearts
- Empowers us, giving us the power to live for Him-
Keeps us, holding us secure in His love and care

May God's grace be our power and salvation today and always!

_Prayer: _ _Dear God_, thank You for Your grace, our power and salvation. Help me to live in the gift of faith and new life. May Your grace be my strength and hope, empowering me to live for You. Amen

## _February 18: Today ask God to remove the mask/masks_

_Scripture: 1 Samuel 16:7 But the Lord said to Samuel, 'Do not consider his appearance or his height, for I have rejected him. The Lord does not look at the things people look at. People look at the outward appearance, but the Lord looks at the heart.

_Devotion: _

Let us remove our masks and reveal our true selves while trusting God's love and acceptance.

A beautiful and vulnerable step! Removing our masks and revealing our true selves requires:
- Courage to be authentic and honest
- Trust in God's unconditional love and acceptance
- Freedom from the need for perfection and approval
- Embracing our imperfections and weaknesses- Living in the security of His grace and mercy

As we remove our masks, we can: - Experience true freedom and liberation- Deepen our relationship with God and others- Find comfort in being ourselves, without pretenses- Receive God's love and acceptance, without condition- Live with authenticity and integrity

Prayer: _ *Dear God, help me to remove my masks and reveal my true self, trusting in Your love and acceptance. May Your grace and mercy empower me to live authentically, free from the need for perfection.* Amen

# ROSE PETALS -- 366 DAYS OF MORNING MUSINGS

**February 19**: Today submit to God

_Scripture:_ Job 22:21, Submit to God and be at peace with Him; in this way, prosperity will come to you"

_Devotion:_

God's faithfulness is our joy and our strength, giving us hope and confidence as we surrender and submit to Him.

A powerful truth! God's faithfulness is indeed our joy and strength, providing us with:
- Hope in His promises and plans
- Confidence in His goodness and love
- Peace that surpasses understanding
- Joy in His presence and guidance

As we surrender and submit to God, we can: - Trust in His sovereignty and wisdom- Rest in His care and provision- Find strength in His faithfulness and love- Experience transformation and growth- Live with purpose and direction

Prayer: _ Dear God, thank You for Your faithfulness, our joy and strength. Help me to surrender and submit to You, trusting in Your goodness and love. May Your faithfulness be my hope and confidence, giving me peace and courage. Amen.

**_February 20:_** God's Renewal- Restoration and Transformation

_Scripture:_ Psalm 23:3-He restores my soul; He leads me in the paths of righteousness for His name's sake.

_Devotion:_

God's renewal, restoration and transformation gives us new life and purpose.

A beautiful theme! God's renewal is a powerful force in our lives, bringing restoration, transformation, and new life. Through His renewal, we experience:

- Refreshed hope and purpose
- Renewed minds and spirits
- Restoration of relationships and dreams
- Transformation from the inside out
- New life and beginnings

May God's renewal be a constant presence in our lives, refreshing and transforming us daily

Prayer: _ *Dear God, thank you for your renewal and hope. Give me the grace to trust in your strength and soar like eagles. Thank You for Your restoration, and transformation, giving me new life and purpose. Help me to surrender to Your work in me, trusting in Your goodness and love. Amen.*

_February 21_: The Hope of God's Salvation_

_Scripture:_ Psalm 3:8 - From the Lord comes deliverance. May your blessing be on your people.
_Devotion:_

God's salvation is our hope and our deliverance, giving us freedom and blessing.

A wonderful truth! God's salvation is indeed our hope and deliverance, offering us:
- Freedom from sin and its consequences
- Freedom from fear, anxiety, and doubt
- Freedom to live for Him and His glory
- Blessings of joy, peace, and abundant life
- Hope for eternity, secure in His promises

Through God's salvation, we can:
- Experience forgiveness and cleansing
- Receive new life and purpose
- Find strength and courage in His presence
- Trust in His goodness and love

May we rejoice in His salvation, bask in His blessing, and share the Good News with a world in need!

_Prayer:_ *Dear God, thank You for Your salvation, our hope and deliverance. Help me to live in the freedom and blessings You offer. May Your salvation be my guiding force, giving me hope and confidence.* Amen.

## February 22: The Strength of God's Power

_Scripture:_ Philippians 4:13 - I can do all this through him who gives me strength.

_Devotion:_

God's power is our strength and our hope, giving us confidence and courage in times of need.

A mighty truth! God's power is indeed our strength and our hope, a rock-solid foundation that anchors our souls in times of turmoil. His power:

- Lifts us up when we are weak
- Gives us courage in the face of fear
- Provides confidence in His promises
- Helps us overcome obstacles and challenges
- Transforms us from the inside out

May we tap into His power, relying on His strength and hope in every situation. May His power be our constant companion, guiding us and empowering us to live a life that honors Him!

_Prayer:_ *Dear God, thank you for your power and strength. Give me the grace to trust in Your might and courage. Amen.*

## _February 23_: The Hope of God's Guidance_

_Scripture:_ Psalm 32:8 - I will instruct you and teach you in the way you should go; I will counsel you with my loving eye on you.

_Devotion:_

God's guidance is our hope and our trust, giving us direction and purpose.

A beautiful expression of faith! God's guidance is indeed our hope and our trust, a steady compass that points us towards His will and purpose for our lives. His guidance:

- Illuminates our path and leads us forward
- Provides wisdom and discernment in decision-making
- Gives us confidence and assurance in uncertain times
- Helps us navigate life's challenges and crossroads
- Reveals His plan and purpose for our lives

May we seek His guidance constantly, trusting in His sovereignty and goodness.

May His guidance be our anchor and our hope!

_Prayer:_ *Dear God, thank you for your guidance and love. Give me the grace to trust in your instruction and counsel. Amen.*

## _February 24:_ Faith and Perseverance _

_Scripture:_ Romans 5:3-4-And not only that, but we also glory in tribulations, knowing that tribulation produces perseverance; and perseverance, character; and character, hope.

_Devotion:_

When we trust God's sovereignty and goodness, we can face difficulties with courage and confidence.

That's a beautiful reflection! Trusting in God's sovereignty and goodness is a powerful foundation for facing life's challenges. When we truly believe that God is in control and that He loves us, we can approach difficulties with courage and confidence. This trust allows us to:

- Face our fears and anxieties with faith
- Endure hardships with perseverance
- Find joy in the midst of trials
- Grow in character and maturity

May we continue to cultivate this trust in God's sovereignty and goodness, that we may glorify Him in every circumstance!

Prayer: *Dear God, help me to trust in Your plan and Your presence, even in the midst of trials. Give me the grace to persevere, that I may grow in character and hope.* Amen.

## _February 25_: Gratitude is Powerful_

_Scripture:_ Psalm 107:1 Give thanks to the Lord, for He is good; His love endures forever.

_Devotion:_

The power of showing gratitude to God is a powerful force that shifts our focus from what's lacking to what we already have. When we cultivate thankfulness, we open our hearts to God's goodness, love, and provision. It transforms our perspective, relationships, and even our circumstances.

A wonderful topic! Showing gratitude to God is a powerful way to cultivate a deeper relationship with Him and experience His blessings in our lives. When we show gratitude to God, we:

- Recognize His sovereignty and provision
- Humble ourselves, acknowledging our dependence on Him
- Experience joy and peace, knowing we are not alone
- Strengthen our trust and faith in Him.

_Prayer:_ *Dear God, thank You for Your countless blessings and love. Help me to cultivate a heart of gratitude, always mindful of Your goodness and grace in my life.* Amen.

# **February 26:** God's Faithfulness

*Scripture:* 1 Corinthians 1:9 God is faithful, by whom you were called into the fellowship of His Son, Jesus Christ our Lord.

*Devotion:*

God's faithfulness is a rock-solid foundation for our lives

Amen to that! God's faithfulness is indeed a rock-solid foundation for our lives. It's a reminder that He is always true to His character, promises, and love for us. It's a reminder that He is:

- Stability in uncertain times
- Security in His unchanging nature
- Strength to face challenges and trials
- Hope in His promises and plans
- Confidence in His love and care

With God's faithfulness as our foundation, we can:
- Stand firm against adversity
- Trust in His sovereignty and wisdom
- Build our lives on His unshakeable promises
- Find peace in His presence and guidance
- Live with courage and assurance

*Prayer:* *Dear God, thank You for Your unwavering faithfulness. Help me to trust in Your promises and presence, even when circumstances seem uncertain. May Your faithfulness be my guiding force, giving me stability and strength. Amen.*

ROSE PETALS -- 366 DAYS OF MORNING MUSINGS

**_February 27_** The Joy of Forgiveness

_Scripture: _ - 1 John 1:9 -If we confess our sins, He is faithful and just to forgive us our sins and to cleanse us from all unrighteousness.

_Devotion: _

Forgiveness is a powerful gift that frees us from the weight of guilt, shame, and resentment.

Well said! Forgiveness is indeed a powerful gift that brings freedom and healing to our lives. When we choose to forgive, we:

- Release the burden of resentment and bitterness
- Break free from the chains of guilt and shame
- Open the door to healing and restoration
- Reflect the love and grace of God to others
- Experience the joy and peace that comes with forgiveness

Forgiveness is not always easy, but it's a choice that can transform our lives and relationships. As Jesus taught us, "Forgive us our debts, as we forgive our debtors" (Matthew 6:12).

_Prayer: _ *Dear God, help me to release the burdens of unforgiveness and embrace the joy of forgiveness, both towards myself and others.* Amen.

_**February 28:** The Guidance of God's Wisdom_

_Scripture:_ James 1:5 - If any of you lacks wisdom, you should ask God, who gives generously to all without finding fault, and it will be given to you.

_Devotion:_

God's wisdom is our guidance and our hope, giving us direction and purpose in times of uncertainty.

Amen to that! God's wisdom is indeed our guidance and hope, providing us with direction and purpose even in the midst of uncertainty. God's wisdom is:

- A treasure to be sought and cherished
- A guide for our decisions and actions
- A source of peace and confidence
- A gift available to us through prayer and seeking Him
- A reminder of His love and care for us

May we continue to seek and trust in God's wisdom, knowing that He is our rock and our salvation.

_Prayer:_ *Dear God, thank you for your wisdom and guidance. Give me the grace to trust in your direction and purpose.* Amen.

## _February 29_ The Power of Prayer in Uncertain Times

_Scripture: Philippians 4:6-7 - Do not be anxious about anything, but in every situation, by prayer and petition, with thanksgiving, present your requests to God. And the peace of God, which transcends all understanding, will guard your hearts and your minds in Christ Jesus.

### _Devotion_

In uncertain times, prayer is our powerful refuge. When anxiety and fear knock on our door, prayer welcomes peace and trust to take their place.

Through prayer, we present our requests to God, and He guards our hearts and minds with His peace. This peace is not the absence of trouble but the presence of God in the midst of trouble.

May we turn to prayer in uncertain times, trusting God's peace to guide us.

_Prayer: *Dear God, I bring my anxieties to you. Please replace them with your peace, which transcends all understanding.* Amen.

ROSE PETALS -- 366 DAYS OF MORNING MUSINGS

As February comes to a close, we reflect on the shortest yet impactful month of the year. We've navigated the ups and downs, celebrated love and friendship, and honored the achievements of remarkable individuals.

February has taught us to:
- Embrace love and kindness in all forms
- Recognize the strength and resilience of marginalized communities
- Stay committed to our passions and pursuits
- Find joy and beauty in the smallest moments

As we step into March, we carry forward the warmth and energy of February. May the lessons learned continue to inspire us to spread love, kindness, and compassion. May we remain steadfast in our commitments, and may the momentum of February propel us towards a brighter, more inclusive, and vibrant future.

Farewell February-your brevity and intensity have left a lasting impact on our hearts and minds.

# MARCH 1-31

1. The Hope of New Beginnings
2. God's Peace: A Calm in Every Storm
3. The Hope of New Life
4. God's Presence: A Constant Companion
5. God's Faithfulness: A Rock in Every Storm
6. The Strength of God's Courage
7. God's Joy: A Treasure That Never Fades
8. The Joy of God's Grace
9. God's Grace: A Gift of Unmerited Favor
10. God's Love: A Never-Ending Fountain
11. The Strength of God's Protection
12. The joy of trust and obedience
13. The Beauty of Humility
14. The Power of Surrender
15. The Armor of Faith
16. The Hope of God's Deliverance
17. The Strength of God's Comfort
18. The Hope of God's Forgiveness
19. The Strength of God's Wisdom
20. The hope of God's renewal
21. The Joy of God's Faithfulness
22. The Joy of God's Salvation
23. Rooted in Endurance
24. The Power of Perseverance
25. Finding Strength in Weakness
26. Hope in the Darkness
27. Perseverance: Fixing Our Eyes on Jesus
28. The Power of Prayer
29. Unshakable Hope
30. Fruitful Endurance
31. Grace for the Journey

## _March 1_: The Hope of New Beginnings_

_Scripture:_ Isaiah 43:19 - Behold, I am doing a new thing; now it springs forth, do you not perceive it?

_Devotion:_

God's new beginnings are our hope and our future, giving us purpose and direction.

Amen! God's new beginnings are indeed our hope and our future, providing us with purpose and direction. As the Bible says, "Forget the former things; do not dwell on the past.

God's new beginnings are:

- A fresh start and a clean slate
- A chance to redeem and restore
- A promise of hope and renewal
- A source of purpose and direction
- A reminder of His love and grace

May we embrace God's new beginnings in our lives, trusting in His plan and provision for our future.

_Prayer:_ *Dear God, thank you for your new beginnings and hope. Give me the grace to trust in your future and purpose.* Amen

_March 2:_ God's Peace: A Calm in Every Storm

Scripture: John 14:27-Peace I leave with you; my peace I give to you. Not as the world gives do I give to you, let not your hearts be troubled, neither let them be afraid.

_Devotion: _

God's peace, a gift that surpasses all understanding.

What a wonderful topic! God's peace is indeed a calm in every storm, a comfort in times of trouble, and a gift that surpasses all understanding.

As we reflect on God's peace, let's remember that:

- Jesus is our Prince of Peace (Isaiah 9:6)
- God's peace guards our hearts and minds (Philippians 4:7)
- We can have peace in the midst of trials (James 1:2-4)
- God's peace is a fruit of the Holy Spirit (Galatians 5:22-23)
- We can trust in God's sovereignty and provision (Romans 8:28)

May God's peace be our anchor in the storms of life, our comfort in times of sorrow, and our guide in times of uncertainty.

_Prayer: _ *Dear God, thank you for the calm in the middle of the storm. Help me to trust you wholeheartedly for your guidance and direction.* Amen.

## REFLECTION

How can you experience the peace in the middle of a storm today? Ask God for His direction.

_Reflection Prompt:_ Write down ways you can allow God to be your peace in the middle of a storm.

## March 3: The Hope of New Life_

_Scripture:_ Romans 6:4 - We were therefore buried with Him through baptism into death in order that, just as Christ was raised from the dead through the glory of the Father, we too may live a new life.

_Devotion:_

God's new life is our hope and our strength, giving us purpose and meaning in Christ.

Amen! God's new life in Christ is indeed our hope and strength, providing us with purpose and meaning. God's new life in Christ is:

- A transformation from the inside out
- A gift of grace and mercy
- A source of purpose and meaning
- A wellspring of hope and strength
- A testament to His love and redemption

May we walk in the newness of life, empowered by God's Spirit and guided by His Word.

_Prayer:_ *Dear God, thank you for your new life and hope. Give me the grace to trust in your strength and purpose.* Amen.

## _March 4:_ God's Presence: A Constant Companion

_Scripture:_ Matthew 28:20-And surely, I am with you always, to the very end of the age.

_Devotion:_

God's Presence is a constant companion to us.

A comforting truth! God's Presence is indeed a constant companion to us, providing:

- Guidance and direction in our journey
- Comfort and peace in times of turmoil
- Strength and courage in the face of challenges
- Wisdom and discernment in decision-making
- Love and acceptance in our weaknesses and failures

With God's Presence as our constant companion, we can:

- Feel His gentle nudges and whispers
- Sense His loving gaze upon us
- Experience His peace that surpasses understanding
- Find solace in His embrace
- Live with hope and confidence

_Prayer:_ *Dear God*, thank You for Your Presence, our constant companion. Help me to cultivate awareness of Your nearness. May Your Presence be my comfort, strength, and guide, empowering me to live for You. Amen.

**March 5**: God's Faithfulness: A Rock in Every Storm

Scripture: Psalm 18:2-3 says The Lord is my rock, my salvation and my deliverer; my God is my rock, in whom I take refuge, my shield and the horn of my salvation, my stronghold.

_Devotion:_

God is our rock in the midst of the storm.

Amen! God is indeed our rock in the midst of the storm, a steadfast and unshakeable presence that anchors us in the midst of turmoil.

God as our rock means:

- He is our solid foundation
- He is our source of strength
- He is our refuge and shelter
- He is our unshakeable hope
- He is our constant companion

May we cling to God as our rock in the midst of life's storms, trusting in His presence, power, and love to carry us through.

Prayer: _ Dear God, thank you for your love and peace. Give me the grace to trust in your presence and refuge in the middle of life's storms._ Amen.

## _March 6:_ The Strength of God's Courage_

_Scripture: _ Joshua 1:9 - Have I not commanded you? Be strong and courageous. Do not be afraid; do not be discouraged, for the Lord your God will be with you wherever you go.

_Devotion: _

God's courage is our strength and our hope, giving us confidence and boldness in times of fear.

Amen! God's courage is indeed our strength and our hope, empowering us with confidence and boldness in times of fear. As the Bible says, "Be strong and courageous. Do not be afraid; do not be discouraged, for the Lord your God will be with you wherever you go." (Joshua 1:9)

God's courage in us means:

- We can face challenges with confidence
- We can overcome obstacles with faith
- We can stand up for what is right with boldness
- We can share our faith with others without fear
- We can trust in God's presence and guidance

May we rely on God's courage to strengthen us in times of fear, and may it flow through us to inspire others.

_Prayer: _ *Dear God, thank you for your courage and strength. Give me the grace to trust in your presence and boldness.* Amen.

## March 7: God's Joy: A Treasure That Never Fades

_Scripture:_ Psalm 16:11 says you make known to me the path of life; you will fill me with joy in your presence, with eternal pleasures at your right hand.

_Devotion:_

**God's joy is:**

- A treasure that overflows from His presence
- A gift that fills our hearts and souls
- A strength that sustains us in trials
- A peace that surpasses all understanding
- A love that never fades or ends

**God's joy is:**

- Unshakeable, unwavering, and unending
- A fountain that bubbles up from within
- A radiance that shines from our faces
- A song that echoes from our hearts
- A celebration that resounds through eternity

May we bask in God's joy, drink from its river, and share its sweetness with a world in need!

_Prayer:_ *Dear God, thank you for your joy, grace and love. Give me the grace to trust in your love, and the peace to stand still and focus.* Amen.

## _March 8_: The Joy of God's Grace_

_Scripture:_ Titus 2:11-12 says for the grace of God has appeared that offers salvation to all people. It teaches us to say no to ungodliness and worldly passions and to live self-controlled, upright and godly lives in this present age."

_Devotion:_

God's grace is our joy and our hope, giving us salvation and new life in Christ.

Amen! God's grace is indeed our joy and our hope, providing us with salvation and new life in Christ.

God's grace in our lives means:

- We are saved by His unmerited favor
- We are forgiven and reconciled to God
- We are given new life and purpose in Christ
- We are empowered to live for Him
- We are filled with joy and hope in His presence

May we bask in the richness of God's grace, and may it flow through us to touch the lives of those around us.

_Prayer:_ *Dear God, thank you for your grace and salvation. Give me the grace to trust in your joy and hope.* Amen.

**March 9:** God's Grace: A Gift of Unmerited Favor

_Scripture:_ Ephesians 2:8-9 says for it is by grace you have been saved, through faith—and this is not from yourselves, it is the gift of God—not by works, so that no one can boast.

_Devotion:_

A Gift of Unmerited Favor.

A beautiful description of God's grace! A Gift of Unmerited Favor, indeed. God's grace is:

- Unearned and undeserved, yet freely given
- A manifestation of His love and kindness
- A gift that opens our hearts to His presence
- A transformative power that changes our lives
- A reminder of His mercy and compassion

With this Gift of Unmerited Favor, we can:

- Receive forgiveness and new life
- Experience the joy of salvation
- Find strength in our weaknesses
- Discover purpose and meaning
- Live with gratitude and praise

_Prayer:_ *Dear God may we always remember to approach you with humility and gratitude, knowing that your grace is a gift that we don't deserve, but that He freely offers to us anyway.* Amen.

### **March 10:** God's Love: A Never-Ending Fountain

_Scripture:_ 1 John 4:8 says, and His love is the very essence of His being. It's a love that is patient, kind, generous, and sacrificial, always seeking our highest good and greatest joy.

_Devotion:_

God's love is:
- A never-ending fountain- A boundless and unconditional gift- A source of strength and inspiration- A reminder of His care and devotion- A treasure to cherish and share

What a beautiful description of God's love! "A Never-Ending Fountain" perfectly captures the boundless, infinite, and eternal nature of His love for us.

Just as a fountain continually flows with fresh water, God's love continually pours out to us, refreshing, renewing, and revitalizing our lives. It's a love that never runs dry, never fades away, and never ceases to amaze us with its depth and richness.

May we drink deeply from the never-ending fountain of God's love, and may it overflow from our lives to touch the lives of those around us.

_Prayer:_ *Dear God, thank you for your never-ending fountain of unconditional redemptive love. Give me the peace to trust in your love.* Amen.

_**March 11:** The Strength of God's Protection_

_Scripture:_ Psalm 91:4 - He will cover you with his feathers, and under His wings you will find refuge; His faithfulness will be your shield and rampart.

_Devotion:_

God's protection is our strength and our hope.

Amen! God's protection is indeed our strength and our hope. It's a shield that guards us from harm, a refuge that shelters us from the storms of life, and a fortress that keeps us safe from the enemy's attacks.

God's protection gives us:

- Courage in the face of danger
- Peace in the midst of turmoil
- Hope in the darkness
- Strength in our weaknesses
- Assurance of His love and care

May we always seek God's protection and trust in His loving care, knowing that He is our Rock, our Savior, and our Lord.

_Prayer:_ *Dear God, thank you for your protection and refuge. Give me the grace to trust in your shield and rampart. Amen.*

## **March 12**: The joy of trust and obedience

_Scripture:_ Psalm 40:8, I delight to do your will, O God; your law is within my heart. May we too delight in trusting and obeying God, and may our lives be filled with the joy that comes from following Him.

_Devotion:_

A beautiful combination! Trust and obedience are essential components of a deepening relationship with God. When we trust God, we:
- Believe in His goodness and sovereignty
- Have faith in His promises and plans
- Rely on His wisdom and guidance
- Surrender our will to His
- Experience peace and confidence

And when we obey God, we:
- Demonstrate our love and commitment
- Show our willingness to follow His lead
- Experience the blessings of His guidance
- Grow in our faith and character
- Reflect His character to others

Trust and obedience are intertwined, as trust leads to obedience, and obedience deepens our trust. May we continue to cultivate both, trusting God's heart and obeying His leading.

_Prayer:_ *Dear God help me to trust and obey you in all circumstances. Give me the deep assurance that I am in your loving hands, and that you are guiding my life's path. Amen.*

## March 13: The Beauty of Humility

_Scripture:_ James 4:6 says, humility is the gateway to greatness, for it is the doorway to God's grace.

_Devotion:_

God beautifies you when you are humble.

What a wonderful truth! God indeed beautifies us when we are humble. Humility is a virtue that God honors and blesses.

Humility is a precious quality that opens us up to God's grace, love, and purpose. When we embrace humility, God:

- Lifts us up in His grace
- Shines His light upon us
- Clothes us with His beauty
- Fills us with His Spirit
- Uses us for His glory

May we seek to humble ourselves before God, that He may beautify us with His loveliness and use us for His purposes.

_Prayer:_ *Dear God, thank you for the spirit of humility in my life. Give me the grace to continue to be grateful and humble knowing you are the Lord of my life. Amen.*

## _March 14_: The Power of Surrender _

_Scripture:_ Romans 12:1 says I beseech you therefore, brethren, by the mercies of God, that you present your bodies a living sacrifice, holy, acceptable to God, which is your reasonable service.

_Devotion:_

The Power of Surrendering to God.

The power of surrendering to God! It's a transformative experience that can change our lives forever. Surrendering to God means:

- Letting go of our control and pride
- Submitting to His will and plans
- Trusting in His goodness and love
- Find peace and joy in His presence
- Become a living sacrifice, pleasing to Him

May we surrender our lives to God, trusting in His love and sovereignty, and experience the power and beauty of His presence in our lives.

_Prayer:_ *Dear God, thank you for your faithfulness and mercy. Give me the grace to trust in your love and strength.* Amen.

# _March 15_: The Armor of Faith_

_Scripture:_ Ephesians 6:11 says, put on the full armor of God, so that you can stand against the schemes of the devil.

## _Devotion:_

Faith is our shield and armor against the enemy's attacks.

Amen! Faith is indeed our shield and armor against the enemy's attacks.

_Our faith in God and His promises:
- Protects us from Satan's lies and deceit
- Guards us against fear and doubt
- Strengthens us for spiritual battle
- Helps us stand firm in the face of adversity
- Reminds us of God's presence and victory

Just as a shield deflects attacks, our faith deflects the enemy's attempts to discourage and defeat us. And as an armor, it covers us with God's righteousness and protection.

May we hold up the shield of faith and wear the armor of God's truth, standing strong against the enemy's schemes and living victorious in Christ.

_Prayer:_ _Dear God, thank you for protecting me from the attracts of the Satan and for the strength you give me to fight against him._ Amen

## ROSE PETALS -- 366 DAYS OF MORNING MUSINGS

**_March 16:_** _The Hope of God's Deliverance_

_Scripture:_ Psalm 124:8 says our help is in the name of the Lord, the Maker of heaven and earth.

_Devotion:_

God's deliverance is our hope and our salvation, giving us freedom and new life in Christ.

Amen! God's deliverance is indeed our hope and our salvation. God's deliverance:

- Rescues us from the grip of sin and darkness
- Frees us from the chains of fear and anxiety
- Lifts us out of the pit of despair and hopelessness
- Brings us into the light of His love and grace

In God's deliverance, we find:
- Hope in the midst of despair
- Salvation from the enemy's snare
- Peace in the midst of turmoil
- Joy in the presence of our Savior

May we trust in God's deliverance and rest in His salvation, knowing that He is our Rock, our Refuge, and our Redeemer.

_Prayer:_ *Dear God, thank you for your deliverance and redemption. Give me the grace to trust in your freedom and salvation.* Amen.

ROSE PETALS -- 366 DAYS OF MORNING MUSINGS

## _March 17_: The Strength of God's Comfort_

_Scripture:_ Psalm 46:1 says God is our refuge and strength, an ever-present help in trouble"

_Devotion:_

God's comfort is our strength and our hope.

Amen! God's comfort is indeed our strength and our hope. giving us peace and consolation in times of need. As the Bible says, God's comfort:

- Wraps us in His loving embrace
- Soothes our sorrows and calms our fears
- Lifts our spirits and renews our hope
- Strengthens us to face life's challenges
- Reminds us of His presence and love

In God's comfort, we find:
- Solace in times of sorrow
- Peace in the midst of turmoil
- Courage in the face of uncertainty
- Hope in the darkness

May we seek God's comfort and find strength in His loving presence, knowing that He is our Comforter, our Savior, and our Lord.

Prayer: _ *Dear God, thank you for your comfort and compassion. Give me the grace to trust in your peace and consolation.* Amen.

## _March 18:_ The Hope of God's Forgiveness_

_Scripture: _ 1 John 1:9 says if we confess our sins, he is faithful and just and will forgive us our sins and purify us from all unrighteousness.

_Devotion: _
God's forgiveness is our hope and our peace, giving us new life and restoration in Christ.

Amen! God's forgiveness is indeed our hope and our peace. As the Bible says, God's forgiveness:

- Cleanses us from the stain of sin
- Restores us to a right relationship with Him
- Brings us peace and tranquility
- Gives us hope for a new beginning

In God's forgiveness, we find:
- Mercy instead of judgment
- Grace instead of condemnation
- Love instead of rejection

May we seek God's forgiveness and experience His peace and hope, knowing that He is our Redeemer, our Savior, and our Lord.

_Prayer: _ *Dear God, thank you for your forgiveness and love. Give me the grace to trust in your compassion and mercy.* Amen.

## _March 19_: The Strength of God's Wisdom

_Scripture:_ James 1:5 - "If any of you lacks wisdom, you should ask God, who gives generously to all without finding fault, and it will be given to you.

_Devotion:_

God's wisdom is our strength and our guide, giving us direction and understanding in times of need.

Amen! God's wisdom is indeed our strength and our guide.

God's wisdom:
- Illuminates our path and guides our decisions
- Gives us discernment and understanding
- Helps us navigate life's challenges and trials
- Provides us with spiritual insight and perspective

In God's wisdom, we find:
- Clarity in the midst of confusion
- Direction in the face of uncertainty
- Confidence in the presence of fear
- Joy in the journey of life

May we seek God's wisdom and trust in His guidance, knowing that He is our Rock, our Refuge, and our Redeemer.

_Prayer:_ *Dear God, thank you for your wisdom and guidance. Give me the grace to trust in your direction and understanding.* Amen.

## ROSE PETALS -- 366 DAYS OF MORNING MUSINGS

_**March 20**: The Hope of God's Renewal_

_Scripture:_ 2 Corinthians 5:17 - Therefore, if anyone is in Christ, the new creation has come: The old has gone, the new is here!

_Devotion:_

God's renewal is our hope and our trust, giving us a new beginning and a fresh start.

Amen! God's renewal is indeed our hope and our trust. God's renewal:
- Restores our spirit and revitalizes our soul
- Brings new life to our weary hearts
- Refreshes our minds and revives our bodies
- Strengthens our faith and trust in Him

In God's renewal, we find:
- New beginnings and second chances
- Forgiveness and fresh starts
- Healing and restoration
- Transformation and growth
- Hope and trust in His loving care

May we seek God's renewal and trust in His loving grace, knowing that He is our Redeemer, our Savior, and our Lord.

_Prayer:_ *Dear God, thank you for your renewal and love. Give me the grace to trust in your newness and care.* Amen.

# _March 21_: The Joy of God's Faithfulness_

_Scripture:_ Psalm 20:5 says, I will rejoice in your salvation, and in the name of the Lord my God, I will set my banner high!

## _Devotion:_

God's faithfulness is our joy and our hope, giving us confidence and assurance in His love. Amen! God's faithfulness is indeed our joy and our hope.

God's faithfulness:
- Provides a foundation for our trust
- Assures us of His love and care
- Keeps His promises and covenant
- Remains steadfast and unchanging
- Offers a hope that anchors our souls

In God's faithfulness, we find:
- Comfort in times of uncertainty
- Strength in the face of adversity
- Peace that surpasses understanding
- Joy that overflows from His presence
- Hope that endures through all trials

May we rest in God's faithfulness, rejoice in His love, and trust in His sovereign care.

_Prayer:_ *Dear God, thank you for the joy of your faithfulness. Please keep me safe to face all trials in the face of adversities. Amen*

## _March 22:_ The Joy of God's Salvation_

_Scripture:_ Psalm 51:12 - Restore to me the joy of your salvation and grant me a willing spirit, that I may be sustained.

_Devotion:_

God's salvation brings us joy and new life, giving us purpose and meaning. Ask Him to show you the joy of His salvation today.

It's a joy that:
- Overflows from the heart of God
- Floods our souls with love and grace
- Lifts us up from the depths of despair
- Transforms our lives with new purpose

In God's salvation, we find:
- Redemption that sets us free from bondage
- Restoration that heals our brokenness
- Renewal that gives us a new heart and spirit

May we rejoice in God's salvation, bask in His joy, and share it with a world in need!

Prayer: _ Dear God, I come before you with grateful hearts, thankful for the joy of your salvation. You have rescued me from the depths of sin and darkness, and brought me into the light of your love. Amen

_March 23_: Rooted in Endurance_

_Scripture:_ Romans 5:3-5 - "Not only so, but we also glory in our sufferings, because we know that suffering produces perseverance; perseverance, character; and character, hope.

_Devotion:_

A tree develops deeper roots during seasons of drought.

What a beautiful analogy! That's so true. Just as a tree develops deeper roots during seasons of drought to access water deep in the earth, our faith can grow stronger and more resilient through life's challenges. This process of spiritual growth and maturation is often referred to as "being refined" or "being pruned" in the Bible.

Just as a tree's roots grow deeper and stronger during drought, our faith can:
- Develop a stronger foundation in God's Word
- Grow more resilient in the face of adversity
- Produce fruit that is more abundant and sweet

May our roots grow deep in God's love and grace, even in the midst of life's challenges!

_Prayer:_ *Dear God, thank you for the promise that suffering produces endurance. Help me trust in your strength when faced with challenges.* Amen.

## _March 24: The Power of Perseverance

_Scripture: _ Hebrews 12:1-3 - Therefore, since we are surrounded by such a great cloud of witnesses, let us throw off everything that hinders and the sin that so easily entangles. And let us run with perseverance the race marked out for us, fixing our eyes on Jesus, the pioneer and perfecter of faith.

_Devotion: _

Perseverance is not about being perfect, but about progressing in our faith. A wonderful truth! Perseverance in our faith journey is indeed about progressing, not perfection. It's about:

- Embracing our imperfections and weaknesses
- Learning from our mistakes and failures
- Growing in our understanding and trust of God
- Developing resilience and character
- Moving forward, even in the face of challenges

Perseverance is not about: - Achieving flawlessness- Never stumbling or struggling- Having all the answers- Being self-sufficient- Giving up in the face of obstacles

But rather, it's about: - Getting back up after falling - Continuing to seek God's guidance- Trusting in His sovereignty and goodness- Finding strength in His presence- Pressing on, even when the journey gets tough

_Prayer: _ *Dear God, help me to persevere in my faith, focusing on progress, not perfection. May Your grace and strength sustain me as I journey with You.* Amen.

## _March 25:_ Finding Strength in Weakness

_Scripture:_ 2 Corinthians 12:9-10 - But he said to me, 'My grace is sufficient for you, for my power is made perfect in weakness.' Therefore, I will boast all the more gladly about my weaknesses, so that Christ's power may rest on me.

_Devotion:_

God's strength is perfected in our weakness. Weaknesses and limitations are opportunities for God to showcase His power and strength. God's strength isn't diminished by our weaknesses; rather, it's magnified through them.

When we acknowledge and surrender our weaknesses, God's power fills the gaps, making us strong in Him, frees us from the pressure to be self-sufficient or perfect and reminds us that God's power is always available, even in our darkest moments.

Remember, God's strength is perfected in our weakness, making us strong in Him, not in ourselves.

_Prayer:_ *Dear God, thank you for your promise to be my strength in weakness. Help me surrender my limitations and rely on your power.* Amen.

### March 26: Hope in the Darkness

*Scripture:* Hebrews 13:5 says, God is our constant companion, never leaving us or forsaking us.

*Devotion:*

God's presence is not limited by our circumstances. Ask Him to be your light in the darkness.

What a powerful reminder! God's presence is indeed not limited by our circumstances, and that truth can bring us comfort, hope, and peace in the midst of challenging situations. This reminds us that: God's presence is our comfort in sorrow, our strength in weakness, and our hope in despair.

God's presence is not bound by physical constraints or circumstances. He is omnipresent, meaning He is always present everywhere, regardless of our situation.

God's presence is not limited by our perceptions, emotions, or understanding. He is always present, even when we're unaware of it

Remember, God's presence is not limited by our circumstances. He is always with us, always for us, and always working in us.

Prayer: *Dear God, thank you for being my light in the darkness. Help me trust in your presence and hope, even in the toughest times.* Amen.

## _March 27_: Perseverance: Fixing Our Eyes on Jesus

_Scripture:_ Hebrews 12:1-3 - Therefore, since we are surrounded by such a great cloud of witnesses, let us throw off everything that hinders and the sin that so easily entangles. And let us run with perseverance the race marked out for us, fixing our eyes on Jesus, the pioneer and perfecter of faith.

_Devotion:_

Perseverance is about fixing our eyes on Jesus and running the race of faith with endurance.

A beautiful reminder! Perseverance in our faith journey is indeed about:

- Fixing our eyes on Jesus, our ultimate goal and prize
- Running the race of faith with endurance, perseverance, and stamina
- Trusting in His presence and guidance every step of the way
- Finding strength in His Word and promises
- Pressing on, even when the journey gets tough and challenging

As the Bible says, "Let us fix our eyes on Jesus, the author and perfecter of our faith, who for the joy set before Him endured the cross, scorning its shame, and sat down at the right hand of the throne of God." (Hebrews 12:2)

_Prayer:_ *Dear God, help me to fix my eyes on Jesus and run the race of faith with endurance. May Your presence and guidance sustain me as I persevere in my journey with You.* Amen

## _March 28_: The Power of Prayer

_Scripture:_ Philippians 4:6-7 - Do not be anxious about anything, but in every situation, by prayer and petition, with thanksgiving, present your requests to God. And the peace of God, which transcends all understanding, will guard your hearts and your minds in Christ Jesus.

_Devotion:_

Prayer is a powerful weapon against anxiety and worry.

Amen to that! Prayer is indeed a powerful weapon against anxiety and worry. When we bring our concerns to God in prayer, we can experience His peace and comfort in a way that surpasses human understanding. Here's a reflection on this truth:

- In prayer, we can surrender our worries and receive God's wisdom, guidance, and strength.

- Regular prayer practice can rewire our brains to default to faith and trust in God, reducing anxiety's grip.

Remember, prayer is a mighty weapon against anxiety and worry. Take your concerns to God, and trust in His loving care and provision.

_Prayer:_ *Dear God, thank you for the promise of peace through prayer. Help me bring all my worries and concerns to you, trusting in your loving care. Amen.*

## March 29: Unshakable Hope

_Scripture:_ Hebrews 6:19 - We have this hope as an anchor for the soul, firm and secure. It enters the inner sanctuary behind the curtain.

_Devotion:_

Hope in God is the anchor that keeps us grounded in life's storms.

What a beautiful metaphor! Hope in God is indeed the anchor that keeps us grounded, stable, and secure in the midst of life's storms. Just as an anchor holds a ship firmly in place, hope in God anchors our souls, providing a sense of calm and assurance. Here's a reflection on this truth:

- It keeps us grounded in God's faithfulness and love, even when circumstances seem uncertain or chaotic.
- This anchor of hope holds us fast, preventing us from drifting away from God's truth and promises.
- It provides a sense of security and stability, allowing us to weather life's challenges with confidence.

May your hope in Him be unshakable!

Prayer: _Dear God, thank you for the hope that anchors my soul. Help me hold onto your promises and trust in your presence, even in uncertain times._ Amen.

# ROSE PETALS -- 366 DAYS OF MORNING MUSINGS

## _March 30_: Fruitful Endurance

_Scripture:_ James 1:12 - Blessed is the one who perseveres under trial because, having stood the test, that person will receive the crown of life that the Lord has promised to those who love him.

_Devotion:_

Endurance produces spiritual fruit and a deeper relationship with God.

A beautiful truth! Endurance indeed produces spiritual fruit, making our lives more fruitful and meaningful. Just as a tree bears fruit after weathering the seasons, our lives bear spiritual fruit when we persevere through life's challenges. Here's a reflection on this truth:

- Endurance helps us develop a deeper root system of faith, anchoring us in God's love and grace.
- Endurance refines our character, making us more like Christ and equipping us for greater ministry and impact.
- It teaches us to rely on God's strength, not our own, and to trust in His sovereignty and goodness.

Remember, endurance is not just about persevering; it's about producing spiritual fruit that brings joy, peace, and glory to God!

May your endurance produce abundant spiritual fruit!

Prayer: _Dear God, thank you for the promise of a crown of life through endurance. Help me trust in your goodness and love, even in difficult times._ Amen

## _March 31_: Grace for the Journey

_Scripture:_ Psalm 84:11 For the Lord God is a sun and shield; the Lord bestows favor and honor; no good thing does He withhold from those who walk uprightly.

_Devotion:_

God's grace is sufficient for our journey, providing all we need to walk with Him.

A beautiful truth! God's grace is indeed sufficient for our journey, providing us with the strength, guidance, and wisdom we need to navigate life's ups and downs. Here's a reflection on this truth:

- God's grace is sufficient for our weaknesses, shortcomings, and failures (2 Corinthians 12:9).
- God's grace is a never-ending supply that we can draw upon daily
- God's grace is our constant companion, guiding us, comforting us, and empowering us (John 16:13).

Remember, God's grace is sufficient for our journey, and it's always available to us. Let's draw upon His grace daily, trusting in His goodness and love. May your heart be filled with joy and gratitude as you walk in His grace!

_Prayer:_ *Dear God, thank you for your abundant grace and guidance. Help me trust in your goodness and provision for my journey.* Amen.

# ROSE PETALS -- 366 DAYS OF MORNING MUSINGS

*As March comes to a close, we reflect on the journey of the past month. We've navigated the transition from winter to spring, symbolizing growth, renewal, and transformation.*

*March has taught us to embrace change, to find strength in uncertainty, and to persevere through challenges. We've celebrated milestones, like International Women's Day, and honored the resilience and contributions of women worldwide.*

*As we bid farewell to March, we carry forward the lessons learned:*

- *The power of transformation and growth*
- *The importance of resilience and adaptability*
- *The value of celebrating diversity and inclusivity*
- *The need to stay curious and keep learning*

*May the momentum of march propel us into April with renewed energy, hope, and determination. may we continue to grow, to learn, and to thrive, making the most of every opportunity that comes our way.*

# APRIL 1-30

1. Rooted in God's Love
2. A Heart of Courage
3. God's Masterpiece
4. Surrender and Trust
5. Abiding in Christ
6. Fearless Trust
7. Unwavering Faith
8. Surrendered Life
9. God's Guiding Hand
10. Unshakeable Confidence
11. Fruitful Obedience
12. God's Faithfulness
13. God's Peaceful Refuge
14. Surrendering Our Fears
15. God's Transforming Power
16. God's Guidance in Uncertainty
17. God's Strength in Weakness
18. God's Peace in Turbulent Times
19. God's Faithfulness in Our Failures
20. God's Love in the Midst of Fear
21. God's Love for the Brokenhearted
22. The Hope of Eternal Life
23. The Freedom of Forgiveness
24. The Hope of Heaven
25. The Love of God's Presence
26. The Peace of God's Protection
27. The Hope of God's Promises
28. The Grace of God's Mercy
29. The Hope of God's Plans
30. The Peace of God's Love

## _April 1_: Rooted in God's Love

_Scripture:_ John 3:1 says, being rooted in God's love gives us a sense of identity, belonging, and purpose.

_Devotion:_

Being rooted in God's love is the foundation of our faith, empowering us to experience His fullness and love others with His grace.

A wonderful truth! Being rooted in God's love is indeed the foundation of our faith, providing a solid base for our spiritual growth and development. Here's a reflection on this truth:

- God's love is the soil in which our faith takes root and flourishes (Ephesians 3:17-19).

- It's the foundation of our spiritual strength, enabling us to weather life's storms (Psalm 31:3).

- Being rooted in God's love helps us to trust His sovereignty, goodness, and grace (Psalm 138:8).

Remember, being rooted in God's love is the foundation of our faith, and it's a truth that can transform our lives and relationships. Also, remember that God's love is not just a feeling, but a reality that transforms our lives. May your heart be filled with His love and grace!

Prayer: _ Dear God, help me to be rooted and grounded in Your love. May it be the foundation of my faith and the source of my strength. Amen

## April 2: A Heart of Courage

_Scripture:_ Joshua 1:9 - Be strong and courageous. Do not be afraid; do not be discouraged, for the Lord your God will be with you wherever you go.

_Devotion:_

God calls us to live with courage and faith, trusting in His presence and guidance.

A beautiful summary! That's the essence of living with courage and faith. Trusting in God's presence and guidance is the foundation of a life that honors Him. Here's a reflection to ponder:

Trusting in God's presence and guidance means:
- Believing He is always with me (Isaiah 43:2)
- Relying on His strength in my weaknesses (2 Corinthians 12:9)
- Surrendering my fears and doubts to His peace and wisdom (Philippians 4:6-7)

May we choose to trust in God's presence and guidance today, living with courage and faith in all we do."

_Prayer:_ Dear God, thank you for your presence and guidance. Help me be strong and courageous, trusting in your faithfulness and love. Amen.

## _April 3_: God's Masterpiece

_Scripture:_ Ephesians 2:10 - For we are his workmanship, created in Christ Jesus for good works, which God prepared beforehand, that we should walk in them.

_Devotion:_

You are God's masterpiece, created for a purpose and empowered by His grace.

What a wonderful truth! You are indeed God's masterpiece, created with love and care. Here's a reflection to ponder. God's masterpiece:

- Means you are a unique and precious work of art (Ephesians 2:10)
- Created with purpose and intention (Psalm 138:8)
- Loved and valued beyond measure (John 3:16)
- Shaped and molded by God's hands (Isaiah 64:8)

Remember, you are a masterpiece, crafted by the Divine Artist. You are a work of art, worthy of love, respect, and admiration.

May this truth inspire you to see yourself and others in a new light!"

_Prayer:_ *Dear God, thank you for creating me in Christ Jesus. Help me embrace my identity as your masterpiece and live out my faith with confidence and joy.* Amen.

## _April 4_: Surrender and Trust

_Scripture:_ Proverbs 3:5-6 - Trust in the Lord with all your heart, and do not lean on your own understanding. In all your ways acknowledge him, and he will make straight your paths.

_Devotion:_

Surrendering our lives to God requires trust and faith, but it's the only way to experience true freedom and guidance.

A beautiful truth! Surrendering our lives to God indeed requires trust and faith, and it's a journey that unfolds day by day. Here's a reflection to ponder. Surrendering our lives to God means:

- Trusting in His goodness and love (Psalm 138:8)
- Having faith in His plans and purposes (Jeremiah 29:11)
- Letting go of control and surrendering to His will (Matthew 16:24)
- Trusting that He has our best interests at heart (Romans 8:28)

Surrender is not a one-time event but a daily choice to trust and follow God. May we choose to surrender our lives to Him, trusting in His love and goodness.

_Prayer:_ *Dear God, help me trust in you with all my heart, surrendering my fears and doubts. Make straight my paths and guide me in your truth.* Amen.

## **April 5:** Abiding in Christ

*Scripture:* John 15:4-5 - Abide in me, and I in you. As the branch cannot bear fruit by itself, unless it abides in the vine, neither can you, unless you abide in me.

*Devotion:*

Abiding in Christ is essential for spiritual growth and fruitfulness. A beautiful truth! Abiding in Christ is indeed a vital concept in Christianity, emphasized by Jesus Himself.

Abiding in Christ means remaining in a state of intimacy and communion with Him, deepening our relationship, and relying on His guidance and strength. It's a continual process of surrender, trust, and dependence on Him, which leads to spiritual growth, fruitfulness, and a life that reflects His character and love. Some ways to abide in Christ include:

- Spending quality time with Him in prayer and meditation
- Studying and applying His Word
- Seeking His guidance and wisdom
- Trusting in His sovereignty and goodness
- Surrendering our will to His

May we continue to abide in His love and grace!

*Prayer:* *Dear God, help me abide in you, trusting in your presence and guidance, and bearing fruit for your glory.* Amen.

## _April: 6.     Fearless Trust

_Scripture:_ Psalm 56:3-4 - When I am afraid, I put my trust in you. In God, whose word I praise, in God I trust; I shall not be afraid. What can flesh do to me?

### _Devotion:_

Trusting God fearlessly requires surrendering our fears, worries, and doubts, and choosing to have faith in His goodness, sovereignty, and love. It means trusting that He is always with us, always for us, and always working everything out for our good, even when we can't see or understand.

When we trust God fearlessly, we can:
- Face challenges with courage
- Rest in His peace
- Live with purpose and hope
- Experience His presence and guidance
- Discover His strength in our weakness

May we continue to trust God fearlessly, surrendering our fears and doubts, and choosing to have faith in His goodness and love!

_Prayer:_ *Dear God, thank you for being my rock and refuge. Help me trust you more than my fears and anxieties.* Amen.

## _April: 7_  Unwavering Faith

_Scripture:_ Hebrews 11:6 - And without faith it is impossible to please God.

_Devotion:_

Unwavering faith pleases God and opens doors to His promises.

That's a beautiful truth! Faith is a powerful force that can bring us closer to God and unlock the doors to His promises.

Having unwavering faith means trusting in God's goodness, sovereignty, and love, even when we can't see the way ahead. It means believing in His promises and holding onto them, even when faced with challenges and doubts.

When we have faith, we open ourselves up to God's blessings, guidance, and protection. We can trust that He is working everything out for our good, even when we can't understand what's happening.

Remember, faith is not about having all the answers or being perfect. It's about trusting in God's character and His love for us.

_Prayer:_ *Dear God, thank you for the gift of faith. Help me trust in your goodness and love, even when I can't see the way ahead.* Amen.

## _April: 8 Surrendered Life

_Scripture:_ Romans 12:1-2 - Therefore, I urge you, brothers and sisters, in view of God's mercy, to offer your bodies as a living sacrifice, holy and pleasing to God—this is your true and proper worship. Do not conform to the pattern of this world, but be transformed by the renewing of your mind. Then you will be able to test and approve what God's will is—his good, pleasing and perfect will.

_Devotion:_

A surrendered life is a transformative life, pleasing to God and impactful in the world.

What a powerful and profound statement! Surrendering can mean letting go of control, ego, and our own limitations, allowing us to tap into a deeper sense of purpose, inner peace, and connection to something greater than ourselves, who is the Almighty God.

When we surrender, we open ourselves to new possibilities, experiences, and growth. We become more receptive to God's word, more resilient in the face of challenges, and more grateful for the present moment.

Remember, surrender is not about giving up or losing control; it's about embracing the present and aligning with our true nature.

_Prayer:_ *Dear God, thank you for your mercy and grace. Help me surrender my life to you, that I may be transformed and pleasing to you.*

# ROSE PETALS -- 366 DAYS OF MORNING MUSINGS

## _April: 9    God's Guiding Hand

_Scripture:_ Psalm 73:24 - Thou shalt guide me with thy counsel, and afterward receive me to glory.

### _Devotion:_

God's guiding hand is always upon us, leading us through life's journey.

A beautiful reminder! The concept of God's guiding hand in our lives, is a comforting idea that brings hope and reassurance to many people. It suggests that a higher power is actively involved in our lives, guiding us through life's challenges and triumphs.

This belief can be a source of strength, comfort, and inspiration, helping us navigate life's ups and downs with faith and confidence. It reminds us that we're not alone, and that a loving and divine presence is always with us, guiding us towards our highest potential.

Remember, faith is a personal journey, and this belief can bring people closer to their spiritual path. Also, remember that God's guidance is not a distant concept, but a present reality that shapes our decisions and steps.

May His hand guide you today and always!

_Prayer:_ *Dear God, thank you for your presence and guidance in my life. Hold me by my right hand and lead me according to your will. Amen.*

## April: 10  Unshakeable Confidence

_Scripture:_ Psalm 27:13-14 - I remain confident of this: I will see the goodness of the Lord in the land of the living. Wait for the Lord; be strong and take heart and wait for the Lord."

_Devotion:_

Unshakeable confidence in God's goodness and love anchors our souls in every storm.

A beautiful reminder! That unshakeable confidence in God's goodness and love is a powerful anchor for our souls, providing stability and hope in the midst of life's challenges.

With unshakeable confidence in God's goodness and love, we can:
- Face challenges with courage and faith
- Trust in God's sovereignty and provision
- Experience peace and calm in the midst of turmoil
- Find hope and strength in God's promises

Remember, God's love and goodness are unshakable, and His anchor holds fast in every storm.

May your confidence in Him be unwavering today!

_Prayer:_ *Dear God, thank you for your unfailing love and goodness. Help me wait for you with confidence and courage, knowing that you are always with me.* Amen.

## April: 11  Fruitful Obedience

_Scripture:_ John 14:15 Jesus said, if you love me, keep my commands.

_Devotion:_

Fruitful obedience to God's Word is a reflection of our love for Him and leads to a deeper relationship with Him.

A beautiful truth! Fruitful obedience to God's Word is indeed a reflection of our love for Him. When we obey God's Word, we demonstrate our love and devotion to Him. Obedience is not just about following rules or commands, but about surrendering our will to His and living out our faith in practical ways.

Fruitful obedience bears witness to:
- Our desire to please God and live according to His plans
- Our trust in His goodness and wisdom
- Our willingness to surrender our own desires and inclinations
- Our love for God and our desire to honor Him

Remember, fruitful obedience is not about earning God's love but about living out our love for Him. Also, remember that fruitful obedience is not about earning God's love, but about living in harmony with His will and experiencing the joy of His presence. May your obedience be fruitful and pleasing to Him!

_Prayer:_ *Dear God, thank you for your Word that guides me. Help me obey your teachings with love and surrender, that I may experience your presence and love in my life.* Amen.

## REFLECTION

Ask God to help you obey His teachings with joy and surrender.

_Reflection Prompt:_ Write about a time when obeying God's Word was challenging, but ultimately led to growth and fruitfulness in your life.

## _April: 12_ God's Faithfulness

_Scripture:_ Lamentations 3:22-23 - Because of the Lord's great love we are not consumed, for his compassions never fail. They are new every morning; great is your faithfulness.

_Devotion:_

God's faithfulness is a constant anchor in our lives, reminding us of His love and care.

What a beautiful reminder! God's faithfulness is indeed a steady and reliable anchor that provides comfort, hope, and strength in the midst of life's challenges and uncertainties. It's a reminder that God's love and care for us are unshakable and unwavering, and that He is always with us, guiding and supporting us through every storm and every calm.

Also, remember that God's faithfulness is not based on our performance, but on His character and promises. May His faithfulness be your rock and comfort today!

May this truth bring you peace and inspiration today!

_Prayer:_ *Dear God, thank you for your faithfulness that never ends. Help me rely on your compassion and love, knowing that you are always with me.* Amen.

## _April: 13    God's Peaceful Refuge

_Scripture:_ Psalm 91:2 says, I will say of the Lord, He is my refuge and my fortress: my God; in him will I trust.

_Devotion:_

God's presence is our refuge and fortress, a peaceful sanctuary from life's storms.

What a powerful reminder! God's presence is indeed our refuge and fortress, a place of safety, protection, and peace. Just as a refuge provides shelter from the storms of life, God's presence shields us from the temptations and trials that we face.

The image of a fortress also reminds us of God's strength and power, a bulwark against the forces of evil and darkness. In Him, we find our security, our comfort, and our hope.

Take a moment to reflect on this truth: God's presence is your refuge and fortress. Say it out loud, and let the assurance of His love and protection fill your heart!

Also, remember that God's refuge is not just a temporary escape, but a permanent dwelling place of peace and security in Him. May His presence be your refuge!

_Prayer:_ *Dear God, thank you for being my refuge and fortress. Help me dwell in your presence and trust in your protection, knowing that you are my rock and salvation. Amen.*

## _April: 14_  Surrendering Our Fears

_Scripture:_ Psalm 34:4 says I sought the Lord, and He answered me and delivered me from all my fears.

_Devotion:_

Surrendering our fears to God allows us to experience His deliverance and peace.

When we surrender our fears to God, we're able to:
- Let go of anxiety and worry
- Trust in His sovereignty and goodness
- Find comfort in His promises and faithfulness
- Live with freedom and confidence, knowing God is in control
- Deepen our relationship with Him, abiding in His love and grace

Remember, surrendering our fears to God is a process, and it may take time. But with each step, we can trust that He is faithful to meet us, guide us, and perfect everything that concerns us (Psalm 138:8). Also, remember that surrender is not a one-time event, but a daily choice to trust God's sovereignty and love.

May your heart be free from fear and filled with His peace!

_Prayer:_ *Dear God, thank you for being my deliverer and refuge. Help me surrender my fears to you, that I may experience your peace and radiate your joy.* Amen.

### April: 15    God's Transforming Power

_Scripture:_ 2 Corinthians 5:17 - Therefore, if anyone is in Christ, the new creation has come: The old has gone, the new is here!

_Devotion:_
God's transforming power creates a new you, renewing your mind, heart, and life.

A beautiful and uplifting sentiment! This reminds me of the Christian belief in the transformative power of faith and spiritual growth. The idea that God's love and grace can renew and transform us, changing us from the inside out, is a powerful message of hope and redemption. It's a reminder that we don't have to be bound by our past or our current struggles, but that we can be made new and live a life of purpose and meaning.

Also, remember that transformation is a lifelong process, and God's grace is sufficient for each step of the journey.

May your life be a testimony to His transforming power!

_Prayer:_ *Dear God, thank you for your transforming power that makes me new in Christ. Help me surrender to your renewal, that I may reflect your glory and grace.* Amen.

## _April:_ 16 God's Guidance in Uncertainty

_Scripture:_ 1 Corinthians 14:33 For God is not *the author* of [a]confusion but of peace, as in all the churches of the saints.

### _Devotion:_

God's guidance is available in times of uncertainty, leading us on the right path.

A comforting reminder! God's guidance is indeed always available, especially in times of uncertainty. When we face unknowns or uncertain paths ahead, we can trust that God is always guiding us. Here are some ways He guides us:

- Through His Word: The Bible
- Through prayer and listening to the Holy Spirit
- Through wise counsel from trusted friends, family, or mentors
- Through circumstances and events that shape our journey
- Through the peace and prompting in our hearts

Remember, God's guidance is not always a loud voice, but often a gentle whisper, a nudge, or a sense of peace. May we seek to listen and follow His guidance with confidence and trust! Also, remember that God's guidance is not a one-time answer, but a continuous process of seeking His will and trust in His sovereignty.

_Prayer:_ *Dear God, thank you for your guidance and counsel. Help me seek your loving eye on me, that I may trust your direction and follow your path.* Amen

## REFLECTION

Ask God to help you remain in His love.

_Reflection Prompt:_ Write about a time when you felt God's love abundant in your life, and how it empowered you to obey His commands.

## _April: 17 God's Strength in Weakness

_Scripture:_ 2 Corinthians 12:9 say but he said to me, 'My grace is sufficient for you, for my power is made perfect in weakness.' Therefore, I will boast all the more gladly about my weaknesses, so that Christ's power may rest on me.

### _Devotion:_

God's strength is perfected in our weaknesses, making us reliant on His grace and power.

A beautiful reminder! Yes, God's strength is indeed perfected in our weaknesses. When we acknowledge our limitations and weaknesses, God's strength and grace can take over, and His power is made perfect in us.

May we embrace our weaknesses as opportunities for God's strength to shine through!

Also, remember that God's strength is not based on our abilities, but on His power that works through our weaknesses.

May your heart be filled with His grace and strength!

_Prayer:_ *Dear God, thank you for your grace that is sufficient for me. Help me embrace my weaknesses, that I may experience your strength and power in my life.* Amen.

## _April: 18 God's Peace in Turbulent Times

_Scripture:_ Isaiah 26:3-4 - You will keep in perfect peace those whose minds are steadfast, because they trust in you. Trust in the Lord forever, for the Lord, the Lord himself, is the Rock eternal.

_Devotion:_

God's peace is a steady anchor in turbulent times, available to those who trust in Him.

What a beautiful and comforting thought! "God's peace is a steady anchor in turbulent times" is a wonderful reminder that even in the midst of chaos and uncertainty, there is a constant and unshakable peace that can be found in faith. This phrase echoes the words of Hebrews 6:19, which says, "We have this hope as an anchor for the soul, firm and secure." May this truth bring comfort and strength to all who need it today!

Also, remember that God's peace is not the absence of storms, but the presence of God in the midst of them.

May your heart be filled with His peace and trust!

_Prayer:_ *Dear God, thank you for your peace that surpasses understanding. Help me fix my mind on you, that I may experience your peace and trust in your sovereignty. Amen.*

## April: 19.  God's Faithfulness in Our Failures

*Scripture:* 2 Timothy 2:13 says, if we are faithless, He remains faithful—for He cannot deny Himself.

*Devotion:*

God's faithfulness is evident even in our failures, using them to teach us valuable lessons and draw us closer to Him.

Amen to that! What a powerful reminder that God's faithfulness is not dependent on our successes or failures, but on His unchanging character. His love and faithfulness are not earned by our achievements, but are freely given to us by grace.

As the Bible says in Even in our failures, God's faithfulness is a constant reminder that He is always with us, always loves us, and is always working for our good. What a comforting truth!

Also, remember that God's faithfulness is not based on our performance, but on His character and love for us.

May your heart be filled with His grace and faithfulness!

*Prayer:* *Dear God, thank you for your faithfulness that never fails. Help me see your hand in my struggles, that I may learn from them and grow in my relationship with you. Amen.*

# ROSE PETALS -- 366 DAYS OF MORNING MUSINGS

## _April: 20_ God's Love in the Midst of Fear

_Scripture:_ 1 John 4:18-19 - There is no fear in love, but perfect love casts out fear because fear has to do with punishment. The one who fears is not made perfect in love. We love because He first loved us.

_Devotion:_

God's love is the antidote to fear, casting it out and replacing it with His perfect love.

So true! God's love is the perfect antidote to fear, anxiety, and doubt. When we experience His love and acceptance, it drives out fear and fills us with peace, courage, and confidence.

God's love is a powerful balm that heals our emotional wounds, calms our fears, and sets us free to live with joy, hope, and faith. When we rest in His love, we can face any challenge or uncertainty with courage and trust.

What a wonderful truth to hold onto! Also, remember that God's love is not based on our performance, but on His character and grace.

May your heart be filled with His love and peace!

_Prayer:_ *Dear God, thank you for your perfect love that casts out fear. Help me experience your love in the midst of uncertainty, that I may trust in your goodness and sovereignty.* Amen

# ROSE PETALS -- 366 DAYS OF MORNING MUSINGS

**April: 21.** God's Love for the Brokenhearted

*Scripture:* Psalm 34:18 - The Lord is near to the brokenhearted and saves the crushed in spirit.

*Devotion:*

God's love is especially close to those who are brokenhearted, offering comfort and healing.

A precious truth! God's love is indeed especially close to those who are brokenhearted, offering:

- Comfort in their sorrow and pain
- Healing for their emotional and spiritual wounds
- Hope in their darkness and despair
- Guidance through their struggles and challenges
- Assurance of His presence and care

As the Bible says, "The Lord is close to the brokenhearted and saves the crushed in spirit." (Psalm 34:18)

God's love is a:
- Safe haven for the hurting
- Gentle touch for the wounded
- Soft whisper for the sorrowful
- Strong embrace for the broken
- Enduring presence for the struggling

*Prayer:* *Dear God Thank You for Your love and comfort in our brokenness. Help me to trust in Your presence and care, especially in my darkest moments. Amen.*

## April: 22    The Hope of Eternal Life

_Scripture:_ John 3:16 - For God so loved the world that he gave his one and only Son, that whoever believes in him shall not perish but have eternal life.

_Devotion:_

The hope of eternal life is a powerful anchor for our souls, giving us purpose and meaning in this life.

What a beautiful and profound statement! The idea of eternal life has been a source of comfort, hope, and inspiration for many people across cultures and centuries. It suggests that our lives have a deeper purpose and meaning that transcends our physical existence.

The concept of eternal life can be interpreted in many ways, depending on one's beliefs, values, and worldview. Some people believe in an afterlife, where the soul continues to exist in a spiritual realm. Others believe in reincarnation, where the soul is reborn into a new life.

Regardless of the specific beliefs, the hope of eternal life can bring a sense of peace, comfort, and significance to our lives. It can inspire us to live with purpose, to cherish every moment, and to cultivate a sense of connection with something greater than ourselves. Also, remember that eternal life is not just a future destination, but a present reality that transforms our lives.

Prayer: _ *Dear God, thank you for the gift of eternal life through Jesus Christ. Help me live with eternity in mind, that I may prioritize what truly matters and share your love with others.* Amen

## REFLECTION

Ask God to help you grasp the depth of His love and the promise of eternal life.

_Reflection Prompt:_ Write about what eternal life means to you and how it impacts your daily life.

### _April: 23     The Freedom of Forgiveness

_Scripture: _ Matthew 6:14-15 - For if you forgive other people when they sin against you, your heavenly Father will also forgive you. But if you refuse to forgive others, your Father will not forgive you.

_Devotion: _

Forgiveness is a powerful tool that sets us free from the bondage of bitterness and resentment.

What a beautiful and profound statement! Forgiveness is indeed a powerful tool that can liberate us from the emotional burdens and negative energies that hold us back. When we choose to forgive, we release ourselves from the shackles of resentment, anger, and hurt, and create space for healing, growth, and renewal.

Forgiveness doesn't mean forgetting or condoning, but rather releasing the negative emotions associated with a past hurt or trauma. It's a process that can be challenging, but ultimately transformative, allowing us to move forward with greater peace, compassion, and understanding. As the saying goes, "Forgiveness is the key to unlocking the door to inner peace."

Also, remember that forgiveness is not a feeling, but a choice to release the debt of others and trust God's justice. May your heart be filled with His freedom and peace!

_Prayer:_ *Dear God, thank you for your forgiveness and grace. Help me extend that same forgiveness to others, that I may experience your freedom and joy.* Amen.

## REFLECTION

Ask God to help you forgive those who have hurt you and experience His freedom.

_Reflection Prompt:_ Write about a time when you struggled with forgiveness, and how God helped you overcome it.

## April: 24 The Hope of Heaven

_Scripture:_ Revelation 21:4 - He will wipe away every tear from their eyes, and death shall be no more, neither shall there be mourning, nor crying, nor pain anymore, for the former things have passed away.

_Devotion:_

The hope of heaven is a powerful anchor for our souls, reminding us that our present struggles are temporary and eternal joy awaits us.

What a wonderful and uplifting sentiment! The hope of heaven can indeed be a powerful anchor for our souls, providing comfort, strength, and guidance in times of uncertainty and darkness.

The idea of a heavenly paradise, where love, joy, and peace reign supreme, can give us a sense of purpose and meaning, and help us navigate life's challenges with grace and resilience. It can also inspire us to live with greater intention, compassion, and kindness, as we strive to create a little bit of heaven right here on earth.

The hope of heaven can be a steady and reassuring presence in our lives, reminding us that we are not alone, and that a brighter future awaits us. Also, remember that heaven is not just a destination, but a present reality that transforms our lives.

_Prayer:_ *Dear God, thank you for the hope of heaven. Help me keep my eyes fixed on eternity, that I may live with purpose and joy, knowing that you are preparing a glorious home for me.* Amen.

## REFLECTION

Ask God to help you fix your eyes on heaven and live with eternity in mind.

_Reflection Prompt:_ Write about what heaven means to you and how it impacts your daily life.

**_April 25_**: The Love of God's Presence

_Scripture:_ Psalm 23:4, says, Yea, though I walk through the valley of the shadow of death, I will fear no evil: for thou art with me; thy rod and thy staff they comfort me.

_Devotion:_

God's presence gives us love and comfort, surrounding us with His love.

What a beautiful truth! God's presence is indeed a source of unconditional love and comfort, enveloping us in a sense of peace and security. When we feel God's presence, we know that we are not alone, and that we are loved beyond measure.

As God's presence is like a warm embrace, wrapping us in love, race, and mercy. It's a reminder that we are cherished, valued, and deeply loved, not just for who we are, but for whose we are – beloved children of God.

In His presence, we find comfort in times of sorrow, strength in times of weakness, and hope in times of uncertainty. We are surrounded by His love, which casts out fear, anxiety, and doubt, and fills us with joy, peace, and confidence.

As you reflect on God's presence in your life, what does it mean to you to be surrounded by His love? How does it impact your thoughts, feelings, and actions?

_Prayer:_ *Dear God, thank you for your loving presence. Give me the grace to feel your love today.* Amen.

## REFLECTION

Ask Him to show you His presence today.

_Reflection Prompt:_ Write down ways you can experience God's presence today.

## ROSE PETALS -- 366 DAYS OF MORNING MUSINGS

_**April 26**: The Peace of God's Protection_

_Scripture:_ Psalm 91:4 - He will cover you with his feathers, and under his wings you will find refuge; his faithfulness will be your shield and rampart.

_Devotion:_

God's protection is our peace and refuge, shielding us from harm.

What a beautiful and comforting sentiment! Indeed, many people find solace in their faith and believe that God's protection provides a sense of peace and refuge in times of uncertainty or hardship. This belief can bring comfort, hope, and strength to navigate life's challenges. May this thought bring you peace and inspiration today!

Here are some additional thoughts related to God's protection and peace:

- "God is our refuge and strength, an ever-present help in trouble." (Psalm 46:1)
- "The Lord will keep you from all harm—he will watch over your life." (Psalm 121:7)
- "Cast your cares on the Lord and he will sustain you; he will never let the righteous be shaken." (Psalm 55:22)

I hope these verses bring you additional comfort and reassurance!

_Prayer:_ *Dear God, thank you for your protection and peace. Give me the grace to trust in your care.* Amen.

*April 27*: The Hope of God's Promises

_Scripture:_ Hebrews 10:23 - Let us hold fast the confession of our hope without wavering, for he who promised is faithful.

_Devotion:_

God's promises give us hope and confidence, assuring us of His love. Amen to that! God's promises are a source of hope and confidence for many people. They provide a sense of assurance and faith, reminding us that God is always with us and has a plan for our lives. Here are some additional thoughts:

- "For I know the plans I have for you," declares the Lord, "plans to prosper you and not harm you, plans to give you hope and a future." (Jeremiah 29:11)
- "God is faithful, who has called you into fellowship with his Son, Jesus Christ our Lord." (1 Corinthians 1:9)
- "Let us hold unswervingly to the hope we profess, for he who promised is faithful." (Hebrews 10:23)

Remembering God's promises can bring us comfort, strength, and courage in our daily lives. If you have a favorite promise or verse that brings you hope and confidence, feel free to share it!

_Prayer:_ *Dear God, thank you for your promises that give me hope and confidence. Your word is a lamp to my feet and a light to my path. Please help me to trust in your faithfulness and to apply your truths to my life. Amen.*

_April 28_: The Grace of God's Mercy_

_Scripture:_ Psalm 103:8-10 - The Lord is compassionate and gracious, slow to anger and abounding in love. He will not always accuse, nor will he harbor his anger forever; he does not treat us as our sins deserve or repay us according to our iniquities.

_Devotion:_

God's mercy is our grace and forgiveness, giving us new life in Him.

A beautiful and profound statement! Indeed, many people believe that God's mercy is a source of grace and forgiveness, offering a chance for redemption and new beginnings. This concept is central to many religious and spiritual traditions, and is often a source of comfort, hope, and inspiration for those seeking guidance and peace.

May this message bring blessings and peace to you and all who reflect on it!

_Prayer:_ *Dear God, thank you for your mercy and grace.* I come before you with a humble heart, grateful for your mercy and forgiveness. Thank you for loving me unconditionally and for sending your Son to die on the cross for my sins.

Thank you for your faithfulness and steadfast love. May I always find refuge in your mercy and grace. Amen.

**April 29**: The Hope of God's Plans

_Scripture:_ Jeremiah 29:11 - For I know the plans I have for you," declares the Lord, "plans to prosper you and not harm you, plans to give you hope and a future."

_Devotion:_

God's plans are our hope and future, giving us confidence in His love.

Amen! That's a beautiful summary! God's plans are the foundation of our hope and future, and they are rooted in His love for us. He wants to give us a hope and a future. Knowing that God has good plans for us gives us confidence in His love and care, even when we can't see what's ahead.

Here's a related verse that encourages me:

"And we know that in all things God works for the good of those who love him, who have been called according to his purpose." - Romans 8:28

May the confidence of God's love and plans guide and encourage you and bring you comfort and inspiration today!

_Prayer:_ *Dear God, thank you for your plans to prosper me, not to harm me. Thank you for giving me hope and a future. Help me to trust in your love and care, even when I can't see what's ahead. Give me confidence in your plans, and guide me according to your purpose. May your love and grace surround me today and always.* Amen.

_April 30: The Peace of God's Love_

_Scripture:_ Colossians 3:14 - And above all this put on love, which binds everything together in perfect harmony.

_Devotion:_

God's love is our peace and harmony, binding everything together.

What a beautiful and uplifting sentiment! You're absolutely right. The love and grace of a higher power can bring people together and provide a sense of peace and harmony, even in the midst of challenges and difficulties. This belief can be a powerful source of comfort, strength, and inspiration for many people.

Just as a symphony consists of diverse notes and melodies that come together to create beautiful music, God's love harmonizes our unique experiences, perspectives, and talents to create a masterpiece of unity and peace. May we celebrate and embrace our differences, just as a conductor celebrates the distinct sounds of each instrument, knowing that together, they create something truly magnificent.

_Prayer:_ *Dear God, thank you for your love that binds us together in peace and harmony. Just as a river flows smoothly when its currents are in harmony, may our lives flow smoothly when our hearts are in harmony with yours. Help us to celebrate our differences and to use our unique gifts and talents to create a beautiful symphony of love and unity. May your love be the melody that fills our hearts and the rhythm that guides our steps. Amen.*

# ROSE PETALS -- 366 DAYS OF MORNING MUSINGS

As April comes to a close, we reflect on the themes that guided us throughout the month: hope, freedom, peace, faithfulness, love, and guidance.

May the hope that bloomed in our hearts continue to inspire us to dream big and work towards a brighter future. May the freedom we've experienced empower us to break free from limitations and soar to new heights.

May the peace that settled in our souls remain a constant presence, guiding us through life's challenges. May our faithfulness to ourselves, others, and our values remain unwavering.

May the love that filled our lives continue to nurture our spirits and connect us with those around us. And may the guidance we've received

from within and from others remain a steady force, illuminating our path forward.

As we step into a new month, may these themes remain a foundation for growth, joy, and fulfillment.

May we carry the light of hope, freedom, peace, faithfulness, love, and guidance with us always, sharing it with the world and making a positive impact on all we meet.

# MAY 1-31

1. Humility: The Key to Spiritual Growth
2. Humility: The Key to God's Strength
3. Humility: The Key to Fruitful Service
4. Humility: The Key to Lasting Legacy
5. Humility: The Key to God's Wisdom
6. Humility: The Key to Divine Guidance
7. Humility: The Key to God's Presence
8. Humility: The Key to Meaningful Relationships
9. Humility: The Key to Lasting Relationships
10. Humility: The Key to God's Blessings
11. Humility in Marriage
12. Humility: The Key to Effective Service
13. Humility: The Root of True Greatness
14. Humility: The Key to True Greatness
15. Humility: The Path to Intimacy with God
16. Humility: The Key to answered Prayer
17. Humility: The Path to Spiritual Growth
18. Humility: The Key to Unity
19. Humility: The Key to Spiritual Freedom
20. Humility: The Key to Effective Prayer
21. Humility: The Key to Hearing God's Voice
22. Humility: The Key to Wisdom
23. Humility: The Key to Servant Leadership
24. Humility: The Path to Spiritual Maturity
25. Humility: The Path to True Wisdom
26. Humility: The Heart of a Servant
27. Humility: The Foundation of Prayer
28. Humility: The Key to Learning
29. Humility: The Path to True Greatness
30. Humility: The Antidote to Pride

## _May 1_: Humility: The Key to Spiritual Growth

_Scripture:_ 2 Peter 3:18 - Grow in the grace and knowledge of our Lord and Savior Jesus Christ. To him be glory both now and forever! Amen.

_Devotion:_

Humility is the key to spiritual growth, allowing us to grow in grace and knowledge of Jesus Christ.

Remember, humility is what allows us to grow in grace and knowledge of Jesus Christ, and it's what allows us to experience spiritual growth. May God's grace continue to guide and empower you each day!

"Humility is the soil that nurtures spiritual growth." - Unknown

I hope this quote inspires you to cultivate humility and grow spiritually!

Prayer: _ Dear God, thank you for teaching me that humility is the key to spiritual growth. Help me to cultivate humility and grow in grace and knowledge of Jesus Christ._ Amen.

**_May 2**  Humility: The Key to God's Strength

_Scripture: _ 2 Corinthians 12:10 - "That is why, for Christ's sake, I delight in weaknesses, in insults, in hardships, in persecutions, in difficulties. For when I am weak, then I am strong.

_Devotion: _

Humility is the key to God's strength, allowing us to acknowledge our weaknesses and rely on His power.

Remember, humility is what allows us to acknowledge our weaknesses and rely on God's power, and it's what allows us to experience His strength. May God's grace continue to guide and empower you each day!

Humility is the vessel that receives God's strength. – Unknown

I hope this quote inspires you to cultivate humility and experience God's strength!

_Prayer: _ *Dear God, thank you for teaching me that humility is the key to Your strength. Help me to cultivate humility and rely on Your power, that I may experience Your strength in my weaknesses.* Amen.

## _May: 3_  Humility: The Key to Fruitful Service

_Scripture:_ John 12:24-26 - Very truly I tell you, unless a kernel of wheat falls to the ground and dies, it remains only a single seed. But if it dies, it produces many seeds. Anyone who loves their life will lose it, while anyone who hates their life in this world will keep it for eternal life.

_Devotion:_

Humility is the key to fruitful service, allowing us to die to ourselves and produce fruit for God's kingdom.

Remember, humility is what allows us to die to ourselves and produce fruit for God's kingdom, and it's what allows us to serve others with a humble heart. May God's grace continue to guide and empower you each day!

"Humility is the fertilizer that makes our service fruitful." Unknown

I hope this quote inspires you to cultivate humility and serve others with a humble heart!

_Prayer:_ *Dear God, thank you for teaching me that humility is the key to fruitful service. Help me to cultivate humility and serve others with a humble heart, that I may produce fruit for Your kingdom. Amen.*

_May: 4_ Humility: The Key to Lasting Legacy

_Scripture: _ Proverbs 22:4 - Humility is the fear of the Lord; its wages are riches and honor and life.

_Devotion: _

Humility is the key to a lasting legacy, allowing us to build a foundation of righteousness and wisdom that will outlast us.

Remember, humility is what allows us to build a foundation of righteousness and wisdom that will outlast us, and it's what allows us to leave a lasting legacy. May God's grace continue to guide and empower you each day!

"Humility is the foundation of a lasting legacy." – Unknown

I hope this quote inspires you to cultivate humility and build a lasting legacy!

_Prayer: _ *Dear God, thank you for teaching me that humility is the key to a lasting legacy. Help me to cultivate humility and build a foundation of righteousness and wisdom that will outlast me. Amen.*

## _May: 5 Humility: The Key to God's Wisdom

_Scripture:_ James 1:5-6 - If any of you lacks wisdom, you should ask God, who gives generously to all without finding fault, and it will be given to you. But when you ask, you must believe and not doubt, because the one who doubts is like a wave of the sea, blown and tossed by the wind.

### _Devotion:_

Humility is the key to God's wisdom, allowing us to ask and receive wisdom from Him.

Remember, humility is what allows us to ask and receive wisdom from God, and it's what allows us to seek His guidance. May God's grace continue to guide and empower you each day!

"Humility is the soil that receives God's wisdom." – Unknown

I hope this quote inspires you to cultivate humility and seek God's wisdom!

_Prayer:_ *Dear God, thank you for teaching me that humility is the key to Your wisdom. Help me to cultivate humility and seek Your wisdom, that I may receive generously from You. Amen.*

**_May: 6**   Humility: The Key to Divine Guidance

_Scripture:_ Psalm 25:9 - He guides the humble in what is right and teaches them his way.

_Devotion:_

Humility is the key to divine guidance, allowing us to seek God's direction and follow His path.

Remember, humility is what allows us to seek God's direction and follow His path, and it's what allows us to experience divine guidance. May God's grace continue to guide and empower you each day!

"Humility is the compass that points us to God's guidance." – Unknown

I hope this quote inspires you to cultivate humility and seek God's guidance!

_Prayer:_ *Dear God, thank you for teaching me that humility is the key to Your guidance. Help me to cultivate humility and seek Your direction, that I may follow Your path.* Amen.

## **May: 7** Humility: The Key to God's Presence

*Scripture:* Psalm 51:17 - My sacrifice, O God, is a broken spirit; a broken and contrite heart you, God, will not despise.

*Devotion:*

Humility is the key to experiencing God's presence, allowing us to come before Him with a broken and contrite heart.

Remember, humility is what allows us to come before God with a broken and contrite heart, and it's what allows us to experience His presence. May God's grace continue to guide and empower you each day!

"Humility is the doorway to God's presence." – Unknown

I hope this quote inspires you to cultivate humility and experience God's presence!

*Prayer:* *Dear God, thank you for teaching me that humility is the key to Your presence. Help me to cultivate humility and come before You with a broken and contrite heart. Amen.*

## _May: 8_ Humility: The Key to Meaningful Relationships

_Scripture: _ Philippians 2:3-4 - Do nothing out of selfish ambition or vain conceit. Rather, in humility value others above yourselves, not looking to your own interests but each of you to the interests of the others.

### _Devotion: _

Humility is the key to meaningful relationships, allowing us to value others above ourselves and build strong, loving connections.

Remember, humility is what allows us to value others above ourselves and build strong, loving connections. May God's grace continue to guide and empower you each day!

"Humility is the glue that holds relationships together." – Unknown

I hope this quote inspires you to cultivate humility and prioritize others in your relationships!

_Prayer: _ *Dear God, thank you for teaching me that humility is the key to meaningful relationships. Help me to cultivate humility and value others above*

### _May: 9 Humility: The Key to Lasting Relationships

_Scripture: _ Proverbs 13:10 - Pride only leads to arguments, but those who are humble will earn respect.

### _Devotion: _

Humility is the key to lasting relationships, allowing us to build bridges of respect and understanding with others.

Remember, humility is what allows us to build strong relationships with others, and it's what allows us to earn respect and understanding. May God's grace continue to guide and empower you each day!

Humility is the glue that holds relationships together. – Unknown

I hope this quote inspires you to cultivate humility and build strong relationships!

_Prayer: _ *Dear God, thank you for teaching me that humility is the key to lasting relationships. Help me to cultivate humility and build strong relationships with others. Amen.*

### _May: 10_ Humility: The Key to God's Blessings

_Scripture:_ Matthew 18:4, Jesus says, whoever humbles themselves like a child is the greatest in the kingdom of heaven.

_Devotion:_

Humility is the key to God's blessings, allowing us to tremble at His word and receive His favor.

What a wonderful insight! Humility is indeed considered a vital virtue in many spiritual and religious traditions. The idea is that by being humble, we open ourselves to divine guidance, wisdom, and grace. When we let go of pride and ego, we create space for God's love and blessings to flow into our lives. Humility allows us to:

- Recognize our limitations and dependence on God
- Listen and learn from others
- Forgive and let go of our need for control
- Cultivate gratitude and appreciation
- Embrace our vulnerabilities and imperfections

By embracing humility, we may indeed become more receptive to God's blessings and guidance in our lives.

_Prayer:_ *Dear God, thank you for teaching me that humility is the key to Your blessings. Help me to cultivate humility and seek Your blessings, that I may tremble at Your word and receive Your favor. Amen.*

# ROSE PETALS -- 366 DAYS OF MORNING MUSINGS

## _May: 11 Humility in Marriage

Scripture: Philippians 2:3-4 Do nothing out of selfish ambition or vain conceit. Rather, in humility value others above yourselves, not looking to your own interests but each of you to the interests of the others.

_Devotion:_

A beautiful topic! Humility in marriage is a vital ingredient for a healthy and fulfilling relationship. When both partners cultivate humility, they create a safe and supportive environment for growth, understanding, and love to flourish. Humility in marriage means:

- Letting go of ego and pride
- Active listening and empathy
- Admitting mistakes and apologizing
- Valuing your partner's perspectives and feelings
- Supporting each other's growth and development
- Forgiving and seeking forgiveness
- Embracing each other's imperfections
- Working together as a team

By embracing humility, couples can build a strong foundation for their relationship, navigate challenges with grace, and create a lifelong bond of love, trust, and mutual respect.

_Prayer_ Dear Lord, help me to put aside my own selfish desires and ambitions, and instead seek to serve and love my partner with humility. May our marriage be a reflection of your love and grace. Amen.

_May: 12 Humility: The Key to Effective Service

_Scripture:_ Matthew 20:26-28 - "Not so with you. Instead, whoever wants to become great among you must be your servant, and whoever wants to be first must be your slave—just as the Son of Man did not come to be served, but to serve, and to give his life as a ransom for many.

_Devotion:_

Humility is the key to effective service, allowing us to put others before ourselves and serve with a willing heart.

Remember, humility is what allows us to put others before ourselves and serve with a willing heart, and it's what allows us to make a meaningful impact in the lives of those around us.

May God's grace continue to guide and empower you each day!

"Humility is the foundation of all true service." – Unknown

I hope this quote inspires you to cultivate humility in your service to others!

_Prayer:_ *Dear God, thank you for teaching me that humility is the key to effective service. Help me to cultivate humility and serve others with love, just as Jesus did.* Amen.

## _May: 13 Humility: The Root of True Greatness

_Scripture:_ Matthew 23:11-12 - The greatest among you will be your servant. For those who exalt themselves will be humbled, and those who humble themselves will be exalted.

_Devotion:_

Humility is the root of true greatness, allowing us to serve others and glorify God.

Beautifully said! Humility is indeed the foundation of true greatness, and it's a quality that enables us to serve others with authenticity and sincerity. By acknowledging our limitations and surrendering our ego, we can focus on lifting others up and pointing them to a higher power.

Your statement reminds me of a quote by C.S. Lewis, who said, "Humility is not thinking less of yourself, it's thinking of yourself less." This mindset shift allows us to prioritize others' needs, build meaningful relationships, and ultimately, bring glory to God.

Remember, humility is what allows us to serve others and glorify God, and it's what allows us to experience true greatness in His eyes.

_Prayer:_ *Dear God, thank you for teaching me that humility is the root of true greatness. Help me to cultivate humility and seek true greatness in your eyes, and may your grace guide me on this journey. Amen.*

# ROSE PETALS -- 366 DAYS OF MORNING MUSINGS

_May: 14 Humility: The Key to True Greatness

_Scripture:_ Luke 14:11 - For all those who exalt themselves will be humbled, and those who humble themselves will be exalted.

_Devotion:_

Humility is the key to true greatness, allowing us to surrender our pride and rely on God's strength.

As we surrender our pride, we open ourselves up to God's guidance and wisdom. We begin to see that our strength comes not from our own abilities, but from His power working through us. Humility allows us to:

- Recognize our limitations and weaknesses
- Seek help and support from others
- Trust in God's sovereignty and provision
- Serve others with a willing and obedient heart

In humility, we find freedom from the need to control and manipulate. We find peace in knowing that God is in control, and that His plans are far greater than our own.

May God's grace continue to guide and empower you each day!

_Prayer:_ *Dear Lord, help us to humble ourselves before You. May we surrender our pride and rely on Your strength. Give us a willingness to serve and a heart that trusts in Your goodness. Amen."*

_**May: 15** Humility: The Path to Intimacy with God

_Scripture: _ Psalm 138:6 - Though the Lord is exalted, he looks with favor on the humble; but the proud he knows from afar.

_Devotion: _

Humility is the path to intimacy with God, allowing us to surrender our pride and draw near to His heart.

Remember, humility is what allows us to surrender our pride and draw near to God's heart, and it's what allows us to experience intimacy with Him.

May God's grace continue to guide and empower you each day!

"Humility is the doorway to the throne room of God." – Unknown

I hope this quote inspires you to cultivate humility and deepen your relationship with God!

_Prayer: _ *Dear God, thank you for teaching me that humility is the path to intimacy with You. Help me to cultivate humility and draw near to Your heart, that I may know You more deeply. Amen.*

**_May: 16.**   Humility: The Key to answered Prayer

_Scripture: _ Matthew 18:4 - Whoever humbles himself
like a child is the greatest in the kingdom of heaven.

_Devotion: _

Humility is the key to answered prayer, allowing us to approach God with a childlike heart.

Beautifully said! With humility, we come to God with a childlike heart, recognizing our dependence on Him and our need for His guidance and provision. We let go of our pride and self-sufficiency, and instead, we:

- Approach God with reverence and awe
- Trust in His goodness and love
- Surrender our worries and concerns to Him
- Receive His answers with gratitude and faith

In humility, we create space for God to work in our lives. We acknowledge that He is the One who knows what's best for us, and we trust in His perfect timing and plan.

_Prayer: _ *Dear Lord, help us to come to You with childlike humility. May we trust in Your goodness and love, and may we receive Your answers with gratitude and faith. Teach us to surrender our worries and concerns to You, and may we find peace in Your presence.* Amen.

### _May: 17 Humility: The Path to Spiritual Growth

_Scripture:_ 1 Peter 2:2-3 - Like newborn babies, crave spiritual milk, so that by it you may grow up in your salvation, now that you have tasted that the Lord is good.

### _Devotion:_

Humility is the path to spiritual growth, allowing us to crave spiritual milk and grow in our salvation.

Through humility, we recognize our need for spiritual nourishment and growth. We crave the pure spiritual milk of God's Word, and we: - Hunger for deeper understanding and insight- Thirst for a closer relationship with God- Seek guidance from spiritual mentors and leaders- Submit ourselves to the transformative power of the Holy Spirit

As we grow in our salvation, we become more like Christ, reflecting His character and love to a world in need. Humility is the soil in which spiritual growth takes root, allowing us to: - Develop a stronger faith and trust in God- Bear fruit that honors Him- Experience the joy and peace of His presence- Become a light in the darkness, shining His love to others

_Prayer:_ Dear Lord, *give us humble hearts that crave spiritual growth. May we hunger for Your Word and thirst for a deeper relationship with You. Help us to submit ourselves to Your transformative power, and may we grow in our salvation, becoming more like You each day.* Amen.

## _May: 18 Humility: The Key to Unity

_Scripture:_ Ephesians 4:2-3 - Be completely humble and gentle; be patient, bearing with one another in love. Make every effort to keep the unity of the Spirit through the bond of peace.

### _Devotion:_

Beautifully said! With humility, we recognize that we are all equal in God's eyes, and that our differences are not as important as our shared identity in Christ. We:

- Let go of pride and self-importance
- Embrace our unique perspectives and gifts
- Listen to and learn from one another
- Seek common ground and shared purpose

In humility, we create space for unity to flourish. We prioritize love and understanding over our own interests and agendas. We become a beautiful tapestry of diverse threads, woven together by the thread of humility.

_Prayer:_ *Dear Lord, help us to put aside our differences and come together in love. May humility be the glue that binds us, and may our unity be a testament to Your power and grace. Teach us to listen, to learn, and to love one another as You love us. Amen."*

## _May: 19_ Humility: The Key to Spiritual Freedom

_Scripture:_ Galatians 5:1 - It is for freedom that Christ has set us free. Stand firm, then, and do not be subject again to a yoke of slavery.

_Devotion:_

With humility, we acknowledge our dependence on God and our need for His liberation.

We:
- Recognize the chains of sin and bondage that once held us captive
- Embrace the truth of our identity in Christ and the freedom He offers
- Surrender our lives to His guidance and wisdom
- Walk in the liberty of His Spirit, unencumbered by pride and self-reliance

In humility, we find the freedom to:

- Live without pretenses and masks
- Be ourselves, authentic and vulnerable
- Serve others without expectation of reward
- Rest in God's sovereignty and provision

_Prayer:_ *Dear Lord, thank You for the gift of spiritual freedom. May humility be the key that unlocks our hearts to walk in the liberty You've given us. Help us to surrender our lives to Your guidance and wisdom, and may we live unencumbered by pride and self-reliance. Amen.*

## _May: 20_ Humility: The Key to Effective Prayer

_Scripture:_ Luke 18:13-14 - But the tax collector stood at a distance. He would not even look up to heaven, but beat his breast and said, 'God, have mercy on me, a sinner.' I tell you that this man, rather than the other, went home justified before God. For all those who exalt themselves will be humbled, and those who humble themselves will be exalted.

_Devotion:_

Humility is the key to effective prayer, allowing us to approach God with a humble heart and receive His mercy and grace.

By the way, I hope you're finding these devotional guides helpful! Remember, humility is what allows us to approach God with a humble heart and receive His mercy and grace. May God's grace continue to guide and empower you each day!

"Humility is the foundation of effective prayer." – Unknown

I hope this quote inspires you to cultivate humility and pray with a humble heart!

_Prayer:_ *Dear God, thank you for teaching me that humility is the key to effective prayer. Help me to cultivate humility and pray with a humble heart, that I may receive Your mercy and grace. Amen.*

## May: 21 Humility: The Key to Hearing God's Voice

_Scripture:_ Psalm 25:14 - The Lord confides in those who fear him; he makes his covenant known to them.

_Devotion:_

Humility is the key to hearing God's voice, allowing us to fear Him and receive His counsel.

Beautifully said! When we humble ourselves before God, we create space to hear His gentle whisper. We become receptive to His guidance, and our hearts become fertile ground for His counsel to take root.

In humility, we:
- Recognize our need for God's direction
- Quiet our minds and listen for His voice
- Submit our will to His wise and loving plan
- Receive His correction and instruction with gratitude

As we fear God in reverence and awe, we open ourselves up to His wisdom and guidance. We begin to see the world through His eyes, and our paths become illuminated by His presence.

_Prayer:_ *Dear Lord, humble us to hear Your voice. May we fear You in reverence and awe, and receive Your counsel with willing hearts. Speak to us, Lord, and may we listen with humility and obedience. Amen.*

**_May 22_**: Humility: The Key to Wisdom

_Scripture:_ Proverbs 9:10 - "The fear of the Lord is the beginning of wisdom, and knowledge of the Holy One is understanding."

_Devotion:_

Humility is the foundation of wisdom. It's the recognition that our understanding is limited, and God's ways are higher than ours. When we humble ourselves before God, we open ourselves to His wisdom.

In Proverbs 9:10, we're reminded that fearing the Lord is the starting point of wisdom. This fear isn't about being afraid; it's about revering God's majesty and acknowledging His sovereignty.

Humility:

Recognizes God's sovereignty
Acknowledges our limitations
Seeks wisdom from above
Cultivates a teachable spirit

_Prayer:_ *Dear Heavenly Father, help us cultivate humility, recognizing our limitations and your sovereignty. Grant us wisdom from above, guiding us to trust and obey You. May our fear of You be the beginning of wisdom, and may we grow in understanding of Your Holy character. In Jesus' name,* Amen.

## _May: 23    Humility: The Key to Servant Leadership

_Scripture:_ Mark 10:42-45 - Jesus called them together and said, 'You know that those who are regarded as rulers of the Gentiles lord it over them, and their high officials exercise authority over them. Not so with you. Instead, whoever wants to become great among you must be your servant, and whoever wants to be first must be slave of all.

_Devotion:_

Humility is the key to servant leadership, allowing us to serve others and put their needs before our own.

Remember, humility is what allows us to serve others and put their needs before our own, and it's what allows us to become true leaders. May God's grace continue to guide and empower you each day!

"Humility is the hallmark of a true leader." – Unknown

I hope this quote inspires you to cultivate humility and become a servant leader!

_Prayer:_ *Dear God, thank you for teaching me that humility is the key to servant leadership. Help me to cultivate humility and become a servant leader, that I may serve others and glorify You.* Amen.

## _May: 24._ Humility: The Path to Spiritual Maturity

_Scripture:_ 1 Peter 5:6-7 - Humble yourselves, therefore, under God's mighty hand, that he may lift you up in due time. Cast all your anxiety on him because he cares for you.

_Devotion:_

Humility is the path to spiritual maturity, allowing us to surrender our pride and rely on God's strength.

As we walk the path of humility, we mature in our faith and become more like Christ. We:

- Recognize our weaknesses and limitations
- Surrender our pride and self-sufficiency
- Rely on God's strength and wisdom

In humility, we:
- Develop a deeper trust in God's goodness and love
- Cultivate a heart of gratitude and thanksgiving
- Learn to submit to His will and timing
- Grow in our understanding of His character and ways

_Prayer:_ *Dear Lord, help us to walk the path of humility, surrendering our pride and relying on Your strength. May we mature in our faith and become more like You each day. Teach us to trust in Your goodness and love, and may we bear fruit that honors You. Amen.*

May we continually seek to humble ourselves before God, and may He lift us up to new heights of spiritual maturity and intimacy with Him.

## REFLECTION

Ask Him to help you cultivate humility and grow in spiritual maturity.

_Reflection Prompt:_ Write about a time when you humbled yourself and relied on God's strength. How did that experience shape your faith?

And here's a verse to meditate on:

"Humble yourselves before the Lord, and He will lift you up." - James 4:10

May we continually seek to humble ourselves before God, and may He lift us up to new heights of spiritual maturity and intimacy with Him.

# ROSE PETALS -- 366 DAYS OF MORNING MUSINGS

_May: 25_ Humility: The Path to True Wisdom.

_Scripture:_ Proverbs 11:2 - When pride comes, then comes disgrace, but with humility comes wisdom.

_Devotion:_

Humility is the path to true wisdom, allowing us to learn from God and others.

"Through humility, we become receptive to wisdom from above. We:
- Recognize our limitations and need for guidance
- Seek knowledge and understanding from God's Word
- Listen to and learn from others' experiences and insights
- Embrace correction and constructive feedback

In humility, we:
- Develop a teachable spirit and a willingness to grow
- Cultivate a heart of curiosity and wonder
- Learn to discern wisdom from folly
- Grow in our understanding of God's ways and character

_Prayer:_ *Dear Lord, grant us humility to learn from You and others. May we be receptive to Your wisdom and guidance, and may we grow in our understanding of Your ways. Teach us to listen, to learn, and to discern wisdom.* Amen.

_May: 26_     Humility: The Heart of a Servant

_Scripture:_ Philippians 2:3-4 - Do nothing out of selfish ambition or vain conceit. Rather, in humility value others above yourselves, not looking to your own interests but each of you to the interests of the others.

_Devotion:_

Humility is the heart of a servant, allowing us to put others before ourselves.

Remember, humility is what allows us to put others before ourselves and serve with a joyful heart. May God's grace continue to guide and empower you each day!

"Humility is the highest form of wisdom, and it is the key to true greatness." – Unknown

I hope this quote inspires you to cultivate humility in your daily life!

_Prayer:_ *Dear God, thank you for teaching me that humility is the heart of a servant. Help me to put others before myself and serve with a humble heart, and may your grace fill me with a desire to serve.* Amen.

## _May: 27    Humility: The Foundation of Prayer

_Scripture:_ Luke 18:13-14 - But the tax collector stood at a distance. He would not even look up to heaven, but beat his breast and said, 'God, have mercy on me, a sinner.' I tell you that this man, rather than the other, went home justified before God. For all those who exalt themselves will be humbled, and those who humble themselves will be exalted.

_Devotion:_

Humility is the foundation of effective prayer, allowing us to approach God with a contrite heart.

Remember, humility is what allows us to come to God with a humble and contrite heart, and it's what allows us to experience His mercy and grace in our lives.

May God's grace continue to guide and empower you each day!

"Humility is the gateway to the throne of grace." – Anonymous

I hope this quote inspires you to cultivate humility in your prayer life!

_Prayer:_ *Dear God, thank you for teaching me that humility is the foundation of effective prayer. Help me to humble myself before you, and may your grace and mercy flow into my life. Amen.*

**_May: 28.**   Humility: The Key to Learning

_Scripture:_ Proverbs 1:7 - The fear of the Lord is the beginning of knowledge, but fools despise wisdom and instruction.

_Devotion:_

Humility is the key to learning and gaining wisdom.

What a wonderful insight! Humility is indeed a vital quality for learning and gaining wisdom. When we approach life with humility, we open ourselves up to new experiences, perspectives, and knowledge. By being willing to listen, ask questions, and acknowledge our limitations, we create space for growth and understanding.

As the ancient Greek philosopher, Aristotle, said, "The wise person is not the one who knows everything, but the one who is willing to learn." Humility allows us to let go of our ego and embrace the idea that there is always more to learn, discover, and explore.

In essence, humility is the gateway to a lifelong journey of learning, self-awareness, and wisdom.

Remember, humility is what allows us to learn and grow in our relationship with God and with others. May God's grace continue to guide and empower you each day!

"Humility is the mark of a great learner, and the gateway to true wisdom." - John Maxwell

I hope this quote inspires you to cultivate humility in your daily life!

Prayer: _ Dear God, thank you for teaching me that humility is the key to learning. Help me to humble myself and be teachable, and may your grace fill me with wisdom and knowledge. Amen.

## _May: 29_     Humility: The Path to True Greatness

_Scripture:_ Luke 14:11 - For everyone who exalts himself will be humbled, and he who humbles himself will be exalted.

### _Devotion:_

Humility is the path to true greatness, as it allows us to surrender our pride and self-interest to God.

A beautiful truth! Humility is indeed the path to true greatness. When we walk the path of humility, we open ourselves up to:

- Deeper connections with others
- Greater self-awareness
- Increased empathy and compassion
- A willingness to learn and grow
- More meaningful relationships

As C.S. Lewis said, "Humility is not thinking less of yourself, but thinking of yourself less." When we let go of our need for recognition and validation, we can focus on what truly matters – making a positive impact, serving others, and leaving a lasting legacy.

True greatness is not about seeking power, status, or fame, but about living a life of purpose, integrity, and service. And humility is the foundation upon which this greatness is built.

Remember humility is what allows us to surrender our pride and self-interest to God, and it's what allows us to truly find greatness in His eyes.

_Prayer:_ *Dear God, thank you for teaching me that humility is the path to true greatness. Help me to humble myself and seek your glory, not mine, and may your grace exalt me in your time.* Amen.

## May: 30  Humility: The Antodote to Pride

_Scripture:_ Proverbs 16:18 - Pride goes before destruction, a haughty spirit before a fall.

### _Devotion:_

Humility is the antidote to pride, which can lead to destruction and separation from God.

A wise insight! Humility is indeed the antidote to pride. Pride can be a corrosive force, leading us to:

- Overestimate our abilities and accomplishments
- Become arrogant and self-centered
- Look down on others and diminish their value
- Become rigid and unwilling to learn or grow
- Focus on our own interests at the expense of others

As Proverbs 11:28 says, "Pride leads to destruction, but humility leads to wisdom." By embracing humility, we can avoid the pitfalls of pride and walk a path that leads to greater wisdom, stronger relationships, and a more fulfilling life.

Remember, humility is a journey, and it's okay to take it one step at a time. May God's grace continue to guide and empower you each day!

"Pride makes us artificial, humility makes us real." – Anonymous

I hope this quote inspires you to cultivate humility in your daily life!

_Prayer:_ *Dear God, thank you for teaching me that humility is the antidote to pride. Help me to recognize and surrender my pride, and may your grace fill me with humility and wisdom.* Amen.

# ROSE PETALS -- 366 DAYS OF MORNING MUSINGS

As May comes to a close, we reflect on a month of renewal, growth, and celebration. We've welcomed warmer weather, blooming flowers, and longer days, symbolizing the beauty and vibrancy of life.

May has taught us to:
- Embrace the beauty of nature and its transformative power
- Honor the resilience and strength of those around us
- Cultivate gratitude and appreciation for life's simple joys
- Stay curious, keep learning, and embrace new experiences

As we step into June, we carry forward the energy and vitality of May. May the warmth and light of the past month continue to inspire us to nurture our relationships, pursue our passions, and stay true to ourselves.

May's lessons will stay with us, reminding us to stay present, mindful, and open to the wonders of life.

Farewell, May – your beauty and vibrancy will be deeply missed, but your impact will continue to bloom in our hearts and minds.

# JUNE 1-30

1. God's Perfect Timing
2. The Gift of Grace
3. Grace in Our Weakness
4. Grace that Transforms
5. Grace that Lifts Us Up
6. Grace that Sets Us Free
7. Grace that Renews Us
8. Grace that Unites Us
9. Grace that Empowers Us
10. Grace that Forgives Us
11. Grace that Sustains Us
12. Grace that Transcends Our Limits
13. Grace that Renews Our Minds
14. Grace that Brings Joy
15. Grace that Gives Us Hope
16. Grace that Strengthens Us
17. Grace that Sets Us Free
18. Grace that Gives Us Humility
19. Grace that Gives Us Boldness
20. Grace that Gives Us Assurance
21. Grace that Transforms Us
22. Grace that Satisfies Our Souls
23. Grace that Helps Us Grow
24. Grace that Helps Us Forgive
25. Grace that Gives Us Purpose
26. Grace that Gives Us Eternal Life
27. Resting in Grace
28. Extending Grace to Others
29. Growing in Grace
30. The Grace of God's Love

**_June 1**: God's Perfect Timing

_Scripture: _ Galatians 4:4-5 - But when the fullness of time had come, God sent forth his Son, born of woman, born under the law, to redeem those under the law, so that we might receive adoption as sons.

_Devotion: _

God's timing is perfect, and His plans are always for our good.

Amen to that! That's a great reminder of God's character and love for us.

God's timing and plans are indeed perfect, and He is always working for our good, even when we can't see the bigger picture. Trusting in His sovereignty and goodness brings peace and hope to our lives.

Here's a short prayer to reflect this truth:

- Dear God, *I thank you that your timing is perfect, and your plans are always for my good. Help me to trust in you and your ways, even when I don't understand. I pray for your guidance and peace to fill my heart today. In Jesus' name.* Amen.

May this truth bring encouragement and hope to your day!

## _June 2: _ The Gift of Grace

_Scripture: _ Ephesians 2:8-9 - For by grace you have been saved through faith. And this is not your own doing; it is the gift of God, not a result of works, so that no one may boast.
_Devotion: _

Grace is a gift that we don't deserve, but God freely gives to us through faith in Jesus Christ.

What a beautiful and profound statement! You're absolutely right. Grace is often defined as unmerited favor or love. It's the idea that we receive something we don't deserve, not because of our own actions or worthiness, but because of the generosity and love of someone else.

This concept is deeply rooted in many religious and philosophical traditions, and it can be a powerful reminder of the importance of humility, gratitude, and compassion. When we recognize that we've received something we don't deserve, it can cultivate a sense of appreciation and wonder, and encourage us to pay it forward to others.

_Prayer: _ *Dear God, I am humbled by the reminder that your grace is a gift that I don't deserve. Thank you for loving me unconditionally and for showing me kindness and mercy that I couldn't earn on my own. Help me to receive your grace with a humble heart and to extend it to others who are in need of your love and forgiveness. May your grace be my anchor, my comfort, and my guide.* Amen

# ROSE PETALS -- 366 DAYS OF MORNING MUSINGS

## _June 3:_ Grace in Our Weakness

_Scripture:_ 2 Corinthians 12:9-10 - But he said to me, 'My grace is sufficient for you, for my power is made perfect in weakness.' Therefore, I will boast all the more gladly of my weaknesses, so that the power of Christ may rest upon me.

_Devotion:_

God's grace is sufficient for us, even in our weakest moments.

Amen to that! That's a powerful truth. God's grace is sufficient for us, even when we feel weak, vulnerable, or inadequate. It's a reminder that we're not alone and that God's strength and power are made perfect in our weakness.

When we are weak, God's strength shines through, it's a paradox that our weaknesses and limitations can become the very platforms for God's power and grace to be displayed.

May we embrace our weaknesses as opportunities for God's strength and power to shine through, and may we find comfort in His promise to be our rock and our refuge in times of need.

_Prayer:_ *Dear God, thank you for your promise to be my strength in weakness. Help me to embrace my vulnerabilities as opportunities for your power and grace to shine through. May I find joy in my weaknesses, knowing that they are platforms for your strength to be displayed. Amen.*

## June 4: Grace that Transforms

*Scripture:* 2 Corinthians 5:17 - Therefore, if anyone is in Christ, he is a new creation. The old has passed away; behold, the new has come.

*Devotion:*

God's grace not only forgives us but also transforms us into new creations. This idea of transformation through grace encourages us to live a life of gratitude, humility, and service to others.

That's a beautiful insight! The concept of transformation through grace is a powerful idea in many spiritual traditions. The idea is that divine grace not only pardons our mistakes and shortcomings but also empowers us to become better versions of ourselves, renewed and revitalized.

*Prayer:* *Dear God, I thank you for your abundant grace, which not only forgives me but also transforms me into new creations. Help me to surrender to your transformative power, that I may be renewed in my minds, hearts, and spirits. As I receive your forgiveness, may I also experience your regenerating love, which makes me new again. May your grace empower me to live a life that reflects your character, a life of love, joy, and service to others. Amen.*

_June 5: _   Grace that Lifts Us Up

_Scripture: _ Psalm 145:14-16 - The Lord upholds all who are falling and lifts up all who are bowed down. The eyes of all look to you, and you give them their food in due season. You open your hand, and satisfy the desire of every living thing.

_Devotion: _

God's grace lifts us up when we are falling and surrounds us with His love and care.

A beautiful truth! Here's a prayer based on the theme "God's grace lifts us up when we are falling. When we are weak, may your grace be our power, is a reminder that God's strength is made perfect in our weakness (2 Corinthians 12:9). It's a truth that can bring us comfort, hope, and courage in the midst of struggles.

May this truth and prayer continue to inspire and uplift you!

_Prayer: _ *Dear God, we thank you for your grace, which is our safety net in times of struggle. When we are falling, your grace lifts us up, catches us, and holds us close. Your love and care for us are unwavering, even when we stumble and fall.* Amen.

Help us to trust in your goodness and your ability to lift us up from the ashes of our mistakes and failures. May your grace be our rock, our refuge, and our strength in times of need.

## June 6: Grace that Sets Us Free

*Scripture:* Romans 6:14 - For sin will have no dominion over you, since you are not under law but under grace.

### Devotion:

God's grace sets us free from the power of sin and the weight of legalism.

That's a beautiful insight! The concept of God's grace is a central theme in many religious traditions, including Christianity. The idea is that God's grace, or unmerited favor, liberates us from the bondage of sin and the constraints of legalism, allowing us to live a life of freedom, joy, and service to others.

Legalism can be a heavy burden, leading to a focus on rules and regulations rather than a relationship with God. But grace, on the other hand, brings freedom, peace, and a sense of acceptance.

*Prayer:* *Dear God, thank you for your abundant grace, which sets me free from the power of sin and the weight of legalism. Help me to live a life that reflects your love and grace, and to extend that grace to others. Amen.*

May our hearts be filled with gratitude and our lives be a reflection of your goodness.

## _June 7_: Grace that Renews Us

_Scripture:_ As 2 Corinthians 3:18 says, and we all, who with unveiled faces contemplate the Lord's glory, are being transformed into his image with ever-increasing glory, which comes from the Lord, who is the Spirit.

_Devotion:_

God's grace renews us daily, transforming us into the image of Christ.

A beautiful truth! God's grace is a continuous and ongoing work in our lives, transforming us daily into the likeness of Jesus Christ. This transformation is a result of His grace at work in us, renewing our minds, hearts, and lives.

This transformation is a lifelong process, and God's grace is always at work in us, even when we're not aware of it. It's a remarkable journey of growth, sanctification, and becoming more like Jesus.

May God's grace continue to transform you daily, and may you experience His love, peace, and guidance in every step of your journey.

_Prayer:_ *Dear God, thank you for your grace that renews me daily. Help me focus on the eternal and not the temporary, and may my life reflect the glory of Christ*

## June 8:   Grace that Unites Us

_Scripture:_ Ephesians 2:19-22 - So then you are no longer strangers and aliens, but you are fellow citizens with the saints and members of the household of God, built on the foundation of the apostles and prophets, Christ Jesus himself being the cornerstone, in whom the whole structure, being joined together, grows into a holy temple in the Lord.

_Devotion:_

God's grace unites us with Himself and with others, creating a community of believers.

That's a beautiful insight! The concept of God's grace uniting us with Himself and others is a central theme in many spiritual traditions. It suggests that God's love and acceptance are the foundation for our connection with ourselves, with others, and with the divine.

This idea resonates with many spiritual and religious teachings, such as: - "Love your neighbor as yourself" (Mark 12:31)- "We love because He first loved us" (1 John 4:19)

The unity and connection that come from God's grace can bring people together, foster empathy and understanding, and transcend differences. It's a powerful reminder of our shared humanity and our deep connection with each other and with the divine.

_Prayer:_ *Dear God, thank you for your grace that unites us. Help me build relationships that reflect your love and grace, and may your grace unite us in our diversity.* Amen.

## REFLECTION

Ask God to help you build relationships that reflect His love and grace.

_Reflection Prompt:_ Write about a time when God's grace helped you connect with someone from a different background or perspective.

## June 9: _ Grace that Empowers Us

_Scripture:_ 2 Timothy 2:1-2 - You then, my child, be strengthened by the grace that is in Christ Jesus, and what you have heard from me in the presence of many witnesses entrust to faithful men who will be able to teach others also.

_Devotion:_

God's grace empowers us to live for Him and to share His love with others.

Amen! That's a beautiful truth! God's grace is a powerful force that enables us to live a life that honors Him and to share His love and kindness with those around us. It's a wonderful reminder that our faith is not just about ourselves, but about serving and loving others in His name.

God's grace is the fuel that ignites our passion to live for Him and share His love with others. With grace, we: - Receive the power to overcome sin and live a life that honors God- Experience the transformation of our hearts and minds- Become ambassadors of God's love and grace to a world in need

In grace, we: - Discover our true identity as beloved children of God- Learn to extend the same grace and forgiveness to others- Grow in our understanding of God's character and love- Become a reflection of His grace and mercy to those around us.

_Prayer:_ *Dear Lord, thank You for Your grace that empowers us to live for You and share Your love with others. May we be vessels of Your grace, pouring out Your love and mercy to a world in need. Amen.*

## REFLECTION

Ask God to help you be a vessel of His grace to those around you.

_Reflection Prompt:_ Write about a way in which God's grace has empowered you to serve or minister to others.

_ **June 10:** _. Grace that Forgives Us

_Scripture: _ Psalm 103:10-12 - He does not deal with us according to our sins, nor repay us according to our iniquities. For as high as the heavens are above the earth, so great is his steadfast love toward those who fear him; as far as the east is from the west, so far does he remove our transgressions from us.

_Devotion: _

God's grace forgives us and removes our sins as far as the east is from the west.

Amen! That's a beautiful truth! God's grace is a gift that forgives us and removes our sins, cleansing us from all unrighteousness. As it says in 1 John 1:9, "If we confess our sins, He is faithful and just to forgive us our sins and to cleanse us from all unrighteousness."

Let's take a moment to reflect on the power of God's grace in our lives. Have you experienced the freedom and peace that comes from knowing your sins are forgiven?

_Prayer: _ *We thank You for Your grace that forgives us and removes our sins. Help us to remember that Your love for us is not based on our past mistakes, but on Your character and faithfulness. Cleanse us from all unrighteousness, and help us to live a life that honors You. May our hearts be filled with gratitude and our lives be a reflection of Your love.* Amen.

## _June 11:_ Grace that Sustains Us

_Scripture:_ Psalm 138:8 - The Lord will fulfill his purpose for me; your steadfast love, O God, endures forever. Do not forsake the work of your hands.

### _Devotion:_

God's grace sustains us and empowers us to fulfill His purpose for our lives.

A beautiful and uplifting sentiment! Faith and spirituality can indeed provide strength and guidance for many people. The concept of God's grace and purpose can be a source of comfort, hope, and inspiration.

Faith and spirituality can be a source of:
- Comfort and solace in times of need
- Guidance and direction for life's challenges
- Strength and resilience for overcoming obstacles
- Hope and inspiration for a brighter future

Faith and spirituality can take many forms and expressions, and can be a deeply personal and individual aspect of one's life.

May you continue to find solace and empowerment in your beliefs!

_Prayer:_ *Dear God, thank you for your grace that sustains me, guides me, and empowers me to fulfill your purpose. Please continue to shine your light in my life, and help me to trust in your love and wisdom. May your grace be my strength in times of need, and may I always reflect your love and grace to those around me. Amen.*

### ROSE PETALS -- 366 DAYS OF MORNING MUSINGS

### _June 12:_ Grace that Transcends Our Limits

_Scripture:_ 2 Corinthians 9:8 - And God is able to make all grace abound to you, so that having all sufficiency in all things at all times, you may abound in every good work.

_Devotion:_

God's grace goes beyond our limitations and empowers us to
abound in good works.

What a beautiful devotion! 2 Corinthians 9:8 is such a powerful reminder of God's abundance and generosity. The idea that God's grace can transcend our limits and empower us to do more than we thought possible is truly uplifting.

Remembering that God's grace is not limited by our own limitations can be a game-changer in our walk of faith. It's a beautiful thing to trust in His power and provision, and to see Him work in and through us in amazing ways.

_Prayer:_ *Dear God, thank you for your grace that transcends our limits. We acknowledge that our abilities and resources are not the only factors that determine our potential. We trust in your power and provision to work in and through us, exceeding our own limitations. Amen.*

## _June 13:_ _ Grace that Renews Our Minds

_Scripture:_ Romans 12:2 - Do not be conformed to this world, but be transformed by the renewal of your mind, that by testing you may discern what is the will of God, what is good and acceptable and perfect.

_Devotion:_

God's grace renews our minds, transforming us to discern His will and live according to His purpose.

A beautiful truth! God's grace has the power to transform our minds, renewing our thoughts and perspectives, and enabling us to discern His will and ways.

This transformation is a result of God's grace at work in our lives, helping us to:

- Discern God's voice and leading
- Live according to His purposes and plans

As we seek to discern God's will, let's remember to:
- Listen for the Holy Spirit's leading
- Trust in God's goodness and sovereignty

May God's grace continue to renew our minds, transforming us to discern and follow His perfect will.

_Prayer:_ *Dear God, thank you for your grace that renews my mind. Help me discern your will and live according to your purpose, and may your grace transform me from the inside out. Amen.*

**REFLECTION POINTS:**

1. How often do you renew your mind with God's Word?

2. What worldly patterns or thoughts do you need to break free from?

3. Ask God to transform your mind, aligning it with His truth.

## June 14: Grace that Brings Joy

_Scripture:_ Acts 11:23 - When he came and saw the grace of God, he was glad, and he exhorted them all to remain faithful to the Lord with steadfast purpose.

_Devotion:_

God's grace brings joy and gladness to our hearts.

Amen! God's grace is a source of joy and gladness, filling our hearts with a sense of wonder, gratitude, and love. Remember the wonders He has done, His miracles, and the judgments He has pronounced."

God's grace brings joy and gladness to our hearts in many ways, including:
- Forgiveness: His grace forgives our sins, lifting the weight of guilt and shame.
- Love: His grace pours out unconditional love, accepting us just as we are.
- Redemption: His grace rescues us from darkness, bringing us into His marvelous light.
- Hope: His grace fills us with hope, promising a future and a purpose.

As we bask in God's grace, may our hearts overflow with joy and gladness, reflecting the goodness and love of our Heavenly Father.

_Prayer:_ *Dear God, thank you for your grace that brings joy. Help me experience the joy of your grace and share it with others, and may my life be a testimony to the gladness of your love.* Amen.

## REFLECTION

Ask God to help you experience the joy of His grace and share it with others.

_Reflection Prompt:_ Write about a time when God's grace filled you with joy and gladness.

## _June 15:_ Grace that Gives Us Hope

_Scripture:_ Romans 5:2 - Through him we have also obtained access by faith into this grace in which we stand, and we rejoice in hope of the glory of God.

_Devotion:_

God's grace gives us hope in the midst of sufferings, producing endurance, character, and ultimately, glory.

Amen! That's so true! God's grace is a beacon of hope in the darkest of times. God's grace gives us hope in the midst of sufferings in many ways, including:

- Providing comfort: His grace comforts us in our pain, reminding us we're not alone.
- Giving perspective: His grace helps us see our struggles in light of eternity.
- Strengthening us: His grace empowers us to persevere, even when we feel weak.
- Reminding us of His presence: His grace assures us that He is always with us, even in the darkest valleys.

As we face various trials and challenges, may God's grace be our constant source of hope, reminding us that He is working everything out for our good and His glory.

_Prayer:_ *Dear God, thank you for your grace that gives me hope. Help me rejoice in the hope of your glory, even in the midst of struggles, and may your grace produce endurance, character, and hope in me.* Amen.

## _June 16:_ Grace that Strengthens Us

_Scripture:_ 2 Timothy 4:17 - But the Lord stood by me and strengthened me, so that through me the message might be fully proclaimed and all the Gentiles might hear it.

### _Devotion:_

God's grace strengthens us to fulfill His purposes, even in the face of challenges.

That's a wonderful truth! God's grace not only saves us but also empowers us to live for Him. As Philippians 2:13 says, for it is God who works in you to will and to act in order to fulfill his good purpose.

God's grace strengthens us to fulfill His purposes in many ways, including:

- Giving us new desires: His grace changes our hearts, giving us a desire to serve and obey Him.
- Providing spiritual gifts: His grace equips us with gifts and talents to serve others and build His kingdom.
- Empowering us to overcome: His grace helps us conquer sin and our flesh, enabling us to live a life pleasing to Him.

Guiding us with wisdom: His grace gives us wisdom and discernment to make decisions aligned with His will.

_Prayer:_ *Dear God, thank you for your grace that strengthens me. Help me rely on your grace to stand firm in the face of challenges, and may your grace empower me to fulfill your purposes.* Amen.

## June 17:  Grace that Sets Us Free

_Scripture:_ Galatians 5:1 - For freedom Christ has set us free; stand firm therefore, and do not submit again to a yoke of slavery.

_Devotion:_

God's grace sets us free from the bondage of sin and legalism, giving us liberty to live for Him. God's grace is a liberating force that sets us free from the shackles of sin and legalism. As Romans 6:14 says, for sin shall no longer be your master, because you are not under law, but under grace.

God's grace frees us from:

- The guilt and shame of sin, forgiving us and declaring us righteous in His sight.
- The burden of trying to earn our way to heaven through good works and legalistic rules.

In its place, God's grace offers us: - Freedom to live a life of joy, peace, and purpose. - The power to overcome sin and temptation, through the Holy Spirit. - The assurance of our salvation, knowing we are secure in Christ's love.

May we bask in the goodness of God's grace, reveling in the freedom and new life He offers us.

_Prayer:_ *Dear God, thank you for your grace that sets me free. Help me walk in the liberty of your grace, and may your grace empower me to live for you alone.* Amen.

## REFLECTION

Ask God to help you walk in the freedom of His grace.

_Reflection Prompt:_ Write about an area of your life where God's grace has set you free.

# _June 18:_ Grace that Gives Us Humility

_Scripture:_ Philippians 2:5-8 - "Have this mind among yourselves, which is yours in Christ Jesus, who, though he was in the form of God, did not count equality with God a thing to be grasped, but emptied Himself, by taking the form of a servant, being born in the likeness of men. And being found in human form, He humbled Himself by becoming obedient to the point of death, even death on a cross.

_Devotion:_

God's grace gives us humility, as we follow Jesus' example of emptying Himself and humbling Himself for our sake.

That's a beautiful sentiment! You're absolutely right, God's grace can cultivate humility in our hearts as we follow Jesus' example. Humility is an important virtue in many spiritual traditions, and it can manifest in various ways, such as:

- Recognizing our limitations and dependence on God- Serving others with kindness and compassion
- Embracing our weaknesses and vulnerabilities as opportunities for growth

As you reflect on this, remember that humility is a journey, and it's okay to take it one step at a time. May God's grace continue to guide and inspire you!

_Prayer:_ *Dear God, thank you for your grace that gives me humility. Help me follow Jesus' example, emptying myself and humbling myself to serve others with grace, and may your grace shine through me.* Amen.

### June 19: _ Grace that Gives Us Boldness

_Scripture:_ Hebrews 4:16 - Let us then with confidence draw near to the throne of grace, that we may receive mercy and find grace to help in time of need.

_Devotion:_

God's grace gives us boldness to approach His throne, receiving mercy and grace in our time of need.

God's grace is not just a gift, but also a source of strength and boldness. When we understand that His grace is sufficient for us, we can approach life's challenges with confidence and courage. Remember that God's power is made perfect in our weaknesses, and that His grace gives us the boldness to face whatever comes our way.

We don't have to earn His love or mercy; He freely offers it to us. Take a moment to thank God for His grace and mercy in your life, and ask for His guidance and strength in your times of need.

Prayer: *Dear God, thank You for Your throne of grace, where I can come to You with confidence and boldness. Help me to remember Your love and mercy, and to seek Your guidance and strength in all I do. Amen."*

_June 20_: Grace that Gives Us Assurance

_Scripture:_ 1 John 5:13 - I write these things to you who believe in the name of the Son of God so that you may know that you have eternal life.

_Devotion:_

God's grace gives us assurance of our salvation and eternal life through faith in Jesus Christ.

That's a beautiful sentiment! The concept of God's grace and its connection to salvation and eternal life is a central belief in many religious traditions. The idea is that God's grace, or unconditional love and forgiveness, provides believers with the assurance of their salvation and eternal life. This belief can bring comfort, hope, and meaning to people's lives.

God's grace is seen as the unmerited gift of salvation, received through faith in Jesus Christ. This belief is often summarized in Ephesians 2:8-9, which states, "For by grace you have been saved through faith, and that not of yourselves; it is the gift of God, not of works, lest anyone should boast."

_Prayer:_ *Dear God, thank you for your grace that gives me assurance of eternal life. Help me rest in the confidence of your love and grace, and may your grace fill me with peace and joy.* Amen.

## June 21: Grace that Transforms Us

_Scripture:_ 2 Corinthians 5:17 - Therefore, if anyone is in Christ, he is a new creation. The old has passed away; behold, the new has come.

_Devotion:_

God's grace transforms us into new creations, renewing our minds and hearts. A wonderful truth! The idea that God's grace transforms us into new creations is a powerful concept in many religious traditions. This transformation is often seen as a spiritual rebirth or renewal, where believers are made new through God's love and grace.

This transformation is not just a one-time event but a continuous process of growth and sanctification. As we surrender to God's grace, we are gradually transformed into the image of Christ, with new thoughts, new desires, and new actions.

This concept is often associated with the idea of regeneration, where God's Spirit renews and transforms our hearts and minds, enabling us to live a life that is pleasing to Him.

_Prayer:_ *Dear God, thank you for your grace that transforms me. Help me surrender to your grace, and may your grace renew my mind and heart, making me a new creation in Christ. Amen.*

## _June 22:_ Grace that Satisfies Our Souls

_Scripture:_ Psalm 107:9 - For he satisfies the thirsty and fills the hungry with good things.

_Devotion:_

God's grace satisfies our souls, quenching our spiritual thirst and hunger.

What a beautiful sentiment! God's grace satisfies our souls is a wonderful reminder of the peace and contentment that can come from faith. It's a great starting point for a conversation about spirituality, personal growth, or simply finding joy in life.

The concept of God's grace quenching our spiritual thirst and hunger is a powerful metaphor. Just as our bodies need nourishment and hydration to survive, our souls need spiritual sustenance to flourish. The idea that God's grace can satisfy our deepest longings and fill the voids in our lives is a comforting and reassuring one.

It's reminiscent of Jesus' words in the Bible, "Whoever drinks the water I give them will never thirst. Indeed, the water I give them will become in them a spring of water welling up to eternal life" (John 4:14).

_Prayer:_ *Dear God, thank you for your grace that satisfies my soul. Help me drink from the well of your grace, and may your grace fill me with joy, peace, and contentment.* Amen.

_June 23:_ Grace that Helps Us Grow

_Scripture:_ 2 Peter 3:18 - But grow in the grace and knowledge of our Lord and Savior Jesus Christ. To him be the glory both now and to the day of eternity.

_Devotion:_

God's grace helps us grow in our faith, increasing our knowledge and love for Jesus Christ.

A beautiful sentiment! Yes, the concept of God's grace is often seen as a guiding force that helps individuals deepen their faith and spiritual growth. It's the idea that God's love and mercy are freely given, and that this gift can inspire and nurture our relationship with the divine.

In many religious traditions, grace is seen as a transformative power that helps us become the best version of ourselves, and grow in our faith and understanding of God's will. It's a reminder that our spiritual journey is not just about our own efforts, but also about surrendering to a higher power and allowing its guidance and wisdom to shape us.

Do you have any specific thoughts about God's grace and its role in your spiritual growth?

_Prayer:_ *Dear God, thank you for your grace that helps me grow. Help me continue to grow in your grace and knowledge, and may your grace produce fruit in my life that honors you.* Amen.

## _June 24:_ Grace that Helps Us Forgive

_Scripture:_ Ephesians 4:32 - Be kind to one another, tenderhearted, forgiving one another, as God in Christ forgave you.

_Devotion:_

God's grace helps us forgive others, just as He forgave us.

What a beautiful sentiment! Forgiveness is indeed a profound aspect of human relationships and spiritual growth. The idea that God's grace helps us forgive others suggests that a higher power guides us towards compassion, understanding, and letting go of grudges.

Forgiveness doesn't mean forgetting or condoning harm, but rather releasing the negative emotions associated with it, allowing us to heal and move forward. It's a powerful reminder of the transformative impact of grace and mercy in our lives.

_Prayer:_ *Dear God, thank you for your grace that helps me forgive. Help me extend grace to others, just as you have extended it to me, and may your grace heal relationships and bring peace.* Amen.

## _June 25:_ Grace that Gives Us Purpose

_Scripture:_ Ephesians 2:10 - For we are his workmanship, created in Christ Jesus for good works, which God prepared beforehand, that we should walk in them.

_Devotion:_

God's grace gives us purpose and equips us for good works.

What a beautiful sentiment! The concept of God's grace giving us purpose is a powerful and comforting idea. It suggests that we are not alone, and that a higher power has a plan for us, even when we may not be able to see it. This belief can bring hope, guidance, and direction to our lives.

In many religious traditions, grace is seen as a gift from God that helps us to find our purpose and live a meaningful life. It's the idea that we are loved and supported, no matter what, and that we have a role to play in the world.

Do you have any personal experiences or thoughts about how God's grace has given you purpose?

_Prayer:_ *Dear God, thank you for your grace that gives me purpose. Help me walk in the good works you have prepared for me, and may your grace empower me to live a life that honors you. Amen.*

## _June 26: Grace that Gives Us Eternal Life

_Scripture: _ John 3:16 - For God so loved the world, that he gave his only Son, that whoever believes in him should not perish but have eternal life.

_Devotion: _

God's grace gives us eternal life through faith in Jesus Christ.

A wonderful reminder! The promise of eternal life through God's grace is a central tenet of many religious beliefs. It offers hope and reassurance that our existence extends beyond our physical lives, and that we will continue to live on in spirit.

The idea of eternal life through grace suggests that our connection with God transcends mortality, and that we will ultimately be reunited with the divine. This belief can bring comfort, peace, and a sense of security, even in the face of life's challenges and uncertainties.

Eternal life is seen as a gift from God, made possible through the sacrifice and love of our Lord and Savior Jesus Christ. It's a reminder that our lives have purpose and meaning beyond our earthly experiences.

May the promise of eternal life through God's grace bring you hope, comfort, and inspiration!

_Prayer: _ *Dear God, thank you for your grace that gives me eternal life. Help me cherish this gift and share it with others, and may your grace shine through me to those around me.* Amen.

## June 27: Resting in Grace

_Scripture:_ Hebrews 4:16 - Let us then approach God's throne of grace with confidence, so that we may receive mercy and find grace to help us in our time of need.

_Devotion:_

God's grace invites us to rest in His presence and find help in times of need.

What a beautiful theme! Let's dive deeper into the concept of resting in God's presence through His grace. "Come to me, all you who are weary and burdened, and I will give you rest." - Matthew 11:28

God's grace invites us to rest in His presence, to lay our worries, fears, and doubts at His feet, and to trust in His love and care for us. When we rest in God's presence, we experience:

1. Peace that surpasses understanding (Philippians 4:7)
3. Renewal and rejuvenation for our souls (Psalm 23:2-3)
4. Guidance and direction for our lives (Proverbs 3:5-6)
5. Assurance of His constant presence and love (Hebrews 13:5)

_Prayer:_ *Dear God, thank you for your throne of grace. Help me to confidently approach you and find rest in your grace. Amen!*

## _June 28:_ Extending Grace to Others

_Scripture:_ Matthew 5:44 - But I say to you, love your enemies and pray for those who persecute you.

_Devotion:_

God's grace teaches us to extend grace to others, even those who may not deserve it.

A wonderful extension of God's grace! "For just as through the disobedience of the one man the many were made sinners, so also through the obedience of the one man the many will be made righteous." - Romans 5:19

God's grace teaches us to:
1. Forgive others as God has forgiven us (Colossians 3:13)
2. Love our enemies and pray for those who persecute us (Matt 5:44)

When we extend grace to others, we:
1. Demonstrate God's love and character to a watching world
2. Create a ripple effect of kindness and compassion

Take a moment to reflect how you can extend grace to someone today.

_Prayer:_ *Dear God, thank you for your grace that teaches me to love and forgive others. Help me to extend your grace to those around me.* Amen!

## _June 29:_ _Growing in Grace

_Scripture:_ 2 Peter 3:18 - Grow in the grace and knowledge of our Lord and Savior Jesus Christ.

_Devotion:_

God's grace invites us to grow and deepen our relationship with Him. What a beautiful sentiment! Cultivating a deeper relationship with a higher power can bring comfort, guidance, and meaning to one's life. Embracing God's grace and invitation to grow can lead to a more profound sense of passion, purpose, and spiritual growth. Here's a brief overview of each:

1. *Purpose*: Your reason for being, the meaning you give to your life, and the sense of direction that guides your actions. It's what drives you and gives you a sense of accomplishment.

2. *Passion*: The enthusiasm and excitement you feel when engaging in activities that bring you joy and fulfillment. Pursuing your passions can help you discover your purpose.

3. *Spiritual growth*: The process of developing a deeper understanding of yourself, the world, and your place in it. It involves cultivating qualities like compassion, empathy, and self-awareness, and can lead to a greater sense of purpose and fulfillment. Cultivating all three can lead to a rich and meaningful life.

Prayer:_ *Dear God, thank you for your grace that helps me grow. Help me to continually deepen my relationship with you.* Amen.

### June 30: The Grace of God's Love

_Scripture:_ Ephesians 2:8-9 - For by grace you have been saved through faith. And this is not your own doing; it is the gift of God, not a result of works, so that no one may boast.

_Devotion:_

God's love is our grace and salvation, giving us new life in Him.

A beautiful sentiment! The concept of God's love being our grace and salvation is a central theme in many religious traditions. It suggests that God's unconditional love and mercy are what save us from our imperfections and guide us towards redemption and spiritual growth. This idea brings comfort and hope to many people around the world.

A beautiful moment for prayer! Here's a simple prayer to reflect on God's love and grace:

_Prayer:_ *Dear God, I come before you with a grateful heart, acknowledging your unconditional love and grace. Thank you for being my salvation and guiding light. Help me to embrace your love fully and share it with others. May your grace inspire me to live a life of compassion, kindness, and forgiveness.*

In times of joy and struggle, remind us of your presence and peace.

# ROSE PETALS -- 366 DAYS OF MORNING MUSINGS

As June, the month of Grace, comes to a close, we reflect on the gentle yet profound impact of this virtue in our lives. We've explored the beauty of elegance, poise, and kindness, and how they can transform our relationships and experiences.

The theme of Grace has taught us to:

- Embody compassion, empathy, and understanding in our interactions
- Move with intention, kindness, and generosity in all we do
- Find beauty in imperfection and strength in vulnerability
- Cultivate humility, gratitude, and a sense of wonder

As we step into July, may the essence of Grace remain with us, guiding us toward a summer of gentle strength, compassionate hearts, and serene resilience. May we continue to embrace the transformative power of Grace, allowing it to shape us into beacons of hope, love, and light.

Farewell, June – your lessons of Grace will stay with us, a reminder to walk in beauty, kindness, and compassion.

May His grace continue to guide, comfort, and empower you each day!

# JULY 1-31

1. God's Perfect Timing
2. The Gift of Grace
3. Grace in Our Weakness
4. Grace that Transforms
5. Grace that Lifts Us Up
6. Grace that Sets Us Free
7. Grace that Renews Us
8. Grace that Unites Us
9. Grace that Empowers Us
10. Grace that Forgives Us
11. Grace that Sustains Us
12. Grace that Transcends Our Limits
13. Grace that Renews Our Minds
14. Grace that Brings Joy
15. Grace that Gives Us Hope
16. Grace that Strengthens Us
17. Grace that Sets Us Free
18. Grace that Gives Us Humility
19. Grace that Gives Us Boldness
20. Grace that Gives Us Assurance
21. Grace that Transforms Us
22. Grace that Satisfies Our Souls
23. Grace that Helps Us Grow
24. Grace that Helps Us Forgive
25. Grace that Gives Us Purpose
26. Grace that Gives Us Eternal Life
27. Resting in Grace
28. Extending Grace to Others
29. Growing in Grace
30. The Grace of God's Love
31. Joy in Grief

### _July 1:_ _ Joy in God's Presence

_Scripture:_ Psalm 16:11 says In Your presence is fullness of joy; at Your right hand are pleasures forevermore.

_Devotional:_

Joy is not found in temporary things, but in the eternal presence of God. When we seek God, we find joy that never fades. His presence fills us with delight, comfort, and peace.

Today, take time to bask in God's presence. Let go of worries and distractions, and simply enjoy Him. Feel His joy filling your heart and soul.

_Prayer:_ *Dear God, I seek Your presence today. Fill me with Your joy and pleasures. Help me let go of distractions and simply enjoy You. May Your joy be my strength and delight.* Amen!

Schedule a quiet time with God today, and intentionally seek His presence. Listen to worship music, read a Psalm, or simply sit in silence, focusing on His joy.

_July 2-:_ The Joy of Gratitude

_Scripture:_ 1 Thessalonians 5:18 - "Give thanks in all circumstances; for this is God's will for you in Christ Jesus."

_Devotion:_

Gratitude unlocks the door to joy. When we focus on what we have, rather than what we lack, we experience the joy of God's goodness.

What a beautiful sentiment! You're absolutely right. Gratitude has the power to shift our focus from what's lacking to what we already have, and that's where the joy is! By cultivating gratitude, we can:

- Appreciate the small things
- Find positivity in challenges
- Strengthen relationships
- Improve mental health
- Live more mindfully

Remember, gratitude is a muscle that grows stronger with practice. Take a moment each day to reflect on the things you're thankful for, no matter how small they may seem. It can be a game-changer!

_Prayer:_ *Dear God, help me to cultivate a heart of gratitude. May thankfulness be my response to your goodness in all circumstances.* Amen

## _July 3: _Joy in Abundance

_Scripture: _ John 10:10 says, have come that they may have life, and have it to the full.

### _Devotional: _

God wants us to experience abundant life, filled with joy, purpose, and meaning. When we trust in Him, we can experience the joy of living life to the full. Today, reflect on areas where you can trust God for abundance.

A wonderful reminder! Yes, many spiritual traditions and beliefs hold that a higher power or divine force desires for us to live a life that is rich in purpose, joy, and fulfillment. This perspective encourages us to:

- Trust in a greater plan
- Seek guidance and wisdom
- Cultivate a sense of connection and oneness
- Embrace our unique talents and gifts
- Live with intention and passion

May this belief inspire you to embrace each day with hope, gratitude, and a sense of wonder! Remember, abundant life is not just about what we have, but about how we live and experience each moment.

_Prayer: _ *Dear God, help me trust You for abundance in all areas of my life. Fill me with joy as I experience life to the full.* Amen!

## _July 4: _Joy in Hope_

_Scripture: _ Romans 15:13 says, May the God of hope fill you with all joy and peace as you trust in Him, so that you may overflow with hope by the power of the Holy Spirit.

_Devotional: _

Hope brings us joy because it reminds us of God's promises and future blessings. When we trust in God's hope, we experience the joy of anticipation and confidence. Today, reflect on areas where you need to trust in God's hope.

What a wonderful reminder! Hope is a powerful force in our lives, and it's amazing how it can bring us joy even in the midst of challenging circumstances.

When we focus on God's promises, we're reminded that He is faithful, loving, and always working for our good. This hope gives us a sense of expectation and anticipation for what's to come, and it can fill us with joy and peace.

Let's take a moment to reflect on God's promises and allow hope to fill our hearts with joy.

_Prayer: _ *Dear God, fill me with joy and peace as I trust in Your hope. Help me overflow with hope by the power of the Holy Spirit.* Amen!

_July 5_: _Joy in Love_

_Scripture:_ 1 Corinthians 13:4 says, Love is patient, love is kind. It does not envy, it does not boast, it is not proud.

_Devotional:_

Love brings us joy because it shows us the beauty of God's character and care. When we love others, we experience the joy of connection and community.

That's a beautiful truth! Love is indeed a reflection of God's character, and it brings us joy because it reveals the depth of His care and compassion for us.

As the Bible says in 1 John 4:8, "Whoever does not love does not know God, because God is love." And in Psalm 136:1-3, "Give thanks to the Lord, for he is good. His love endures forever. Give thanks to the God of gods. His love endures forever."

When we experience love, whether it's through our relationships with others or through our relationship with God, we catch a glimpse of God's beautiful character. We see that He is kind, merciful, and gracious, and that He delights in blessing us and giving us joy.

_Prayer:_ *Dear God, help me love others with patience and kindness. Fill me with joy as I show Your love.* Amen!

## _July 6_: _Joy in Simplicity_

_Scripture:_ Philippians 4:6 says, do not be anxious about anything, but in every situation, by prayer and petition, with thanksgiving, present your requests to God.

_Devotional:_

Simplicity brings us joy because it helps us focus on what's truly important. When we simplify our lives, we can experience the joy of clarity and peace.

What a wonderful insight! Simplicity can indeed bring joy by allowing us to prioritize what truly matters, free from unnecessary distractions and clutter. By embracing simplicity, we can:

- Clarify our values and goals
- Reduce stress and mental overwhelm
- Cultivate mindfulness and presence
- Foster deeper connections with others
- Find contentment and gratitude in everyday moments

Prayer: _ Dear God, help me simplify my life and focus on what's truly important. Fill me with joy as I experience clarity and peace. Amen!_

# _July 7:_ _Joy in Forgiveness_

_Scripture:_ Colossians 3:13 Says, Bear with each other and forgive one another if any of you has a grievance against someone. Forgive as the Lord forgave you.

_Devotional:_

Forgiveness brings us joy because it frees us from the weight of resentment and anger. When we forgive, we experience the joy of release and peace. Today, reflect on areas where you need to forgive others or yourself.

What a beautiful and profound statement! Forgiveness indeed has the power to bring us joy by releasing us from the burdens of resentment and anger. When we hold onto these negative emotions, they can consume us and weigh us down, making it hard to move forward and find happiness.

Forgiveness allows us to let go of the past and release the energy we've been expending on holding onto grudges. It's not about forgetting or condoning hurtful actions, but rather about releasing the hold they have on us. By doing so, we open ourselves up to healing, peace, and a sense of liberation.

As the saying goes, "To forgive is to set a prisoner free and discover that the prisoner was you." Forgiveness brings joy because it sets us free from the prison of our own negativity, allowing us to live more fully and authentically.

_Prayer:_ *Dear God, help me forgive as You forgave me. Fill me with joy as I experience release and peace.* Amen!

# ROSE PETALS -- 366 DAYS OF MORNING MUSINGS

### July 8: _Joy in Service_

_Scripture:_ Ephesians 6:7 says, serve wholeheartedly, as if you were serving the Lord, not people.

_Devotional:_

Serving others brings us joy because it allows us to demonstrate God's love and care. When we serve wholeheartedly, we experience the joy of making a difference and bringing glory to God. Today, look for opportunities to serve others.

That's a wonderful insight! Serving others can indeed bring us joy because it allows us to be a vessel for God's love and care. When we serve others, we're not just meeting their physical or emotional needs, but also showing them that they're valued, seen, and loved. This can be a powerful way to demonstrate God's love and care in a tangible way.

By serving others, we're able to put our faith into action, and experience the joy that comes from being a part of something bigger than ourselves. It's a way to live out our values and beliefs, and to make a positive impact on the world around us.

_Prayer:_ *Dear God, help me serve others with a whole heart, as if I were serving You. Fill me with joy as I demonstrate Your love. Amen!*

### _July 9:_ _Joy in Generosity_

_Scripture:_ 2 Corinthians 9:6 says, remember this: Whoever sows sparingly will also reap sparingly, and whoever sows generously will also reap generously.

_Devotional:_

Generosity brings us joy because it allows us to bless others and experience God's abundance. When we give generously, we experience the joy of sharing and seeing God's impact.

What a beautiful perspective! You're absolutely right, generosity can bring us joy and a sense of fulfillment. When we focus on blessing others, it shifts our attention away from our own needs and worries, and allows us to experience a sense of connection and purpose. The idea of experiencing God's abundance through generosity is a lovely way to frame it - it suggests that there's a deeper, spiritual dimension to giving and sharing with others.

By being generous, we may feel more connected to something greater than ourselves, and experience a sense of joy and contentment that goes beyond material possessions.

_Prayer:_ *Dear God, help me sow generously and trust Your abundance. Fill me with joy as I bless others.* Amen!

## ROSE PETALS -- 366 DAYS OF MORNING MUSINGS

**_July 10: _Joy in Contentment_**

_Scripture: _ Philippians 4:11 says, I have learned to be content whatever the circumstances.

_Devotional: _

Contentment brings us joy because it allows us to trust God's sovereignty and provision. When we are content, we experience the joy of peace and satisfaction. Today, reflect on areas where you need to trust God's provision.

What a great point! Contentment can indeed bring us joy because it allows us to trust in God's sovereignty and provision. When we're content, we're acknowledging that God is in control and that He's provided everything we need.

Contentment isn't about getting what we want, but about being satisfied with what we have. It's a mindset that says, "God, I trust that You've given me exactly what I need, and I'm grateful for it."

By trusting in God's sovereignty and provision, we're able to find joy in the present moment, regardless of our circumstances. We're not constantly striving for more or worrying about what we don't have.

As the apostle Paul wrote, "I have learned to be content whatever the circumstances" (Philippians 4:11).

May we all learn to cultivate this kind of contentment, and find joy in trusting God's sovereignty and provision!

_Prayer: _ *Dear God, help me learn to be content in all circumstances. Fill me with joy as I trust Your provision. Amen!*

## REFLECTION

_Action Step: _ Take a few minutes to write down areas where you need to trust God's provision. Pray over each one, asking God to help you experience contentment and joy.

_Reflection Questions: _

1. What's one area where you need to trust God's provision?
2. How has contentment impacted your life and joy?
3. What's one step you can take today to trust God's sovereignty?

## July 11: _Joy in Worship_

_Scripture:_ Psalm 100:2 says, Worship the Lord with gladness; come before him with joyful songs.

_Devotional:_

Worship brings us joy because it allows us to express our love and gratitude to God. When we worship, we experience the joy of connection and intimacy with Him.

Worship is a powerful way to connect with God and experience joy! When we worship, we're able to express our love and gratitude to God, and that expression brings us joy.

Worship allows us to:
- Acknowledge God's goodness and greatness
- Thank Him for His blessings and provision
- Praise Him for His character and attributes
- Surrender our hearts and lives to Him

As we express our love and gratitude to God through worship, we're reminded of His presence, power, and love. This reminder fills us with joy, peace, and contentment.

The Bible says, "Worship the Lord with gladness; come before Him with joyful songs" (Psalm 100:2). Whether through music, prayer, or simply quiet reflection, worship is a powerful way to experience joy and deepen our relationship with God.

_Prayer:_ *Dear God, help me worship You with gladness and joyful songs. Fill me with joy as I connect with You. Amen!*

## REFLECTION

_Action Step:_ Take a few minutes to worship God through music, prayer, or reading His Word. Express your gratitude and love to Him.

_Reflection Questions:_

1. What's one way you can worship God today?
2. How has worship impacted your life and joy?
3. What's one thing you're grateful to God for?

## _July 12_: _Joy in Obedience_

_Scripture:_ John 15:10 says, if you obey My commands, you will remain in My love, just as I have obeyed My Father's commands and remain in His love.

_Devotional:_

Obedience brings us joy because it allows us to experience God's love and guidance. When we obey God's commands, we experience the joy of intimacy and direction. Today, reflect on areas where you need to obey God.

What a beautiful truth! Obedience to God's will and ways can indeed bring us joy, and here's why:

- When we obey God, we demonstrate our love and trust in Him.
- Obedience shows that we value His guidance and wisdom more than our own desires and understanding.
- As we follow God's commands and principles, we experience His love and care in our lives.
- Obedience allows us to live in harmony with God's plan and purpose, which brings a sense of peace and contentment.

Remember, obedience isn't about following rules or regulations; it's about surrendering to God's love and allowing Him to guide us into the best life possible. And that's where true joy is found!

_Prayer:_ *Dear God, help me obey Your commands and remain in Your love. Fill me with joy as I experience Your guidance. Amen!*

## July 13: _Joy in Humility_

_Scripture:_ James 4:10 says, humble yourselves before the Lord, and He will lift you up.

_Devotional:_

Humility brings us joy because it allows us to surrender our pride and self-reliance. When we humble ourselves, we experience the joy of freedom and dependence on God. Today, reflect on areas where you need to humble yourself.

What a beautiful insight! Humility can indeed bring joy by allowing us to let go of our ego and self-reliance, which can be a heavy burden to carry. When we surrender our pride, we open ourselves up to:

- Deeper connections with others, built on mutual respect and understanding
- A greater sense of belonging and community
- Increased empathy and compassion for ourselves and others
- A willingness to learn and grow, unencumbered by the need to be "right"
- A sense of freedom from the constant need to prove ourselves

By embracing humility, we can find joy in the simplicity of being present, authentic, and connected to others. It's a beautiful paradox – by surrendering our pride, we gain so much more!

_Prayer:_ _Dear God, help me humble myself before You. Fill me with joy as I surrender my pride. Amen!_

## _July 14_: _Joy in Perseverance_

_Scripture:_ Hebrews 12:1-2 says, let us run with perseverance the race marked out for us, fixing our eyes on Jesus, the pioneer and perfecter of faith.

_Devotional:_

Perseverance brings us joy because it helps us stay focused on our goal and trust God's plan. When we persevere, we experience the joy of progress and hope. Today, reflect on areas where you need to persevere.

That's a beautiful perspective! Perseverance indeed plays a crucial role in our journey towards achieving our goals and living a fulfilling life. By staying focused and committed, we build resilience and character, and trust in a higher power can provide comfort and guidance.

Perseverance helps us develop a growth mindset, learn from our mistakes, and appreciate the small victories along the way. It's a reminder that success is not always immediate, but with persistence and faith, we can overcome obstacles and reach our full potential.

_Prayer:_ *Dear God, help me persevere in the race marked out for me. Fill me with joy as I fix my eyes on Jesus.* Amen!

## July 15: Joy in the Little Things

_Scripture:_ Philippians 4:4 says, Rejoice in the Lord always. I will say it again: Rejoice!

_Devotional:_

Joy can be found in the little things in life. When we focus on the small blessings and pleasures, we can experience great joy. Today, reflect on the little things in your life that bring you joy and thank God for them.

What a wonderful perspective! Yes, joy can indeed be found in the little things in life. It's often the small, everyday moments and experiences that bring us the most happiness and fulfillment.

Things like:
- A beautiful sunset or a stunning view
- A good cup of coffee or tea
- A warm conversation with a friend or loved one
- A great book or a fascinating article
- A relaxing walk or a fun workout
- A home-cooked meal or a favorite dessert
- A moment of quiet reflection or meditation

These small joys can add up and bring a sense of contentment and happiness to our lives. And the best part is, they're often right in front of us, waiting to be appreciated and savored!

_Prayer:_ *Dear God, help me rejoice in the little things. Fill me with joy as I focus on Your blessings.* Amen!

# ROSE PETALS -- 366 DAYS OF MORNING MUSINGS

## July 16: _Joy in the Journey_

_Scripture:_ Psalm 16:11 Say, you make known to me the path of life; you will fill me with joy in your presence, with eternal pleasures at your right hand.

_Devotional:_

Joy is not just a destination, but a journey. When we walk with God, He fills us with joy in His presence and gives us eternal pleasures.

That's a beautiful way to put it! Joy is not just a feeling we arrive at, but a mindset we can cultivate and experience throughout our lives. It's a journey of embracing the present moment, finding beauty in everyday experiences, and appreciating the small pleasures.

When we view joy as a journey, we:
- Focus on the process, not just the outcome
- Learn to appreciate the ups and downs
- Cultivate gratitude and positivity
- Savor each moment, rather than rushing to the next

By embracing joy as a journey, we can:
- Experience more happiness and fulfillment
- Develop a more optimistic outlook
- Find meaning and purpose
- Live more mindfully and intentionally

_Prayer:_ *Dear God, fill me with joy in Your presence. Help me see the eternal pleasures at Your right hand.* Amen!

# ROSE PETALS -- 366 DAYS OF MORNING MUSINGS

## July 17: _Joy in Surrender_

_Scripture:_ James 4:10 says, humble yourselves before the Lord, and He will lift you up.

_Devotional:_

Surrendering our lives to God can bring us great joy. When we let go of control and trust in His goodness, we experience freedom and peace.

Surrendering our lives to God can indeed bring us great joy! When we let go of control and trust in a higher power, we can experience a sense of peace, freedom, and contentment. This surrender can:

- Release us from the weight of our own expectations
- Allow us to trust in a plan greater than our own
- Give us hope and reassurance in uncertain times
- Help us find purpose and meaning
- Bring us closer to our spiritual selves

In surrendering to God, we can experience: - A sense of calm and inner peace- Guidance and direction- Strength and courage- Forgiveness and redemption

As the Bible says, "Delight yourself in the Lord, and He will give you the desires of your heart" (Psalm 37:4). When we surrender to God, we can find joy in His presence, His love, and His plan for our lives.

_Prayer:_ *Dear God, help me surrender my life to You. Fill me with joy as I trust in Your goodness. Amen!*

## _July 18_: _Joy in Unity_

_Scripture:_ Psalm 133:1 says, how good and pleasant it is when God's people live together in unity!

_Devotional:_

Unity with others brings joy because it reflects the unity we have with God. When we come together in love and harmony, we experience a sense of belonging and connection that fills our hearts with happiness.

What a beautiful truth! Unity with others indeed brings joy because it reflects the unity we have with God. When we come together in love, acceptance, and understanding, we experience a glimpse of the divine connection that exists between us and God. This unity:

- Mirrors the harmony and oneness that exists within the Trinity (Father, Son, and Holy Spirit)
- Demonstrates our shared humanity and common purpose
  - Fosters empathy, compassion, and support
  - Reflects God's love and grace in our relationships

As the Bible says, "For just as each of us has one body with many members, and these members do not all have the same function, so in Christ we, though many, form one body, and each member belongs to all the others" (Romans 12:4-5).

_Prayer:_ Dear God, help me cultivate unity with others. Fill me with joy as I love and serve those around me. Amen!

## July 19: Joy in Serving Others

_Scripture:_ Ephesians 6:7 says, serve wholeheartedly, as if you were serving the Lord, not people.

_Devotional:_

Joy is often found in serving others. When we focus on meeting the needs of those around us, we take our eyes off our own struggles and find happiness in making a difference.

What a wonderful truth! Joy is indeed often found in serving others. When we focus on serving others, we experience a sense of purpose, fulfillment, and happiness. Serving others: Shifts our focus from ourselves to others, breaking the cycle of self-centeredness. Fosters gratitude, humility, and empathy, leading to personal growth.

As Jesus said, "For even the Son of Man came not to be served but to serve, and to give his life as a ransom for many" (Mark 10:45).

Remember, joy is not just a feeling but a choice. Choose to serve others, and you'll likely discover a deeper sense of joy and fulfillment in your life!

_Prayer:_ *Dear God, help me find joy in serving others. Give me opportunities to make a difference and fill me with happiness as I serve.* Men!

## July 20: Joy in Freedom

*Scripture:* 2 Corinthians 3:17 says, where the Spirit of the Lord is, there is freedom.

*Devotional:*

Today, we celebrate freedom in many countries, but as believers, we know that true freedom comes from Jesus. He sets us free from sin, shame, and fear, and fills us with His joy. A profound truth! True freedom indeed comes from Jesus. In Him, we find liberation from:

1. Sin's bondage: Jesus' sacrifice sets us free from the power of sin (Romans 6:6-7).
2. Guilt and shame: His forgiveness cleanses us from guilt and shame (1 John 1:9).
3. Fear and anxiety: Jesus' peace and love dispel fear and anxiety (John 14:27, 1 John 4:18).

In Jesus, we find true freedom to:
1. Live for God and others (2 Corinthians 5:15).
2. Become our authentic selves (Galatians 2:20).
3. Love unconditionally (John 13:34).
4. Forgive and be forgiven (Matthew 6:14-15).

May we embrace this freedom and live a life that reflects the liberty we have in Christ!

*Prayer:* *Dear God, thank You for the gift of freedom in Christ. Fill me with Your joy and help me live out my freedom in a way that honors You. Amen!*

## July 21: Joy in God's Promises

_Scripture:_ Romans 15:13 says, may the God of hope fill you with all joy and peace as you trust in Him, so that you may overflow with hope by the power of the Holy Spirit.

_Devotional:_

God's promises bring us joy because they remind us of His faithfulness and love. When we trust in His promises, we experience joy and peace that overflows into hope.

What a beautiful truth! God's promises indeed bring us joy because they:

1. Reveal His love: God's promises show us the depth of His love and care for us, filling us with joy and gratitude (Jeremiah 31:3, Romans 8:38-39).

2. Encourage trust: God's promises invite us to trust Him, even when circumstances are uncertain, and that trust brings joy (Proverbs 3:5-6, Psalm 37:4-5).

Some of God's promises that bring joy include:
- "I will never leave you nor forsake you" (Hebrews 13:5)
- "I will give you strength in times of weakness" (Isaiah 40:29)
- "I will be with you always" (Matthew 28:20)

May God's promises fill your heart with joy, hope, and confidence in His love and faithfulness!

# ROSE PETALS -- 366 DAYS OF MORNING MUSINGS

**_July 22:_** _Joy is a powerful force_

Scripture: Nehemiah 8:10 says, the joy of the Lord is your strength.

_Devotional:_

Joy is a powerful force that can transform our lives. When we experience joy, we feel alive, energized, and motivated. But joy isn't just a feeling; it's a choice. We can choose to focus on God's goodness, His love, and His presence in our lives, and that choice can bring us joy even in difficult times.

What a profound perspective! You're absolutely right – joy is not just a fleeting emotion, but a conscious choice we can make every day. By choosing joy, we can:

- Focus on the good things in life, no matter how small
- Practice gratitude and appreciation
- Reframe challenges as opportunities for growth
- Take care of ourselves and prioritize our well-being

Choosing joy doesn't mean ignoring difficulties or hardships, but rather approaching life with a sense of hope, resilience, and determination. It's a mindset shift that can have a profound impact on our lives and relationships. As the saying goes, "Joy is not in things; it is in us.

_Prayer:_ *Dear God, fill me with Your joy today. Help me to see the good things You are doing in my life, and to choose joy even when things are tough. May Your joy be my strength. Amen.*

## _July 23_: The Power of Joy_

_Scripture:_ Nehemiah 8:10 - The joy of the Lord is your strength.

### _Devotion:_

Joy is not just a feeling, but a powerful force that can transform our lives. When we choose joy, we tap into God's strength and resilience.

What a beautiful perspective! You're absolutely right. Joy can have a profound impact on our well-being, relationships, and overall outlook on life.

By recognizing joy as a powerful force, we can make a conscious effort to prioritize it in our lives. This might involve practicing gratitude, seeking out activities that bring us delight, or simply slowing down to appreciate the small pleasures.

By choosing joy, we can shift our focus away from fear, worry, and doubt, and instead, align ourselves with faith, hope, and love. This can lead to a deeper sense of trust, peace, and confidence in God's plan for our lives.

As the Bible says, "The joy of the Lord is your strength" (Nehemiah 8:10). May we continue to choose joy and tap into God's strength and resilience in our lives.

_Prayer:_ *Dear God, help me to choose joy, even when it's hard. Fill me with your strength and resilience.* Amen.

_July 24_: Unlocking Joy_

_Scripture:_ Psalm 51:12 - Restore to me the joy of your salvation and grant me a willing spirit, to sustain me.

_Devotion:_

Joy can get locked away by sin, shame, and regret. But God's restoration and forgiveness can unlock it again, bringing us back to the joy of our salvation.

What a profound and poignant statement! Yes, joy can indeed become obscured and locked away by the weights of sin, shame, and regret. These emotions can cast a shadow over our lives, making it difficult to experience joy and happiness.

Sin can lead to feelings of guilt and self-condemnation, causing us to withdraw from joy. Shame can make us feel unworthy of joy, as if we don't deserve it. Regret can haunt us with "what ifs" and "if onlys," preventing us from embracing the present moment and finding joy in it.

But here's the beautiful thing: joy can be unlocked again! Through self-reflection, forgiveness (of ourselves and others), and the practice of self-compassion, we can begin to release the burdens of sin, shame, and regret. We can learn to reframe our experiences, find the lessons in them, and discover the beauty of redemption.

_ Dear God, restore to me the joy of your salvation. Grant me a willing spirit, and sustain me with your joy._ Amen

### **June 25**: Joy in Servantship

_Scripture:_ Mark 9:35 - If anyone wants to be first, he must be the very last, and the servant of all.

_Devotion:_

Joy in servantship is about finding joy in serving others, putting their needs before our own, and reflecting God's heart of service.

What a wonderful topic! Joy in servantship is indeed about finding happiness and fulfillment in serving others. It's about prioritizing the needs of others, being selfless, and taking pleasure in making a positive impact in their lives.

When we focus on serving others, we can experience a sense of purpose, meaning, and joy that goes beyond our own individual interests. It's a mindset shift from "what can I gain?" to "what can I give?"

Joy in servantship can manifest in various ways, such as: - Showing kindness, empathy, and compassion to others- Putting others' needs before our own

By embracing joy in servantship, we can cultivate a more altruistic and compassionate approach to life, leading to deeper connections, a sense of belonging, and a more fulfilling existence.

_Prayer:_ *Dear God, help me to find joy in serving others. Show me Your heart of service.* Amen

### REFLECTION

_Look for opportunities to serve in your daily life, such as holding the door for someone or offering to help with a task._

Ways to practice joy in servantship:

- Reflect God's heart of service
- Celebrate the joy of serving
- Trust in God's sovereignty

_June 26_: Joy in Grace_

_Scripture:_ Romans 5:2 - We rejoice in the hope of the glory of God...and rejoice in God through our Lord Jesus Christ, through whom we have now received reconciliation.

_Devotion:_

Joy in grace is about finding joy in the unearned, undeserved favor of God, who loves and accepts us just as we are.

A beautiful and profound topic! Joy in grace is indeed about finding joy and delight in the unearned, undeserved favor of God. It's about recognizing and embracing the love, mercy, and kindness that God extends to us, even when we don't deserve it.

This concept is rooted in the idea that God's grace is a gift, freely given and not based on our actions or worthiness. When we grasp this truth, it can bring immense joy, freedom, and peace to our lives.

Joy in grace can manifest in various ways, such as:
- A deep sense of gratitude for God's unwavering love and acceptance
- Trust and confidence in God's sovereignty and goodness

Embracing joy in grace can transform our lives, allowing us to live with hope, humility, and a heart full of praise and thanksgiving. It's a reminder that our worth and identity are rooted in God's love, not our own efforts or achievements.

_Prayer:_ *Dear God, help me to rejoice in Your grace. Show me Your favor and love.* Amen.

## REFLECTION

_Write down three ways God's grace has impacted your life and reflect on them throughout the day._

Ways to practice joy in grace:

- Focus on God's unearned favor and love
- Celebrate His acceptance and forgiveness
- Practice humility and gratitude
- Share God's grace with others
- Trust in His goodness and sovereignty

## July 27: Joy in Every Season

_Scripture:_ Ecclesiastes 3:1-4 - There is a time for everything, and a season for every activity under the heavens...a time to weep and a time to laugh, a time to mourn and a time to dance.

_Devotion:_

Joy is not limited to happy times. God's joy can be present in every season, even in difficult ones. Trusting Him and finding joy in His presence can help us navigate life's ups and downs.

What a profound statement! You're absolutely right. Joy can be found in unexpected places and moments, even in difficult or challenging times. It's a mindset and a choice to find the beauty, lesson, or silver lining in every situation.

Joy can be a sense of peace, contentment, or gratitude that comes from within, regardless of external circumstances. It's about appreciating the small things, finding meaning and purpose, and cultivating a sense of wonder and awe.

As the Japanese proverb says, "Fall seven times, stand up eight." Joy can be found in the resilience and strength that comes from navigating life's ups and downs.

_Prayer:_ Dear God, help me to find joy in your presence, no matter the season. Give me trust and hope in your goodness. Amen.

## _July 28_: Radiating Joy_

_Scripture:_ Matthew 5:16 - Let your light shine before others, that they may see your good deeds and glorify your Father in heaven.

### _Devotion:_

Joy is contagious! When we radiate joy, we reflect God's love and light, inspiring others to seek Him. Let your joy shine brightly, and watch how it impacts those around you.

Joy is indeed contagious! When we experience joy, it can spread to those around us, creating a ripple effect of happiness and positivity.

Research has shown that joy can be transmitted through social connections, facial expressions, and even mirror neurons in our brains. When we see someone else experiencing joy, it can trigger a response in our own brain, making us feel more joyful too!

Moreover, joy can be contagious through:

- Smiles: Seeing someone smile can brighten our day and make us feel more joyful.
- Actions: Witnessing acts of kindness and generosity can spread joy and encourage others to do the same.

_Prayer:_ *Dear God, help me to radiate your joy and love. Let my life be a reflection of your light, shining brightly for all to see.* Amen.

## _July 29_: Joyful Witness_

_Scripture:_ 1 Peter 3:15 - Always be prepared to give an answer to everyone who asks you to give the reason for the hope that you have. But do this with gentleness and respect.

_Devotion:_

Our joy can be a powerful witness to others, pointing them to God's love and hope.

What a beautiful truth! Our joy can be a powerful testimony to the world around us, reflecting God's love and hope.

When we radiate joy, it can:

- Attract others to God's love and grace
- Showcase the transformative power of faith
- Offer hope in a world filled with challenges and darkness
- Demonstrate the fruit of the Spirit, as described in Galatians 5:22-23

May our joy be a beacon of God's love, shining brightly for all to see!

_Prayer:_ *Dear God, help me to share my joyful witness with others. Give me opportunities to share your love and hope. Amen.*

## _July 30_: Joyful Trust_

_Scripture:_ Proverbs 3:5-6 - Trust in the Lord with all your heart and lean not on your own understanding; in all your ways submit to him, and he will make your paths straight.

_Devotion:_

Joyful trust is rooted in confidence in God's goodness and sovereignty. When we trust Him fully, we can experience joy even in uncertain times.

A wonderful reminder! Joyful trust is indeed rooted in confidence in God's goodness. When we trust in God's goodness, we can:

- Rest in His sovereignty, knowing He's in control
- Find peace in His promises, which are always true
- Experience joy, even in difficult circumstances
- See challenges as opportunities for growth and refinement
- Receive strength and courage to face each new day

This confidence in God's goodness also helps us to:- Trust His plans, even when we don't understand- Believe in His provision, even in uncertainty- Hope in His presence, even in darkness- See His love, even in difficult circumstances

May our trust in God's goodness be the foundation of our joy, and may we radiate His love and hope to those around us!

_Prayer:_ *Dear God, help me to trust you fully and lean not on my own understanding. Make my paths straight and fill me with joyful trust. Amen.*

## REFLECTION

Ways to cultivate joyful trust:

- Practice surrender and letting go
- Focus on God's character and promises
- Seek guidance from Scripture and prayer
- Share your struggles with a trusted friend or mentor

_Reflection Prompt:_ What area of your life do you need to trust God with more fully? How can you submit your ways to Him?

_July 31_: Joy in Grief_

_Scripture:_ Psalm 126:5-6 - Those who sow with tears will reap with songs of joy. Those who go out weeping, carrying seed to sow, will return with songs of joy, carrying sheaves with them.

_Devotion:_

Joy and grief can coexist. Even in the midst of sorrow, we can find joy in God's presence, promises, and purposes.

What a profound truth! Joy and grief can indeed coexist. It's a paradox that may seem contradictory, but it's a reality that many of us have experienced. *Joy and grief can coexist because:*

- Our hearts are capable of holding multiple emotions simultaneously
- Joy doesn't negate our grief, but rather, it can help us navigate it
- Grief doesn't erase our joy, but rather, it can make it more precious and meaningful

*This coexistence of joy and grief can manifest in various ways, such as*: Finding joy in memories of a loved one who has passed away, while still grieving their loss. Experiencing joy in the present moment, while still carrying the weight of past traumas or difficulties.

*Embracing this paradox allows us to*: Live with authenticity and honesty. Acknowledge the complexity of our emotions. Find ways to heal and navigate our grief, even as we hold onto joy

_Prayer: _ *Dear God, help me to find joy in grief. Show me your presence and promises.* Amen.

## REFLECTION

Ways to practice joy in grief:

- Focus on God's presence and comfort
- Celebrate the life and legacy of loved ones
- Find community and support
- Practice gratitude and praise
- Trust God's sovereignty and purposes

_Reflection Prompt: _ How can you find joy in the midst of grief? What seeds of hope and promise can you sow today?

May we learn to hold space for both joy and grief, allowing them to coexist and inform each other, as we navigate the complexities of life.

As we conclude our July journey through the theme of joy, take a moment to reflect on the happiness and positivity you've experienced. Remember the moments that made you smile, the people who brought you joy, and the experiences that lifted your spirit.

As you move forward, continue to seek joy in the simple things, in the beauty of creation, and in the love of those around you. And when the tough times come, draw on the joy that is rooted in your relationship with God. May the joy of the Lord be your portion now and forevermore!

Carry the lessons and feelings of this month with you, and let them guide you into the next chapter. And when the tough times come, draw on the joy that is rooted in your relationship with God.

May the joy and warmth of this month stay with you always, and may you continue to spread love, kindness, and happiness to those around you.

I hope this captures the essence of your devotional guide on joy!

# AUGUST 1-31

1. The Love of God's Sacrifice
2. The Power of Unconditional Love
3. God's Unconditional Love
4. God's Love is Our Identity
5. God's Love Casts Out Fear
6. Resting in God's Love
7. God's Love is Our Strength
8. God's Love is Our Hope
9. God's Love Transforms Us
10. God's Love is Faithful
11. God's Love is Our Comfort
12. God's Love Restores Us
13. God's Love is Merciful
14. God's Love is Patient
15. The Depth of God's Love
16. Love Forgives
17. Love is a Gift!
18. Love Incarnate
19. Love's Forgiveness
20. Love's Kindness
21. Love's Self-Control
22. Love's Gentleness
23. Love's Humility
24. Love's Compassion
25. Anchored in Love
26. Love is a Choice
27. Love's Legacy
28. Love Never Fails
29. Love Shines Brighter
30. Love Restores
31. The Depth of God's Love

# ROSE PETALS -- 366 DAYS OF MORNING MUSINGS

_August 1: The Love of God's Sacrifice_

Scripture: _ John 3:16 - For God so loved the world that he gave his only Son, that whoever believes in him should not perish but have eternal life.

_Devotion: _

God's sacrifice is our love and salvation, giving us eternal life in Him.

A beautiful reflection! Yes, God's sacrifice is indeed the ultimate expression of His love and our salvation. The willingness to give up His only Son, Jesus Christ, for the redemption of humanity is a profound demonstration of God's boundless love and mercy.

God's sacrifice is not just about what He did for us, but also about what He wants to do in us. His love and mercy are meant to transform us, to make us more like Him. As we receive His gift of salvation, may we also allow Him to shape our hearts, our thoughts, and our actions.

May we always remember and cherish the depth of God's love and the sacrifice He made for us. May it inspire us to share that love with others and live a life that honors His sacrifice.

_Prayer: _ *Dear God, we come before You with grateful hearts, acknowledging the immense sacrifice You made for us through Jesus Christ. Your love knows no bounds, and we are humbled by the depth of Your mercy. May our lives be a reflection of Your grace and love. Give us the strength to follow in Jesus' footsteps, to love unconditionally, and to serve others selflessly.* Amen

## August 2: The Power of Unconditional Love

Scripture: 1 Corinthians 13:4-5 - "Love is patient, love is kind. It does not envy, it does not boast, it is not proud. It does not dishonor others, it is not self-seeking, it is not easily angered, it keeps no record of wrongs."

Devotion:

Love is the foundation of our relationship with God and with others.

What a beautiful sentiment! Love is indeed a fundamental aspect of many spiritual beliefs and practices. It's often seen as a powerful force that connects us with something greater than ourselves, whether that's a higher power, the universe, or a sense of transcendence.

In many religious traditions, love is considered a key attribute of God or the divine, and is often described as unconditional, merciful, and all-encompassing. Cultivating a sense of love and devotion is seen as a way to deepen one's relationship with God and to live a life of purpose, compassion, and service to others.

Prayer: *Dear God, help me to understand and demonstrate unconditional love. May I be patient, kind, and selfless in my interactions with others. Show me opportunities to love others as you love me. Amen!*

**August 3**: _God's Unconditional Love

_Scripture:_ Romans 5:8 - But God demonstrates his own love for us in this: While we were still sinners, Christ died for us.

_Devotion:_

God's love is unconditional and unwavering.

A wonderful reminder! The concept of God's unconditional love is a comforting and liberating truth for many people. It means that God's love is not based on our performance, achievements, or worthiness, but rather on His nature and character.

Unconditional love means that God loves us without any strings attached, regardless of our flaws, mistakes, or circumstances. His love is not earned or deserved, but rather freely given, like a gift.

This understanding of God's love can bring immense peace, freedom, and joy to our lives. It allows us to:

- Let go of self-criticism and self-doubt
- Embrace our true identity and worth
- Trust in God's goodness and sovereignty
- Extend love and grace to others

_Prayer:_ *Dear God, thank you for your unconditional love. Help me to receive your love and extend it to others.* Amen

### August 4: God's Love is Our Identity

*Scripture:* 1 John 3:1 - See what great love the Father has lavished on us, that we should be called children of God! And that is what we are!

*Devotion:*

God's love defines our identity as His beloved children. What a beautiful truth! God's love indeed defines our identity as His beloved children. When we understand and accept this love, it transforms our sense of self and purpose.

*As God's beloved children, we are:*
- Adopted into His family (Ephesians 1:5)
- Chosen and cherished (1 John 3:1)
- Forgiven and redeemed (Ephesians 1:7)
- Empowered and equipped (2 Timothy 1:7)

*This identity shapes our lives in profound ways, helping us to:*
- Embrace our unique purpose and calling
- Trust in God's guidance and provision
- Extend love and compassion to others
- Live with hope and confidence

Remember, our identity is not defined by our past, present, or future, but by God's unwavering love and acceptance. We are loved, not because of who we are, but because of who He is!

*Prayer:* *Dear God, thank you for loving me and calling me Your child. Help me to live out of my true identity in You. Amen!*

### _August 5_: _ God's Love Casts Out Fear!

_Scripture: _ 1 John 4:18 - There is no fear in love. But perfect love drives out fear, because fear has to do with punishment. The one who fears is not made perfect in love.

#### _Devotion: _

God's love is perfect and casts out fear. Reflect on how His love can bring you peace and confidence.

That's a beautiful quote! 1 John 4:18. This verse highlights the transformative power of God's love, which can dispel fear and bring a sense of security and confidence. When we experience God's perfect love, it can free us from the grip of fear and anxiety, and fill us with a sense of peace and trust.

God's love is not based on our performance or worthiness, but on His character and nature. When we understand and experience God's perfect love, it can change our perspective and response to challenging situations.

Fear often holds us back from experiencing God's best for our lives, but His perfect love can empower us to overcome fear and live with courage and faith. God's love is not just a feeling, but a choice and a commitment He has made to us.

_Prayer: _ *Dear God, thank you for your perfect love. Help me to receive your love and let go of fear.* Amen

**August 6**: _Resting in God's Love_

_Scripture:_ Psalm 62:5-6 - My soul finds rest in God alone; my salvation comes from him. He alone is my rock and my salvation; he is my fortress; I will not be shaken.

_Devotion:_

Rest in God's love and find peace in His presence.

Beautifully said! Resting in God's love and finding peace in His presence is a powerful way to experience His comfort, guidance, and strength. It's a reminder to:

- Trust in His goodness and sovereignty
- Let go of worries, fears, and doubts
- Bask in the warmth of His acceptance and care
- Find solace in His promise to work all things for good
- Be still and know that He is God, always with us

As you rest in God's love and find peace in His presence, may you feel:
- His gentle whisper calming your mind and heart
- His loving arms embracing you in times of need
- His joy that fills your soul, overflowing into every area of life
- His love that heals, restores, and renews you, making you whole

May God's love and peace be your constant companion, guiding and sustaining you each day!

Prayer: _ Dear God, thank you for your loving presence. Help me to rest in your love and find peace in your arms._ Amen!

_August 7:_ _God's Love is Our Strength

_Scripture:_ Psalm 28:7 - The Lord is my strength and my shield; my heart trusts in him, and he helps me. My heart leaps for joy, and with my song I praise him.

_Devotion:_

God's love is our strength and shield. Reflect on how His love can empower and equip you for life's challenges.

Amen! God's love is indeed our strength and shield. It's a powerful reminder that:

- His love protects us from harm and danger
- His love shields us from the enemy's attacks and lies
- His love strengthens us in times of weakness and uncertainty
- His love equips us to walk in faith, hope, and victory

As the Bible says, "Love is as strong as death, and jealousy is as cruel as the grave" (Song of Solomon 8:6). God's love is a mighty fortress that surrounds and upholds us, giving us:

- Unshakeable hope- Unwavering faith- Unbreakable peace- Unrelenting joy
- Unconditional acceptance

May God's love be your strength and shield today, and every day!

_Prayer:_ *Dear God, thank you for your loving strength. Help me to trust in your power and praise your name.* Amen!

## **August 8:** God's Love is Our Hope

_Scripture:_ Psalm 39:7 - And now, Lord, what do I wait for? My hope is in you.

_Devotion:_

God's love is our hope and anchor in life's storms.

Beautifully said! God's love is indeed our hope and anchor in life's storms. It's a reassuring reminder that:

- His love holds us secure when waves of adversity crash against us
- His love keeps us grounded when turbulent circumstances seek to uproot us
- His love shines as a beacon of light in the darkness, guiding us through treacherous waters
- His love calms the tempests that rage within and around us
- His love anchors our souls, giving us stability and peace in the midst of chaos

As Hebrews 6:19 says, "We have this hope as an anchor for the soul, firm and secure." God's love is the anchor that: - Keeps us from drifting away from His presence- Holds us fast in times of turmoil- Secures our hearts and minds in His peace- Gives us a firm foundation to stand on- Reminds us that we are not alone, but are held by His loving hands

May God's love be your anchor and hope in the midst of life's storms!

_Prayer:_ *Dear God, thank you for your loving hope. Help me to wait on you and trust in your goodness.* Amen!

## _August 9:_ _God's Love Transforms Us

_Scripture:_ 2 Corinthians 3:18 - And we all, who with unveiled faces contemplate the Lord's glory, are being transformed into his image with ever-increasing glory, which comes from the Lord, who is the Spirit.

_Devotion:_

God's love transforms us into His image.

The phrase "God's love transforms us into His image" is a beautiful expression of a central idea in many spiritual traditions. It suggests that as we experience and accept God's love, we are transformed and become more like God, reflecting His qualities and character. This concept is echoed in the above verse.

In essence, this transformation is a process of spiritual growth, where we become more loving, compassionate, and wise, mirroring the attributes of God. It's a journey of becoming the best version of ourselves, aligned with God's will and purpose.

Here are some additional thoughts on the concept:
*Reflection of God's character*: As we are transformed into God's image, we begin to reflect His character traits like love, kindness, patience, and forgiveness.
*Inner transformation*: This change is not just external but a deep inner transformation, where our

thoughts, emotions, and actions align with God's will, becoming like Christ.

_Prayer:_ *Dear God, thank you for your transforming love. Help me to reflect your glory and become more like you.* Amen!

## REFLECTION

_Reflection Prompt:_ Write about a time when God's love transformed your heart or mind. How did it impact your life?

_Additional Thoughts:_

- Consider how God's love can give you a new perspective and understanding.
- Think about how this truth can help you let go of old patterns and habits.
- Reflect on how God's love can be a source of growth and renewal.

**August 10:** _God's Love is Faithful!

_Scripture:_ Psalm 100:5 - For the Lord is good and his love endures forever; his faithfulness continues through all generations.

_Devotion:_

God's love is faithful and constant.

A beautiful reminder! Yes, God's love is indeed faithful and constant, a steadfast and unwavering presence in our lives. It's a love that endures through every moment, every joy, and every struggle. As the Bible says, "God is love" (1 John 4:8) and "His love endures forever" (Psalm 136:1).

Here are some additional reflections on God's faithful and constant love:
- Unconditional: God's love accepts us just as we are, without judgment or expectation.
- Unwavering: His love remains steadfast, even when we stumble or fall.
- Eternal: God's love has no beginning or end; it simply is and always will be.
- Personal: His love is tailored to each individual, meeting us right where we are.
- Transformative: God's love has the power to change us from the inside out.

May these reminders of God's faithful and constant love bring you peace, comfort, and joy!

May this truth bring comfort, peace, and hope to your heart today!

_Prayer: _ *Dear God, thank you for your faithful love. Help me to trust in your goodness and rely on your presence. Amen!*

## REFLECTION

_Reflection Prompt: _ Write about a time when God's faithfulness gave you hope and reassurance. How did it impact
your life?

_Additional Thoughts: _

- Consider how God's faithfulness can give you a sense of security and peace.
- Think about how this truth can help you navigate uncertain times.
- Reflect on how God's faithfulness can be a source of strength and courage.

## _August 11:_ _God's Love is Our Comfort!_

_Scripture:_ Psalm 119:76 - May your unfailing love be my comfort, according to your promise to your servant.

_Devotion:_

God's love is our comfort in times of trouble or sorrow.

Amen! God's love is indeed our comfort in times of trouble or sorrow. It's a love that:

- Surrounds us with peace and calm
- Lifts us up when we're feeling down
- Provides strength in our weaknesses
- Offers hope in the midst of despair
- Reminds us we're never alone

As Psalm 34:18 says, "The Lord is close to the brokenhearted and saves the crushed in spirit." And in John 14:27, Jesus says, "Peace I leave with you; my peace I give you. I do not give to you as the world gives. Do not let your hearts be troubled and do not be afraid."

May God's love be your comfort and peace today and always!

_Prayer:_ *Dear God, thank you for your comforting love. Help me to find peace and solace in your presence. Amen!*

## _August 12_: _God's Love Restores Us!_

_Scripture:_ Psalm 23:3 - He restores my soul. He leads me in paths of righteousness for his name's sake.

_Devotion:_

God's love restores and revives us.

Yes, God's love has the power to restore and revive us! It:

- Heals our emotional and spiritual wounds
- Renews our minds and hearts
- Brings us back to life when we feel drained or empty
- Revitalizes our relationship with Him and others
- Gives us a fresh start and a new beginning

And in Isaiah 40:31, "But those who hope in the Lord will renew their strength. They will soar on wings like eagles; they will run and not grow weary; they will walk and not be faint."

May God's restoring and reviving love be your portion today!

_Prayer:_ *Dear God, thank you for your restoring love. Help me to receive your healing and guidance.* Amen!

## _August 13_ God's Love is Merciful

_Scripture:_ Psalm 103:8 - The Lord is compassionate and gracious, slow to anger, abounding in love.

_Devotion:_

God's love is merciful and forgiving.

A beautiful reminder! Yes, God's love is often described as merciful and forgiving in many spiritual traditions. It's a love that encompasses compassion, understanding, and kindness, offering second chances and new beginnings. This love is not based on our worthiness or actions, but rather on God's nature and character.

As the Bible says, "God is love" (1 John 4:8) and "His mercy endures forever" (Psalm 136). In Islam, Allah is described as "Al-Rahman" (The Most Merciful) and "Al-Ghaffar" (The Forgiving). Similarly, in other faiths and spiritual beliefs, the concept of a higher power is often associated with mercy, forgiveness, and unconditional love.

Remembering God's merciful and forgiving love can bring comfort, hope, and peace to our lives, encouraging us to extend the same love and kindness to others.

_Prayer:_ *Dear God, thank you for your merciful love. Help me to receive your forgiveness and extend it to others.* Amen!

## **August 14**: God's Love is Patient

*Scripture:* 1 John 4:8 - Whoever does not love does not know God, because God is love.

*Devotion:*

God's love is patient and kind, it can teach you to love others with patience and understanding.

A beautiful reminder! That's a quote from 1 Corinthians 13:4, which describes the characteristics of love. The full quote is:

"Love is patient, love is kind. It does not envy, it does not boast, it is not proud." Love is a powerful and complex emotion that can bring so much joy and fulfillment to our lives.

This passage is often referred to as the "Love Chapter" in the Bible and is a wonderful description of the qualities of unconditional love, including God's love.

- "Love is the master key that opens the gates of happiness." - Oliver Wendell Holmes

*Prayer:* *Dear God, thank you for your patient love. Help me to love others with the same patience and kindness. Amen!*

## _August 15_: _The Depth of God's Love

_Scripture:_ Ephesians 3:18-19 - And I pray that you, being rooted and established in love, may have power, together with all the Lord's holy people, to grasp how wide and long and high and deep is the love of Christ.

_Devotion:_

God's love is immeasurable and beyond human comprehension. It's a love that surpasses knowledge and understanding.

What a beautiful truth! God's love is indeed immeasurable and beyond human comprehension. It's a love that transcends our understanding and exceeds our wildest imagination. This love that surpasses knowledge that you may be filled to the measure of all the fullness of God."

God's love is like an endless ocean, and we are like tiny vessels trying to comprehend its vastness. But even though we can't fully understand it, we can still experience its depth and richness in our lives.

_Prayer: Dear God, thank You for Your boundless love. Help me to understand the width, length, height, and depth of Your love._ Amen:

May you be rooted and established in God's love, and may it transform your life and relationships.

## _August 16:_ _Love Forgives!

_Scripture:_ Colossians 3:13 - Bear with each other and forgive one another if any of you has a grievance against someone. Forgive as the Lord forgave you.

### _Devotion:_

Forgiveness is a fundamental aspect of love. It's the ability to let go of grudges, resentments, and hurt, just as God forgave us through Jesus Christ. And over all these virtues put on love, which binds them all together in perfect unity

A beautiful truth! Forgiveness is indeed a fundamental aspect of love. When we love, we choose to let go of grudges, resentments, and hurts. Forgiveness allows us to release the past and create space for healing, understanding, and deeper connection.

As Mahatma Gandhi said, "The weak can never forgive. Forgiveness is the attribute of the strong." Forgiveness doesn't mean forgetting or condoning hurtful actions, but rather releasing the hold they have on our hearts.

Forgiveness is a choice, a process, and a journey. It's not always easy, but it's essential for our own liberation and the cultivation of love.

_Prayer: Dear God, thank You for forgiving me through Jesus Christ. Help me to extend that same forgiveness to others, letting go of grudges and resentments. Amen!_

## _August 17:_ Love is a Gift!

_Scripture:_ John 3:16 - For God so loved the world that he gave his one and only Son, that whoever believes in him shall not perish but have eternal life.

_Devotion:_

Love is the greatest gift we can give and receive. God demonstrated this by giving His only Son, Jesus Christ, to save humanity.

What a wonderful truth! Love is indeed the greatest gift we can give and receive. It has the power to transform lives, heal wounds, and bring joy and fulfillment.

As the famous quote by Robert Louis Stevenson goes, "The greatest happiness of life is the conviction that we are loved; loved for ourselves, or rather, loved in spite of ourselves."

Love is a gift that:
- Accepts us for who we are
- Encourages us to grow and thrive
- Forgives us when we make mistakes
- Celebrates our triumphs and accomplishments

When we give love, we receive it back multiplied. It creates a beautiful cycle of kindness, compassion, and connection.

_Prayer:_ *Dear God, thank You for the gift of love and salvation through Jesus Christ. Help me to share Your love with others, being a vessel of Your kindness and generosity. Amen!*

## _August 18_: _Love Incarnate!

_Scripture:_ John 1:14 - The Word became flesh and made his dwelling among us. We have seen his glory, the glory of the one and only Son, who came from the Father, full of grace and truth.

_Devotion:_

Today, we celebrate the birth of Jesus Christ, Love Incarnate. God's love took on human form, dwelling among us, and showing us the depth of His grace and truth. A beautiful phrase! "Love Incarnate" suggests a physical embodiment or manifestation of love. It's a powerful concept that can take many forms, **such as:**

1. Jesus Christ: In Christianity, Jesus is often referred to as "Love Incarnate" because He embodied unconditional love and sacrificed Himself for humanity.
2. Selfless acts: When we put others' needs before our own, we become love incarnate, showing compassion and kindness in tangible ways.
3. Unconditional acceptance: Embracing someone for who they are, without judgment, is a manifestation of love incarnate.

The idea of love incarnate reminds us that love is not just a feeling but a choice, a commitment, and a way of being. It inspires us to become the embodiment of love in our own lives, spreading joy, hope, and kindness wherever we go.

_Prayer:_ *Dear God, thank You for sending Your Son, Jesus Christ, to demonstrate Your love. Help me to embrace Your love and share it with others, that they may know Your grace and truth. Amen!*

## _August 19_: Love's Forgiveness

_Scripture:_ Ephesians: 4:32 - "Be kind and compassionate to one another, forgiving each other, just as God forgave you."

_Devotion:_

God's love is forgiving, and He calls us to reflect that forgiveness in our relationships. Forgiveness is a fundamental aspect of God's character, demonstrated through:

God's love is not only unconditional but also forgiving. He doesn't hold our mistakes against us, and His mercy is new every morning (Lamentations 3:22-23).

God's forgiveness:
- Unconditional pardon: God forgives our sins without condition.
- Unrelenting compassion: God's forgiveness is motivated by love, not obligation.
- Unwavering commitment: God's forgiveness is rooted in His faithfulness.
- Redemptive purpose: Forgiveness restores us to a right relationship with Him.

As we experience God's forgiveness, we're empowered to extend forgiveness to others. This transforms our relationships and frees us from bitterness.

_Prayer_ Dear God, thank You for Your forgiving love. Help me to extend forgiveness to others, just as You have forgiven me. May Your love and compassion guide my interactions, bringing healing and restoration to my relationships. Amen!

## August 20: Love's Kindness

Scripture: Ephesians 4:32 - Be kind and compassionate to one another, forgiving each other, just as in Christ God forgave you.

### Devotion:

God's love is kind, and He wants us to reflect that kindness in our lives.

Amen! God's love is indeed kind, and He desires for us to mirror that kindness in our interactions with others. Kindness is a fundamental aspect of God's character, and it's a key part of our relationship with Him.

When we experience God's kindness, it transforms us and enables us to show kindness to others. Kindness:

1. Touches hearts and changes lives
2. Breaks down barriers and builds bridges
3. Reflects God's love and compassion to those around us

As we embrace God's kindness, we become more like Him, and our lives become a testament to His love and care. By showing kindness to others, we:

1. Demonstrate our trust in God's goodness and sovereignty
2. Show that we value people over circumstances
3. Create a ripple effect of compassion and empathy

May we embrace God's kindness and extend it to others.

_Prayer: *Dear God, thank You for Your kindness and love. Help me to reflect Your kindness in my life, showing compassion and forgiveness to those around me.* Amen!

## REFLECTION

Take a moment to reflect on how you can show kindness to those around you.

_Reflection Prompt: _

Write about a time when someone showed kindness to you. How can you extend that same kindness to someone else?

## August 21: Love's Self-Control

_Scripture:_ Galatians 5:22-23 -But the fruit of the Spirit is love, joy, peace, patience, kindness, goodness, faithfulness, gentleness, self-control; against such things there is no law.

_Devotion:_

God's love is self-controlled, and He wants us to reflect that self-control in our lives.

A wonderful aspect of God's love! Self-control is indeed a hallmark of God's love, and it's a quality He desires for us to emulate.

God's self-controlled love means He:
1. Doesn't act impulsively or emotionally
2. Isn't swayed by circumstances or our behavior
3. Always chooses to love, even when we're unlovable

As we grow in understanding God's self-controlled love, we can develop this quality in our own lives. Self-control helps us:

1. Respond thoughtfully, rather than reacting impulsively
2. Treat others with kindness, even when they're difficult
3. Reflect God's character more accurately

By embracing self-control, we become more like Christ and demonstrate His love to those around us.

*Prayer:* *Dear God, thank You for Your self-control and love. Help me to reflect Your self-control in my life, guiding my thoughts, words, and actions.* Amen!

## REFLECTION

*Questions to Ponder:*
- When am I most likely to act impulsively or emotionally? How can I practice self-control in those moments?
- Are there circumstances or people that trigger me to react negatively? How can I choose to love and respond thoughtfully instead?

*Action Step:*
- Take a pause before reacting to a challenging situation or person. Breathe deeply, pray for guidance, and choose a thoughtful response that reflects God's self-controlled love.

Remember, self-control is a fruit of the Spirit, and it's developed through practice, prayer, and surrender to God's guidance. Keep growing and reflecting His love!

### **August 22**: _Love's Gentleness!

_Scripture:_ Galatians 5:22-23 - But the fruit of the Spirit is love, joy, peace, patience, kindness, goodness, faithfulness, gentleness, self-control; against such things there is no law.

_Devotion:_

God's love is gentle, and He wants us to reflect that gentleness in our lives.

A beautiful sentiment! "God's love is gentle" reminds us of the compassionate, caring, and tender nature of God's love. It's a love that nurtures, comforts, and uplifts us, rather than judging or condemning us. This gentle love is often described in scripture and is a source of peace, hope, and strength for many people.

A wonderful reference to Galatians 5:22-23! "But the fruit of the Spirit is love, joy, peace, patience, kindness, goodness, faithfulness, gentleness, self-control; against such things there is no law."

This passage highlights the characteristics of a person who is living a life guided by the Holy Spirit. Love is listed first, emphasizing its importance as the foundation of all the other qualities.

The "fruit of the Spirit" represents the positive traits that grow and develop in our lives when we allow the Holy Spirit to work in us. It's a beautiful reminder of the transformative power of God's presence in our lives.

Prayer: *Dear God, thank You for Your gentleness and love. Help me to reflect Your gentleness in my life, showing kindness and compassion to those around me.* Amen!

## REFLECTION

Take a moment to reflect on how you can demonstrate self-control in your thoughts, words, and actions.

_Reflection Prompt:_

Write about a time when you struggled with self-control. How did you overcome it? What strategies can you use to practice self-control in your daily life?

### _August 23_: _Love's Humility!

_Scripture:_ Philippians 2:3-4 - "Do nothing out of selfish ambition or vain conceit. Rather, in humility value others above yourselves, not looking to your own interests but each of you to the interests of the others."

_Devotion:_

God's love is humble, and He calls us to reflect that humility in our lives.

What a beautiful reminder! Yes, God's love is indeed humble, and He calls us to embody that same humility in our lives. Humility is a vital virtue that allows us to love and serve others selflessly, just as God loves and serves us. By embracing humility, we can:

- Recognize our dependence on God and others
- Listen and learn from those around us
- Serve with kindness and compassion
- Embrace our weaknesses and limitations
- Glorify God rather than ourselves

May we strive to reflect God's humble love in our thoughts, words, and actions today and every day!

_Prayer:_ *Dear God, thank You for Your humility and love. Help me to reflect Your humility in my life, valuing others above myself and looking to their interests. Amen!*

## _August 24: _Love's Compassion!

_Scripture: _ Colossians 3:12 - Therefore, as God's chosen people, holy and dearly loved, clothe yourselves with compassion, kindness, humility, gentleness and patience.

### _Devotion: _

God's love is compassionate, and He calls us to reflect that compassion in our lives.

What a beautiful reminder! Yes, God's love is indeed compassionate, and He encourages us to show empathy and kindness towards others. Reflecting God's compassion in our lives can take many forms, such as:

- Showing understanding and patience towards those who may be struggling
- Offering a helping hand or listening ear to those in need
- Practicing forgiveness and letting go of grudges
- Advocating for justice and standing up for those who are marginalized
- Simply being present and showing care for those around us

May we strive to embody God's compassion in our daily lives and spread love, kindness, and understanding to those around us!

_Prayer: *Dear God, thank You for Your compassion and love. Help me to reflect Your compassion in my life, showing kindness and empathy to those around me.* Amen!

## August 25: Anchored in Love

Scripture: 1 Corinthians 13:13. Says, and now these three remain: faith, hope and love. But the greatest of these is love.

### Devotion:

Life is full of uncertainties, and it's easy to feel adrift in the midst of unknowns. But today, let's anchor our hearts in the one thing that remains constant: God's love.

Beautiful! That's a wonderful reminder. Here's a possible expansion on that thought:

When everything around us seems to be shifting and uncertain, let's anchor our hearts in the one thing that remains constant: God's love. His love is the rock that stands firm, the anchor that holds us fast, and the safe haven where we can find peace.

In a world that's constantly changing, God's love remains steadfast and true. It's the one thing that never fades, never fails, and never falters. His love is the constant that we can cling to, the foundation that we can build on, and the hope that we can hold onto.

So, let's anchor our hearts in God's love today. Let's let it be the guiding force in our lives, the calming presence in our storms, and the reassuring whisper in our doubts.

May His love be our constant companion, our source of strength, and our beacon of hope."

Prayer: *Dear God, thank You for Your unfailing love. Help me to anchor my heart in Your love today, and every day. When uncertainty knocks, may Your love be the rock that keeps me grounded.* Amen.

## REFLECTION PAGE

Take a moment to pray and ask God to help you focus on His love in the midst of uncertainty.

Reflection Prompt:

- How has God's love been a constant in your life?
- In what areas of uncertainty do you need to anchor yourself in God's love today?

# _August 26: _ Love is a Choice!

_Scripture: _ 1 John 4:19 says, Love is not because of who you are, but because of who I am.

## _Devotion: _

Love is often seen as a feeling, but it's also a choice. It's a decision to put someone else's needs before our own, to forgive when we'd rather hold onto hurt, and to show kindness when we'd rather show anger.

God chose to love us, not because we deserved it, but because of His own character. He chose to love us when we were unlovable, and He continues to love us even when we fail.

That's a powerful truth! The Bible says, "But God demonstrates his own love for us in this: While we were still sinners, Christ died for us." (Romans 5:8)

God's love for us is not based on our worthiness or deservingness. He doesn't love us because of our good deeds, our accomplishments, or our strengths. He loves us simply because He chooses to.

This is called unconditional love, and it's a love that: - Doesn't depend on our performance- Isn't earned by our efforts- Can't be lost by our failures

God's love is a gift, freely given, and it's available to us all.

_Prayer: _ *Dear God, help me to choose love today, even when it's hard. Give me the strength to put others first, to forgive freely, and to show kindness generously. May Your love flow through me and touch the lives of those around me. Amen.*

## _August 27_: _Love's Legacy

Scripture: _ 1 Corinthians 13:13 says, and now these three remain: faith, hope and love. But the greatest of these is love.

_Devotion: _

As we approach the end of this month, reflect on the legacy of love you've experienced and shared with others. Remember that love is the greatest legacy we can leave behind.

What a beautiful sentiment! Leaving a legacy of love is indeed one of the most profound and lasting impacts we can have on the world.

Love has the power to: - Transcend time and generations- Heal wounds and mend relationships- Inspire hope and resilience- Create a ripple effect of kindness and compassion

When we prioritize love and make it a core part of our lives, we can: - Build strong, supportive relationships- Create a sense of belonging and connection- Make a positive difference in our communities- Leave a lasting impact on the hearts of those around us

As the saying goes, "Love is the master key that opens the gates of happiness." By choosing to love and be loved, we can create a legacy that continues to inspire and uplift others long after we're gone.

_Prayer: *Dear God, thank You for the legacy of love You've shown me. Help me to share that love with others, leaving a lasting impact that honors You.* Amen!

## REFLECTION

What are some ways you're leaving a legacy of love in your own life?

_Reflection Prompt: _

Write about a time when someone showed you love and kindness, leaving a lasting impact on your life. How can you pay that forward and leave a legacy of love for others?

Remember, love is the greatest legacy we can leave behind, and it's a gift that keeps on giving.

**_August 28: _Love Never Fails!**

_Scripture: _ 1 Corinthians 13:8 - Love never fails. But where there are prophecies, they will cease; where there are tongues, they will be stilled; where there is knowledge, it will pass away.

_Devotion: _

God's love never fails, even when everything else does. It's a constant and enduring force that sustains us through life's challenges.

Amen to that! God's love is indeed unwavering, unrelenting, and unending. It's a constant source of comfort, strength, and hope in our lives.

As the Bible says love never fails. God's love is not limited by our circumstances, emotions, or actions. It's a love that:

- Endures through every trial and challenge
- Forgives and redeems us time and time again
- Lifts us up when we're broken and restores us to wholeness
- Guides us through uncertain times and gives us wisdom
- Surrounds us with an unshakeable sense of peace and joy.

God's love is the foundation of our faith, the anchor of our souls, and the safe haven where we can always find refuge. It's a love that transforms us from the inside out, empowering us to love others with the same depth and sincerity.

May we always remember and rest in the assurance of God's unfailing love!

_Prayer: *Dear God, thank You for Your love that never fails. Help me to trust in Your constant presence and rely on Your love to carry me through life's ups and downs. Amen!*

## REFLECTION

Reflect on how God's love has been a steady presence in your life.

_Reflection Prompt: _

Write about a time when God's love helped you through a difficult situation. How did His love sustain you? How can you rely on His love to carry you through future challenges?

### _August 29_: _Love Shines Brighter

_Scripture:_ 1 John 4:7-8 - "Dear friends, let us love one another, for love comes from God. Everyone who loves has been born of God and knows God."

_Devotion:_

God's love shines brighter in the darkest moments. As we reflect on the past and the present, let us remember how God's love guided and sustained us.

What a beautiful truth! God's love has a way of illuminating even the darkest of times, bringing hope and light to our lives when we need it most.

In the midst of struggles, heartaches, and uncertainties, God's love shines like a beacon, guiding us through the darkness and reminding us that we are never alone. It's a love that:
- Comforts us in our sorrow
- Strengthens us in our weakness- Whispers hope in our despair
- Lifts us up when we're broken- Surrounds us with an unshakeable peace

As Psalm 23:4 says, "Even though I walk through the darkest valley, I will fear no evil, for you are with me; your rod and your staff comfort me."

God's love is the light that pierces the darkness, reminding us that even in the most challenging moments, we are loved, we are seen, and we are cherished. May we always look to Him as our source of hope, comfort, and strength!

_ Prayer: _*Dear God, thank You for Your love that shines brighter in the darkest moments. Help me to reflect Your love, making it shine brighter in the lives of those around me.* Amen!

## REFLECTION

Let His love inspires you to shine brighter in the lives of those around you.

_Reflection Prompt: _

Write about a challenging time when God's love shone brighter. How did you experience His love? How can you share that love with others, making it shine brighter in their lives?

## _August 30_: _Love Restores

_Scripture:_ Romans 5:8 - But God demonstrates his own love for us in this: While we were still sinners, Christ died for us.

_Devotion:_

God's love restores us to Himself, even when we were far from Him. Jesus' sacrifice on the cross bridged the gap between God and humanity, offering forgiveness and reconciliation.

Amen! God's love is a redeeming force that pursues us, even when we've wandered far from Him.
It's a love that:
- Seeks us out in our brokenness
- Calls us back to Himself with gentleness and kindness
- Forgives our mistakes and shortcomings
- Restores our relationship with Him, making us whole again

As the parable of the prodigal son illustrates (Luke 15:11-32), God's love is like a father who waits with open arms, welcoming us back home, no matter how far we've strayed. He celebrates our return, erasing our past mistakes, and embracing us with unconditional love.

God's love restores us to Himself, reviving our spirit, and renewing our purpose. It's a love that transforms us, making us more like Him, and empowering us to live a life that reflects His grace, mercy, and love.

Prayer: *Dear God, thank You for Your restoring love, demonstrated through Jesus' sacrifice. Help me to receive and share that love, bringing restoration and forgiveness to those around me. Amen!*

## REFLECTION

Reflect on how God's love has restored you and how you can extend that restoration to others.

_Reflection Prompt:_

Write about a time when you experienced God's restoring love. How did it change your life or relationship with Him? How can you be an instrument of restoration and forgiveness in someone else's life?

May we always remember that God's love is a restoring force, capable of healing our deepest wounds and bringing us back to Himself, where we belong.

**August 31**: _The Depth of God's Love

_Scripture:_ Ephesians 3:18-19 - And I pray that you, being rooted and established in love, may have power, together with all the Lord's holy people, to grasp how wide and long and high and deep is the love of Christ.

_Devotion:_

God's love is immeasurable and beyond human comprehension. It's a love that surpasses knowledge and understanding.

Amen! God's love is indeed immeasurable and beyond human comprehension. It's a love that:

- Transcends our understanding (Ephesians 3:19)
- Surpasses our wildest imagination (1 Corinthians 2:9)
- Knows no bounds or limits (Psalm 103:11-12)
- Extends far beyond our mistakes and failures (Romans 5:8)
- Encompasses every moment of our lives (Psalm 139:1-4)

God's love is like a vast ocean, infinite and uncharted, with depths we can't fully fathom. It's a love that: - Forgives the unforgivable- Heals the unhealable- Redeems the unredeemable
- Restores the broken

May we humbly acknowledge the vastness of God's love, surrendering to its mystery and majesty, and allowing it to transform us more and more into His likeness.

_Prayer: *Dear God, thank You for Your boundless love. Help me to understand the width, length, height, and depth of Your love. May I be rooted and established in Your love, and may it transform my life and relationships.* Amen!

## REFLECTION

Reflect on the depth of God's love and how it can transform your life.

_Reflection Prompt: _

Write about a time when you experienced God's love in a profound way. How did it impact your life and relationships? How can you continue to grasp the depth of God's love?

As we conclude our reflection on love this August, remember that God's love is the foundation of all love. His love is the anchor that holds us fast, the rock that keeps us grounded, and the safe haven where we can find peace.

May the abundance of God's goodness and love be our guiding force, shaping our relationships, interactions, and daily lives. May we continue to taste and see the goodness of God's love, and may it overflow from our hearts to those around us.

As we move forward, let us carry the lessons of love with us:

- Love is a choice, not just a feeling.
- God's love is patient, kind, and selfless.
- We are called to love others as God loves us.

May God's love be our constant companion, our source of strength, and our beacon of hope. May we love like He loves, and may His love change the world through us.

I hope this conclusion brings a sense of closure and inspiration to your reflection on love this August!

# SEPTEMBER 1-30

1. Gratitude
2. Trust
3. Love
4. Peace
5. Humility
6. Perseverance
7. Courage
8. Forgiveness
9. Hope
10. Faith
11. Generosity
12. Faithfulness
13. Joy
14. Obedience
15. Thankfulness
16. Contentment
17. Peace
18. Long Suffering
19. Renewing Your Mind and Heart
20. Trusting God's Sovereignty
21. The Power of Honesty
22. Serving Others, Serving God
23. Embracing Brokenness, Finding Healing
24. Redeemed and Restored
25. Pressing On
26. The Power of Perseverance
27. The Mystery of God's Sovereignty
28. The Miracle of Spiritual Renewal
29. The Mystery of God's Presence
30. The Secret to Unshakeable Peace

## _September 1:_ Gratitude

_Scripture:_ Psalm 107:1 says, give thanks to the Lord, for he is good; His love endures forever!

_Devotion:_

Gratitude changes our perspective and helps us to see God's goodness in our lives. I choose to cultivate gratitude and trust in God's goodness today. Gratitude is a decision to focus on God's goodness and love, even in the midst of challenges."

What a beautiful sentiment! Practicing gratitude can indeed shift our focus and help us recognize the good things in our lives, no matter how small they may seem. It's a powerful way to cultivate a positive mindset and appreciate the blessings we often take for granted.

Focusing on gratitude can also help us:

- Develop a more optimistic outlook
- Build stronger relationships
- Improve our mental and emotional well-being
- Find joy in everyday moments
- Trust in a higher power or divine guidance

As stated above, gratitude can help us see God's goodness in our lives, and that's a truly wonderful thing!

Prayer: *Dear God, thank you for your goodness and love. Help me to cultivate gratitude and to trust in your care.* Amen.

# _September 2: _Trust

Scripture: Proverbs 3:5-6 says, trust in the Lord with all your heart and lean not on your own understanding; in all your ways submit to him, and he will make your paths straight.

## _Devotion: _

Trust is not just a feeling, but a choice - it's not just an emotion, but an action that changes our lives.

What a profound statement! Trust is indeed a choice, a conscious decision we make to believe in someone or something. It's an action that can lead to deeper connections, stronger relationships, and a more fulfilling life.

Trusting in God can bring a sense of comfort, peace, and guidance to our lives. It's a profound way to cultivate faith and hope, even in challenging times.

When we choose to trust in God or a higher power, we're acknowledging that there's something greater than ourselves at work in the universe. It's a surrendering of our worries,fears, and doubts to a power that's beyond our control.

Trusting in God can also give us the strength to persevere through difficult situations, knowing that we're not alone and that there's a greater plan at work. It's a reminder that we're part of something bigger than ourselves, and that our lives have purpose and meaning.

Prayer: *Dear God, thank you for your guidance and care. Help me to trust in your love and your plans, and to rest in your care.* Amen.

## _September 3: _Love

Scripture: 1 John 4:16 says, and we have known and believed the love that God hath to us. God is love; and he that dwelleth in love dwelleth in God, and God in him.

### _Devotion: _

God's love is not just a feeling.

A beautiful topic! God's love is not just a feeling, but a profound and unwavering commitment to humanity. It's a love that is constant, unchanging, and unconditional, surpassing human emotions and circumstances.

In Christianity, God's love is often described as agape love, which is selfless, sacrificial, and enduring. It's a love that seeks the well-being and salvation of others, regardless of their actions or worthiness.

God's love is also demonstrated through His actions, such as sending His Son Jesus Christ to redeem humanity, providing for our needs, and offering guidance and wisdom through the Bible and the Holy Spirit.

While feelings of love and affection may come and go, God's love remains a steady and reliable foundation for our lives, offering hope, comfort, and strength in times of joy and struggle alike.

_Prayer: _ *A love that is unconditional, unwavering, and true. May my life be a reflection of Your love, a love that shines brightly for all to see.* Amen!

## _September 4: _Peace

Scripture: John 14:27 says, peace I leave with you; my peace I give you. I do not give to you as the world gives. Do not let your hearts be troubled and do not be afraid.

_Devotion: _

What a powerful statement! You're absolutely right, peace is not just an emotion or a feeling, but a conscious choice we can make every day. It's a mindset, an attitude, and a way of living.

Choosing peace means:
- Letting go of worries and fears
- Embracing calmness and serenity
- Practicing forgiveness and understanding
- Cultivating gratitude and positivity
- Being present in the moment

By choosing peace, we can create a sense of inner tranquility, even in the midst of chaos. We can learn to navigate life's challenges with grace, clarity, and confidence.

Remember, peace is a journey, not a destination. And it starts with a simple choice: to prioritize love, kindness, and understanding in our thoughts, words, and actions.

May we all choose peace today and every day.

_Prayer: _ *Dear God, thank you for your peace and strength. Help me to trust in your peace and to rest in your care. Amen.*

## September 5: _Humility

Scripture: James 4:10 says, humble yourselves before the Lord, and He will lift you up.

_Devotion:_

Humility is not just a virtue, but a choice - it's a decision to put aside our pride and seek God's guidance.

What a beautiful and profound statement! Humility is indeed a choice and a decision that requires intentional effort. By choosing humility, we open ourselves up to guidance, wisdom, and growth, and acknowledge that we don't have all the answers.

- Guidance: We become more receptive to advice, correction, and direction from others, including spiritual guidance.
- Wisdom: We gain a deeper understanding of ourselves, others, and the world around us, leading to wiser decisions and actions.
- Growth: We become more open to learning, self-reflection, and personal development, allowing us to evolve and improve.

Humility is a powerful way to cultivate a sense of surrender, self-awareness, and connection with something greater than ourselves. By embracing humility, we essentially unlock the doors to new experiences, knowledge, and self-awareness, leading to a more fulfilling and purposeful life. *Say a prayer.*

### _September 6:_ Perseverance

Scripture: Galatians 6:9 says, let us not become weary in doing good, for at the proper time we will reap a harvest if we do not give up.

#### _Devotion:_

Perseverance is not just a trait, but a choice - it's a decision to keep going and to trust in God's strength.

What a powerful and inspiring perspective! Perseverance is not just an innate trait, but a conscious choice we make every day. It's the decision to push forward, even when faced with challenges and obstacles, and to trust in God or our own inner strength to carry us through.

Perseverance is what separates those who give up from those who keep going, and it's often the key to achieving our goals and realizing our dreams. By choosing to persevere, we build resilience, develop our character, and grow stronger in the face of adversity.

And I love the added words, "to trust in God's strength" - faith and trust can be a powerful source of motivation and comfort when we're feeling overwhelmed or uncertain. Whatever our beliefs or values, perseverance is a quality that can help us navigate life's ups and downs with courage and determination. *Say a prayer.*

## _September 7:_ Courage

Scripture: Joshua 1:9 says, be strong and courageous. Do not be afraid; do not be discouraged, for the Lord your God will be with you wherever you go.

_Devotion:_

Courage is not the absence of fear, but the willingness to trust in God's strength and guidance.

That's a beautiful and inspiring quote! It highlights the idea that courage is about trusting in God or a higher power, and having faith that you will be guided and supported. It's a mindset that allows us to move forward even when we're uncertain or afraid, because we know we're not alone, and that with trust and faith, we can find the strength to overcome them.

Trusting in a higher power can give us the strength to face challenges that might otherwise seem insurmountable. It's a reminder that we don't have to rely solely on our own abilities, but can tap into a deeper source of wisdom, guidance, and power.

_Prayer:_ _Dear thank you for your unwavering strength and courage that guides me through life's challenges. Help me to be brave and to trust in your loving care, even when the path ahead seems uncertain. Give me the confidence to face my fears and to rely on your wisdom and guidance. Grant me the courage to take steps of faith, to follow your lead, and to trust in your goodness. May my heart be filled with your hope and my spirit be lifted by your promises._ Amen.

## _September 8:_ Forgiveness

Scripture: Colossians 3:13 says, bear with each other and forgive one another if any of you has a grievance against someone. Forgive as the Lord forgave you.

_Devotion:_

Forgiveness is not just a feeling, but a choice - it's not just an emotion, but an action that changes our lives and sets us free. What a powerful truth! Forgiveness is indeed a choice, a deliberate decision to let go of resentment, anger, and hurt. It's not always easy, but it's a crucial step towards healing, freedom, and inner peace.

When we choose to forgive, we're not saying that what happened was okay or that the hurt didn't matter. Rather, we're releasing the hold that the hurt has on us, and breaking free from the chains of bitterness and resentment.

Forgiveness is an action that:
- Allows us to heal and move forward
- Brings peace and calm to our minds and hearts
- Reflects the love and grace of God in our lives

Remember, forgiveness is a journey, and it may take time. But with each step, we can experience the liberating power of forgiveness and discover a life of greater freedom, joy, and love.

Prayer: *Dear God, thank you for your forgiveness. Help me to forgive others and to let go of bitterness.* Amen

## _September 9:_ Hope

Scripture: Hebrews 6:19 says, we have this hope as an anchor for the soul, firm and secure.

### _Devotion:_

Hope is not just a feeling, but a choice - it's not just an emotion, but an action that changes our lives.

What a powerful statement! Hope is not just a feeling that comes and goes, but a conscious choice that we can make every day. It's an action that can transform our lives and help us navigate through challenges and difficulties.

As the Bible says, "Rejoice in hope, be patient in tribulation, be constant in prayer." (Romans 12:12).

Choosing hope means:
- Trusting in God's goodness and sovereignty
- Holding onto His promises, even when circumstances seem bleak
- Taking action towards a better future, despite current difficulties

Hope is not a passive emotion but an active decision that can bring light into our darkness, strength to our weaknesses, and joy to our struggles.

Prayer: *Dear God, thank you for your love. Help me to hold onto hope and to trust in your care, and to rest in your guidance.* Amen.

## September 10: Faith

Scripture: Hebrews 11:6 says, and without faith, it is impossible to please God, because anyone who comes to him must believe that he exists and that he rewards those who earnestly seek him.

### Devotion:

Faith is not just a feeling, but a choice - it's a decision to trust in God's love and care, even when we can't see the way ahead.

What a beautiful and profound statement! Faith is not just an emotional feeling, but a conscious choice to trust and have confidence in something greater than ourselves, even when we can't see the outcome or understand the circumstances. It's a decision to put our trust in God's love, care, and sovereignty, even in the midst of uncertainty or difficulty.

As the Bible says, "Faith is the substance of things hoped for, the evidence of things not seen" (Hebrews 11:1). It's a choice to believe and trust, even when we can't see the way ahead, and to trust that God is working everything out for our good (Romans 8:28).

Prayer: *Dear God, thank you for your faithfulness and love. Help me to trust in your care and to seek you with all my heart.* Amen.

How has your faith journey evolved over time, and what significant experiences have shaped it?

## _September 11:_ Generosity

Scripture: Luke 6:38 says, give generously, and you will receive generously. You will be given a full and generous measure, pressed down, shaken together, and running over.

_Devotion:_

Generosity is not just about giving, but about trusting in God's provision and care.

What a beautiful perspective! Generosity is not just about giving, but also about trusting in a higher power's provision and care. This mindset shift can bring a sense of freedom and joy to giving.

When we trust that God will provide for us, we're more likely to:
- Let go of attachment to material possessions
- Feel grateful for what we have
- Recognize the abundance in our lives
- Experience the joy of giving without expectation of return

This trust also acknowledges that our true security and worth come from a power greater than ourselves, rather than just our material possessions.

Prayer: *Dear God, thank you for your generosity and provision. Help me to be generous and to trust in your care.* Amen.

## September 12: Faithfulness

Scripture: 1 Corinthians 1:9 says, God is faithful, who has called you into fellowship with his Son, Jesus Christ our Lord.

### Devotion:

Faithfulness is not just about our actions, but about trusting in God's promises and care.

That's a beautiful insight! You're absolutely right, faithfulness encompasses not only our actions but also our trust in God's promises and care. It's about having confidence in His goodness, sovereignty, and love, even when we can't see the outcome or understand His ways.

Trusting in God's promises and care allows us to:

- Rest in His presence, even in uncertain times
- Find peace amidst chaos
- Persevere through trials and challenges
- Experience joy and hope, regardless of circumstances

May we cultivate a deeper trust in God's promises and care, and may it inspire us to live faithfully, with hearts full of hope and confidence in His goodness.

Prayer: *Dear God, thank you for your faithfulness and promises. Help me to be faithful and to trust in your care.* Amen.

## _September 13: _ Joy

Scripture: Psalm 16:11 says, you make known to me the path of life; You will fill me with joy in Your presence, with eternal pleasures at Your right hand.

## _Devotion: _

Joy is not just a feeling, but a choice - it's a decision to focus on God's presence and love, even in the midst of challenges.

What a beautiful reminder! Joy is not just an emotion that happens to us, but a conscious choice we can make every day. It's a mindset shift that helps us focus on God's goodness, love, and presence, even when circumstances are tough.

By choosing joy, we're not ignoring or denying the difficulties, but rather, we're acknowledging that God is bigger than our struggles. We're declaring that His love, grace, and mercy are more powerful than any challenge we face.

Let's make a conscious effort to choose joy today, and every day, by:

- Practicing gratitude
- Fixing our eyes on God's goodness
- Trusting in His sovereignty

Remember, joy is contagious! When we choose joy, we can spread it to those around us and create a ripple effect of happiness and hope.

Prayer: *Dear God, thank you for your presence and love. Help me to find joy in your care and guidance.* Amen

## _September 14:_ Obedience

Scripture: John 14:15 says, if you love me, keep my commands.

## _Devotion:_

Obedience is not just about our actions, but about our attitude - it's not just about what we do, but about why we do it. That's a profound insight! Obedience is often misunderstood as simply following rules or commands, but it's so much deeper than that. Our attitude and motivation behind our actions are just as important as the actions themselves.

When we obey with the right attitude, we're not just checking boxes or going through the motions; we're demonstrating our love, trust, and surrender to God. We're acknowledging that His ways are higher than ours, and that His plans are better than our own.

A right attitude in obedience involves:
- Humility: Recognizing our limitations and God's sovereignty
- Gratitude: Appreciating God's goodness and guidance
- Trust: Believing in God's wisdom and love
- Surrender: Letting go of our own desires and agendas
- Joy: Finding delight in pleasing God, even when it's hard

When our attitude is right, our obedience becomes an act of worship, a demonstration of our love and devotion to God. It's not just about what we do, but about why we do it – to honor, glorify, and please Him.

Prayer: *Dear God, thank you for your commands and plans. Help me to obey your commands and to trust in your guidance.* Amen.

## REFLECTION

_Action Step:_

"What is my motivation for obeying God? Is it out of love, fear, obligation, or something else?"

- Why do I choose to follow God's commands?
- Is it because I want to earn His approval or avoid punishment?
- Or is it because I genuinely love and trust Him, and want to please Him?
- Are there areas where I'm obeying out of obligation or habit, rather than a genuine desire to follow God?

Reflection: Today, I choose to obey God's commands and trust in His plans, knowing that He desires to guide me and use me for His purposes. I will rest in His care and lean on His guidance.

## _September 15:_ Thankfulness

Scripture: Psalm 107:1 says, give thanks to the Lord, for he is good; his love endures forever!

### _Devotion:_

Thankfulness is not just a feeling, but a choice - it's a decision to thank God for His blessings and provision, even in the midst of challenges.

What a beautiful perspective! Thankfulness is indeed a choice. It's a mindset and an attitude that can be cultivated and practiced, even in difficult times.

Thankfulness has the power to transform our lives and help us see the good in every situation. It's a choice that can lead to a more positive, hopeful, and resilient life. Thankfulness helps us focus on the good things in our lives, rather than dwelling on negative thoughts or circumstances. Practicing thankfulness can change our perspective, helping us see challenges as opportunities for growth and learning. Thankfulness can bring joy and happiness, even in difficult times.

Remember, thankfulness is a choice, and it's a powerful tool for transforming our lives!

Prayer: *Dear God, thank you for your goodness and love. Help me to cultivate a heart of thankfulness and gratitude.* Amen.

## _September 16_: Contentment

Scripture: Philippians 4:12 says, I have learned the secret of being content in any and every situation, whether well fed or hungry, whether living in plenty or in want.

### _Devotion:_

Contentment is not just a feeling, but a choice - it's a decision to trust in God's presence and provision, even in the midst of uncertainty.

What a beautiful and profound statement! Contentment is a choice that requires trust, faith, and surrender. It's about acknowledging that God is in control, even when we can't see the bigger picture or understand what's happening around us.

Choosing contentment means letting go of anxiety, worry, and fear, and instead, embracing peace, hope, and joy. It's a mindset shift that allows us to find rest and satisfaction in God's presence, regardless of our circumstances.

Contentment is not the same as happiness_: Happiness is an emotion that comes and goes, while contentment is a deeper sense of peace and satisfaction that can exist even in difficult circumstances.

Prayer: *Dear God, thank you for your presence and provision. Help me to be content in your care and trust in your goodness.* Amen.

### _September 17:_ Peace in God's Presence!

Scripture: Philippians 4:12 says, I have learned the secret of being content in any and every situation, whether well fed or hungry, whether living in plenty or in want.

_Devotion:_

Peace is not just a feeling, but a choice - it's a decision to trust in God's presence and provision, even in the midst of uncertainty.

What a beautiful and profound statement! Peace is a choice that we can make every day, regardless of our circumstances. It's a decision to trust in a higher power, let go of worry and anxiety, and have faith that everything will work out for our good.

Choosing peace doesn't mean that we won't face challenges or uncertainties, but it means that we'll face them with a sense of calm, clarity, and confidence. It's a mindset shift that allows us to focus on the present moment, rather than getting caught up in worries about the future or regrets about the past.

As you said, trusting in God's presence and provision is a powerful way to choose peace. It's a reminder that we're not alone, and that we have a loving and guiding force in our lives. By choosing peace, we can live with more joy, hope, and resilience, even in the midst of uncertainty.

_Prayer:_ *Dear God, thank you for your presence and provision. Help me to trust in your care and goodness, and to find peace in you, no matter what circumstances I face.* Amen.

## REFLECTION

Action Step:
- Take a few minutes each day to sit in silence, focusing on your breath and God's presence.
- Write down things you're grateful for, no matter how small they may seem.
- Share with a friend or family member how you're seeking peace in God's presence.

Reflection: Read Philippians 4:12 and reflect on what it means to be content in God's presence and provision.
- Think about areas in your life where you struggle with peace and contentment.
- Consider how trusting in God's care and goodness can bring peace to those areas.

Remember, peace is a journey, and it's okay to take it one step at a time. May this devotional guide inspire and encourage you to seek peace in God's presence!

### September 18: Long Suffering

Scripture: Galatians 5:22-23 - But the fruit of the Spirit is patience, kindness, goodness, faithfulness, gentleness, self-control.

### Devotion:

Long suffering is not about tolerating difficult circumstances, but about trusting God's sovereignty and goodness in the midst of them.

What a powerful and insightful perspective on long suffering! It's not just about enduring or tolerating difficult circumstances, but about trusting in God's sovereignty and goodness even when we don't understand what's happening.

Long suffering is about cultivating a deep trust that God is working everything out for our good, even when we can't see it. It's about believing that He is sovereign over every circumstance, and that His goodness and love are never faltering.

This kind of trust allows us to persevere through difficult times with hope and confidence, rather than just trying to "get through" them. It's a beautiful expression of faith, and a testament to the strength and depth of our relationship with God.

May we learn to trust in God's sovereignty and goodness, even in the midst of challenging circumstances.

Prayer: - *Dear God, help me to cultivate long suffering in my life. Give me patience and understanding in difficult circumstances. May I reflect Your love and mercy to those around me.* Amen.

## REFLECTION

Action Step:

- Take a few minutes each day to practice deep breathing exercises, calming your mind and spirit.
- Write down situations where you feel impatient or frustrated, and pray for patience and understanding.
- Share with a friend or family member how you're working on cultivating long suffering.

Reflection: - Read Galatians 5:22-23 and reflect on the fruit of the Spirit, specifically long suffering (patience).
- Think about areas in your life where you struggle with impatience or frustration.
- Consider how practicing long suffering can help you grow in spiritual maturity and character.

## _September 19_: _Renewing Your Mind and Heart

Scripture: _ Romans 12:2 - Do not conform to the pattern of this world, but be transformed by the renewing of your mind. Then you will be able to test and approve what God's will is—his good, pleasing and perfect will.

_Devotion:_

Spiritual renewal is a daily process, and it starts with surrendering to God's transformative power.

What a beautiful and powerful truth! Spiritual renewal is indeed a daily process, and surrendering to God's transformative power is the first step towards experiencing that renewal. It's about acknowledging that we can't do it on our own and inviting God to work in and through us.

Prayer: -*Dear God, I come to you today, seeking your transformative power to renew my mind and spirit. Help me to let go of old patterns, thoughts, and habits that no longer serve me.*

*Renew my mind with your truth, that I may see myself, others, and the world around me through your eyes. Give me a fresh perspective, a clean slate, and a heart that is open to your guidance.*

*Renew my spirit with your presence, that I may be filled with your joy, peace, and love. Help me to walk in the freedom and victory that you have already won for me. May my mind and spirit be renewed daily, that I may reflect your glory and live a life that honors you.* Amen.

## _September 20: _Trusting God's Sovereignty

_Scripture: _ Psalm 103:19 - The Lord has established his throne in heaven, and his kingdom rules over all.

_Devotion: _

God's sovereignty is not just about control, but about His goodness and love for us.

What a beautiful perspective! God's sovereignty is often misunderstood as only being about control or power, but it's so much more than that. It's about His goodness, love, and care for us. It's about Him working everything out for our good, even in the midst of difficult circumstances.

As the Bible says, and we know that for those who love God all things work together for good, for those who are called according to his purpose. (Romans 8:28)

God's sovereignty is a comforting reminder that He is always working for our benefit, even when we can't see the bigger picture. It's a testament to His love and goodness, and a reason to trust and praise Him.

*_Prayer: _- Dear God, help me to trust Your sovereignty in all circumstances. May I rest in Your goodness and wisdom, knowing that You are in control.* Amen.

## _September 21: _The Power of Honesty

_Scripture: _ Proverbs 10:9 - Whoever walks in integrity walks securely, but he who makes his ways crooked will be found out.

### _Devotion: _

Honesty is not just about telling the truth, but about living a life of authenticity and integrity.

What a profound statement! Honesty goes beyond just speaking the truth; it's about being genuine, transparent, and consistent in our words and actions. Living a life of authenticity and integrity means being true to ourselves and others, without pretenses or hidden agendas. It's about aligning our values, beliefs, and actions, and being accountable for who we are and what we do.

This kind of honesty builds trust, respect, and strong relationships. It's not always easy, but it's essential for personal growth, self-respect, and making a positive impact in the world.

Remove any temptation to deceive or manipulate, and fill me with a desire to be transparent and authentic. Help me to admit when I'm wrong and to make amends when necessary.

May my honesty bring me peace, respect, and strong relationships. May I be a role model for others and a reflection of your truth and light.

_Prayer: _- *Dear God, help me to be truthful in all my words and actions. Give me the courage to speak from my heart and to act with integrity. May I be honest with myself and others, even when it's difficult. Amen.*

## REFLECTION

Action Step: _
- Write down areas where you need to practice honesty and integrity.
- Share with a friend or family member how honesty has positively impacted a relationship.
- Take a few minutes each day to meditate on Proverbs 10:9 and ask God to increase your commitment to honesty.

_Reflection: _- Read Proverbs 10:9 and reflect on the importance of integrity and honesty.
- Think about areas in your life where honesty may be challenging or lacking.
- Consider how honesty can build trust, respect, and strong relationships.

# _September 22_: _Serving Others, Serving God

_Scripture:_ Matthew 25:40 - Truly I tell you, whatever you did for one of the least of these brothers and sisters of mine, you did for me.

## _Devotion:_

Serving others is not just a task, but an act of worship and love for God.

What a beautiful perspective! Serving others can indeed be a powerful way to express love, compassion, and devotion to a higher power. Many spiritual traditions emphasize the importance of selfless service as a means of connecting with the divine and cultivating a sense of inner peace and fulfillment.

By viewing service as an act of worship and love, we can transform our interactions with others into opportunities for spiritual growth and meaningful connection. This mindset can help us approach service with a sense of reverence, humility, and joy, leading to a deeper sense of purpose and fulfillment.

May we all strive to serve others with love, kindness, and compassion, and may our actions be a reflection of our devotion to something greater than ourselves.

_Prayer:_ _Dear God, help me to have a heart of service, putting others' needs before my own. Give me opportunities to serve and the humility to do so with joy._ Amen.

### September 23: Embracing Brokenness, Finding Healing

_Scripture:_ Psalm 51:17 - My sacrifice, O God, is a broken spirit; a broken and contrite heart you, God, will not despise.

_Devotion:_

Brokenness is not something to be ashamed of, but an opportunity for God's grace and healing to shine through.

What a powerful and liberating truth! Brokenness is an inherent part of the human experience, and often, we try to hide or deny our weaknesses and vulnerabilities. However, as you so beautifully put it, brokenness can indeed be an opportunity for God's grace and healing to shine through.

By acknowledging and embracing our brokenness, we can:

- Let go of the need for perfection and self-sufficiency
- Open ourselves to receive divine guidance, comfort, and strength
- Experience the transformative power of grace and healing
- Become a testament to the redemptive work of God in our lives

May we learn to view our brokenness as a canvas for God's masterpiece of restoration, rather than something to be ashamed of. May His grace and healing pour into our lives, making us whole and radiant once more.

_Prayer: _- *Dear God, I acknowledge my brokenness and surrender it to You. Please heal and restore me, and help me to find wholeness in You.* Amen.

## REFLECTION

_Action Step: _

- Write down areas of brokenness you're willing to surrender to God.
- Share with a trusted friend or mentor how you're seeking healing and restoration.
- Take a few minutes each day to meditate on Psalm 51:17 and ask God to work in your brokenness.

_Reflection: - Think about areas in your life where you may be struggling with brokenness, such as relationships, emotions, or past experiences.
- Consider how surrendering your brokenness to God can lead to healing and restoration.

May this devotional guide inspire and encourage you to embrace your brokenness and find healing in God today!

## _September 24_: _Redeemed and Restored

_Scripture:_ Ephesians 1:7-8 - In him we have redemption through his blood, the forgiveness of sins, in accordance with the riches of God's grace that he lavished on us.

_Devotion:_

God not only redeems us from our past, but He also restores us for our future. He takes the broken pieces of our lives and puts them back together again, making us whole and new. Just like the psalmist said, 'He restores my soul' (Psalm 23:3).

When we accept Jesus as our Lord and Savior, He begins a work of redemption and restoration in our lives. He frees us from the shackles of sin and shame, and He starts to repair the damage that has been done.

But redemption and restoration are not one-time events - they are ongoing processes. God continually works in us, transforming us into the image of Christ.

As we walk with Him, He restores our hope, our joy, and our purpose. He gives us a new identity and a new destiny.

So, no matter what you've been through or where you are today, know that God is able to redeem and restore you. He is able to take the broken pieces of your life and turn them into something beautiful.

_Prayer:_ - *Dear God, thank You for redeeming me from my past and restoring me for my future. Continue to work in me, transforming me into the image of Christ. Give me hope, joy, and purpose, and use me for Your glory.* Amen.

## _September 25: Pressing On

_Scripture:_ Philippians 3:14 - I press on toward the goal to win the prize for which God has called me heavenward in Christ Jesus.

_Devotion:_

Perseverance is not about being perfect, but about being persistent in our pursuit of God's purposes.

What a wonderful reminder! Perseverance is not about achieving perfection, but about consistently and persistently striving towards our goals and God's purposes, even in the face of challenges and setbacks. It's about getting back up, learning from our mistakes, and keeping moving forward with faith, hope, and determination.

I love that phrase! "Pressing On" is a great way to describe perseverance in action. It's about continuing to move forward, even when the journey gets tough, and not giving up on our goals, dreams, and aspirations. It's a mindset that says, "I will not be deterred, I will not be discouraged, I will keep pressing on, no matter what."

May we all be inspired to press on, even when the going gets tough!

_Prayer:_ - *Dear God, help me to press on in the face of challenges, trusting in Your strength and guidance. Give me perseverance to reach my goals and fulfill Your purposes.* Amen.

## September 26: The Power of Perseverance

_Scripture:_ Galatians 6:9 - Let us not become weary in doing good, for at the proper time we will reap a harvest if we do not give up.

_Devotion:_

Perseverance is not about being perfect.

Exactly! Perseverance is not about being perfect; it's about being persistent and consistent in our efforts, even when we face obstacles and challenges. It's about learning from our mistakes and using them as opportunities for growth and improvement.

Perseverance is about trusting in God's power and sovereignty, even when the journey gets tough or uncertain. It's about relying on His strength and wisdom to carry us through challenges and obstacles, and being open to His creative solutions and guidance.

Perseverance reflects God's boundless power and imagination, and it's a testament to His faithfulness and love for us. When we persevere, we demonstrate our trust in Him and His plans, and we open ourselves up to experiencing His glory and goodness in our lives.

Remember, perseverance is a journey, not a destination. It's a mindset and a heart attitude that says, "I will keep going, no matter what.

_Prayer: _- *Dear God, help me to persevere in the face of challenges and doubts. Give me the strength to keep going, even when the journey gets tough.* Amen.

## REFLECTION

_Action Step: _

- Write down areas in your life where you need to persevere.
- Share with a friend or mentor how this devotional has impacted your understanding of perseverance.
- Take a few minutes each day to meditate on Galatians 6:9 and ask God to give you the strength to keep going.

Reflection: _- Read Galatians 6:9 and reflect on the power of perseverance in your life.
- Think about how perseverance can lead to spiritual growth, stronger relationships, and a deeper trust in God.
- Consider how giving up can lead to missed opportunities and unrealized potential.

## _September 27_: The Mystery of God's Sovereignty

_Scripture:_ Isaiah 55:8-9 - For my thoughts are not your thoughts, neither are your ways my ways, declares the Lord. For as the heavens are higher than the earth, so are my ways higher than your ways and my thoughts than your thoughts.

_Devotion:_

God's sovereignty is a mystery that invites us to trust, surrender, and rest in His infinite wisdom and goodness.

Beautifully said! God's sovereignty is indeed a profound mystery that transcends human understanding. It's a reminder that God is infinitely wise, all-knowing, and all-powerful, and that His ways are higher than ours. Embracing God's sovereignty invites us to:

- Trust in His goodness and love, even when we don't understand
- Surrender our control and desires to His will
- Rest in His infinite wisdom and guidance
- Find peace and comfort in His presence, regardless of circumstances

May we humbly acknowledge God's sovereignty, trust in His goodness, and find rest in His presence.

_Prayer: _- *Dear, we come before You in awe and reverence, acknowledging Your sovereignty over all things. Your ways are mysterious and beyond our understanding, yet we trust in Your goodness and love.*

*Help us to embrace the mystery of Your sovereignty, even when circumstances seem uncertain or difficult. May our faith be rooted in Your unshakeable character and promises.*

*As believers, we pray for wisdom to trust You with the lives of our loved ones, knowing that You are working all things together for good. May our prayers be a reflection of our trust in Your sovereignty. In Jesus' name, we pray. Amen.*

## R EFLECTION PAGE

_Action Step:_
.- Take a few minutes each day to meditate on Isaiah 55:8-9 and ask God to reveal more of His mysterious ways to you.

_Reflection:_ _Think about how God's ways and thoughts are beyond human comprehension, yet He works everything out for our good.
- Consider how surrendering to God's sovereignty can lead to deeper trust and peace.

Additional Mind-Blowing Fact:

The concept of God's sovereignty is rooted in the biblical idea of "providence," which means that God is actively involved in guiding and directing all things, from the smallest details to the largest events.

## _September 28:_ The Miracle of Spiritual Renewal

_Scripture:_ 2 Corinthians 5:17 - Therefore, if anyone is in Christ, the new creation has come: The old has gone, the new is here!

_Devotion:_

Spiritual renewal is not just a one-time event, but a continuous process of growth and transformation, reflecting God's boundless love and grace.

Amen to that! Spiritual renewal is indeed an ongoing journey, not a one-time destination. It's a lifelong process of growth, transformation, and deepening our relationship with God.

This continuous process involves:

- Seeking God's presence and guidance daily
- Embracing His love and grace in every circumstance
- Surrendering to His will and purposes
- Being transformed by His Word and Spirit
- Growing in faith, hope, and love

May we embrace this ongoing journey of spiritual renewal, allowing God's boundless love and grace to shape us into His likeness, day by day.

_Prayer_ Dear Heavenly Father, we come to You, seeking spiritual renewal and revival. Refresh our spirits, revive our hearts, and renew our minds.

*Just as You send rain to revive the parched earth, send Your Holy Spirit to revive our souls. Quench our thirst for You, and satisfy our hunger for Your presence.*

*As believers, we pray for a miracle of spiritual renewal in our own lives and in the lives of those we influence. May our hearts be revitalized, our faith be strengthened, and our love for You be rekindled.*

*May this renewal empower us to live for You, to pray with fervor, and to love others with Your unconditional love. In Jesus' name, we pray. Amen.*

## REFLECTION

_Action Step:_

- Write down areas in your life where you've experienced spiritual renewal.
- Share with a friend or mentor how this devotional has impacted your understanding of new creation.
- Take a few minutes each day to meditate on 2 Corinthians 5:17 and ask God to continue transforming you.

_Reflection:_ -- Think about how becoming a new creation in Christ means leaving old patterns and habits behind.

## _September 29:_ The Mystery of God's Presence

_Scripture:_ Psalm 139:7-10 - "Where can I go from your Spirit? Where can I flee from your presence? If I go up to the heavens, you are there; if I make my bed in the depths, you are there. If I rise on the wings of the dawn, if I settle on the far side of the sea, even there your hand will guide me, your right hand will hold me fast."

_Devotion:_

God's presence is not limited by space or time, but is always available to us, reflecting His boundless love and care.

That's a profound truth! God's presence is indeed not limited by space or time. He is omnipresent, meaning He is present everywhere at all times. This truth has significant implications for our lives:

- God is always with us, no matter where we go or what we do.
- We can never escape His presence, and He is always available to us.
- He transcends spatial boundaries, so we can experience His presence in every location.
- He transcends time, so He is present in every moment, past, present, and future.

May we embrace the reality of God's omnipresent love and guidance, finding comfort, peace, and strength in His constant presence.

_Prayer: _- *Dear God, Thank You for being always present with me. Help me to sense Your presence and trust in Your guidance.* Amen.

## REFLECTION

_Action Step: _

- Write down times when you've felt God's presence in your life.
- Share with a friend or mentor how this devotional has impacted your understanding of God's presence.

_Reflection: _- Think about how God is always with you, no matter where you go or what you do.
- Consider how this truth can bring comfort, peace, and guidance in times of uncertainty.

Additional Mind-Blowing Fact:

- The concept of God's presence is rooted in the biblical idea of "omnipresence," which

## September 30: The Secret to Unshakeable Peace

_Scripture:_ Philippians 4:6-7 - Do not be anxious about anything, but in every situation, by prayer and petition, with thanksgiving, present your requests to God. And the peace of God, which transcends all understanding, will guard your hearts and your minds in Christ Jesus.

_Devotion:_

Unshakeable peace is not the absence of problems, but the presence of God's peace that guards our hearts and minds.

What a powerful truth! Unshakeable peace is not about having a problem-free life, but about having a deep and abiding sense of God's peace that sustains us through life's challenges. This peace:

- Transcends circumstances, remaining steadfast despite turmoil
- Guards our hearts and minds, protecting us from anxiety and fear
- Is rooted in God's presence, love, and sovereignty
- Is available to us through faith, prayer, and surrender
- Empowers us to face challenges with courage, hope, and confidence

May we experience this unshakeable peace, knowing that God's presence and love are always with us, guiding us through life's ups and downs.

_Prayer: _- *Dear God, I bring my worries and fears to You. Please replace them with Your peace, which surpasses all understanding.* Amen.

As we've journeyed through September's devotions, we've explored the depths of God's love, grace, and peace. We've seen that:

- Perseverance is not about being perfect, but about being persistent in our pursuit of God's purposes.
- God's sovereignty is a mystery that invites us to trust, surrender, and rest in His infinite wisdom and goodness.
- Spiritual renewal is a continuous process of growth and transformation, reflecting God's boundless love and grace.
- God's presence is not limited by space or time, and He is always with us.
- Unshakeable peace is not the absence of problems, but the presence of God's peace that guards our hearts and minds.

May these truths anchor us in the midst of life's storms, and may we continue to seek God's guidance, wisdom, and peace in every aspect of our lives. Remember, God's love and grace are always available to us, and His peace is just a prayer away.

Go forth with hope, courage, and confidence, knowing that God is with you every step of the way!

# OCTOBER 1-31

1. Forgiveness: A Choice
2. Forgiveness: A Process
3. Freedom of Forgiveness
4. Forgiving Others, Forgiving Ourselves
5. The Power of Forgiveness
6. The Power of Unconditional Forgiveness
7. Forgiveness and Trust
8. Forgiveness and Release
9. Forgiveness and Renewal
10. The Fruit of Forgiveness
11. Forgiveness and Healing
12. A Forgiving Heart
13. Forgiveness and Humility
14. Forgiveness and Freedom
15. Forgiveness and Love
16. Forgiveness and Mercy
17. Forgiveness and Restoration
18. Forgiveness and Gratitude
19. Forgiveness After Hurt
20. Forgiveness and Surrender
21. Forgiveness After Abuse
22. Forgiveness After Hate
23. Forgiveness and Compassion
24. Gratitude and Forgiveness
25. Serenity and Forgiveness
26. Forgiveness and Joy
27. Forgiveness and Love's Triumph
28. Forgiveness and New Beginnings"
29. Forgiveness and Personal Growth
30. Forgiveness and Love's Generosity
31. The Power of Forgiveness and Empathy

## _October 1_ Forgiveness: A Choice

_Scripture:_ Matthew 6:14-15 - For if you forgive other people when they sin against you, your heavenly Father will also forgive you. But if you do not forgive others their sins, your Father will not forgive your sins.

### _Devotion_

Forgiveness is a choice that can free us from the weight of resentment and bitterness. Reflect on how holding onto unforgiveness can affect your relationships and heart.

What a powerful truth! Forgiveness is indeed a choice that can liberate us from the burdens of resentment and bitterness. When we choose to forgive, we:

- Release the hold that offense has on us
- Break free from the cycle of hurt and anger
- Open ourselves to healing and restoration

Remember, forgiveness doesn't:
- Erase the past or justify wrongdoing
- Mean reconciliation or forgetting what happened
- Excuse or condone hurtful behavior

Forgiveness is a courageous decision to release the negative emotions associated with a past hurt, and to choose love and mercy instead. May we embrace the freedom and peace that comes from choosing forgiveness!

_Prayer:_ *Dear God, help me to choose forgiveness and let go of unforgiveness. Give me the strength to release the hurt and trust in your healing. Amen!*

## _October 2_ Forgiveness: A Process

_Scripture:_ Ephesians 4:32 - "Be kind and compassionate to one another, forgiving each other, just as in Christ God forgave you."

### _Devotion_

Forgiveness is a process that takes time, effort, and grace. Reflect on how God's forgiveness of your sins can help you extend forgiveness to others.

A beautiful reminder! Forgiveness is indeed a process that:
- Unfolds over time, with each step forward
- Requires effort and commitment to let go
- Depends on God's grace and strength to sustain us

This process involves:
- Acknowledging the hurt and its impact
- Confronting our emotions and reactions
- Choosing to release resentment and bitterness
- Cultivating empathy and understanding
- Extending mercy and compassion

Remember, forgiveness is not a one-time event, but a journey of growth, healing, and transformation. It's okay to take your time, to stumble, and to seek help along the way.

May His grace and peace guide you every step of the way!

_Prayer:_ *Dear God, help me to extend forgiveness to others just as you have forgiven me. Give me the grace to work through the process of forgiveness.* Amen

### October 3 — The Freedom of Forgiveness

_Scripture:_ Isaiah 43:25 - I, even I, am he who blots out your transgressions, for my own sake, and remembers your sins no more.

_Devotion_

Forgiveness brings freedom from the weight of resentment and bitterness. Reflect on how God's forgiveness of your sins can give you the freedom to forgive others.

The sweet release of forgiveness! When we choose to forgive, we experience:

- Liberation from the burden of resentment
- Freedom from the toxic grip of bitterness
- Healing of emotional wounds

Forgiveness breaks the chains that bind us to:
- Past hurts and painful memories
- Negative emotions and reactions
- Unhealthy relationships and dynamics

As we forgive, we create space for:
- Love and compassion to flourish
- God's grace and mercy to abound

Remember, forgiveness doesn't change the past, but it can transform our present and future. May forgiveness bring you freedom, peace, and a fresh start!

_Prayer:_ *Dear God, thank you for the freedom of forgiveness. Help me to extend that same freedom to others and release the hold of unforgiveness.* Amen!

## REFLECTION

_Additional Thoughts:_

- Consider how unforgiveness can hold you back from experiencing God's fullness.
- Think about how forgiveness can restore relationships and bring peace.
- Reflect on how God's forgiveness is not based on your worthiness, but on His mercy and love.

_Reflection Prompt:_ Write about a time when you experienced the freedom of forgiveness. How did it impact your life and relationships?

## October 4 — Forgiving Others, Forgiving Ourselves

_Scripture:_ Colossians 3:13 - "Bear with each other and forgive one another if any of you has a grievance against someone. Forgive as the Lord forgave you."

_Devotion:_

Forgiveness is not just about others, but also about ourselves. Reflect on how God's forgiveness can help you forgive yourself and release self-condemnation.

A profound truth! Forgiveness is indeed a two-fold process:
- Forgiving others for their wrongdoing and hurtful actions
- Forgiving ourselves for our own mistakes, shortcomings, and perceived failures

Self-forgiveness is just as important as forgiving others, as it:
- Releases us from self-criticism and self-condemnation
- Frees us from guilt, shame, and regret
- Enables us to embrace our humanity and imperfections

Remember, we are often our own worst critics, and self-forgiveness is essential for:

- Healing emotional wounds
- Restoring self-esteem and confidence

As you practice forgiveness, don't forget to include yourself in the process. You are deserving of love, grace, and mercy – just as much as others.

_Prayer:_ *Dear God, help me to extend your forgiveness to myself and others. Give me the grace to release self-condemnation and walk in your freedom.* Amen!

### REFLECTION

_Additional Thoughts:_

- Consider how self-condemnation can hold you back from experiencing God's fullness.
- Think about how forgiveness can bring healing and restoration to your heart.
- Reflect on how God's forgiveness is not based on your performance, but on His mercy and love.

_Reflection Prompt:_ Write about a time when you struggled to forgive yourself. How did God's forgiveness help you overcome self-condemnation?

## _October 5_ The Power of Forgiveness

_Scripture:_ Matthew 18:21-22 - "Then Peter came to Jesus and asked, 'Lord, how many times shall I forgive my brother or sister who sins against me? Up to seven times?' Jesus answered, 'I tell you, not seven times, but seventy-seven times.'"

_Devotion:_

Forgiveness is a powerful tool that can break cycles of hurt and pain. Reflect on how God's forgiveness can empower you to forgive others and experience His healing.

A beautiful truth! Forgiveness is a powerful tool that can:
- Shatter chains of resentment and bitterness
- Release us from the grip of negativity and anger
- Create space for healing, love, and compassion

By choosing forgiveness, we can:
- Interrupt patterns of revenge and retaliation
- End the perpetuation of hurt and harm
- Create a new narrative of love, mercy, and grace
- Open doors to reconciliation and restoration
- Experience the freedom and peace that comes with release

Forgiveness is about releasing the hold that hurt has on us, and choosing to move forward with love, compassion, and understanding.

_Prayer:_ *Dear God, help me to tap into the power of forgiveness and extend it to others. Give me the strength to forgive and experience your healing.* Amen!

## REFLECTION

_Additional Thoughts:_

- Consider how unforgiveness can create a cycle of hurt and pain.
- Think about how forgiveness can bring restoration and reconciliation to relationships.

- Reflect on how God's forgiveness is not limited, but abundant and overflowing.

_Reflection Prompt:_ Write about a situation where you chose to forgive someone. How did it impact your life and relationships?

## _October 6_ The Power of Unconditional Forgiveness

_Scripture:_ Luke 6:27-28 - "But to you who are listening I say: Love your enemies, do good to those who hate you, bless those who curse you, pray for those who mistreat you."

_Devotion:_

Unconditional forgiveness is a powerful demonstration of God's love and grace. Reflect on how you can extend unconditional forgiveness to others, just as God has forgiven you.

A profound truth! Unconditional forgiveness is indeed a powerful demonstration of God's love and grace, as it:

- Reflects God's character and nature
- Shows us the depth of God's love
- Demonstrates the power of grace to transform lives

Unconditional forgiveness means:
- Forgiveness that is offered freely and generously
- Forgiveness that reflects God's unwavering love and grace

As we experience and extend unconditional forgiveness, we:
- Encounter the transformative power of God's love
- Grow in our understanding of grace and mercy

May we embrace and share the beauty of unconditional forgiveness, reflecting God's love and grace to a world in need!

_Prayer:_ *Dear God, help me to extend unconditional forgiveness to others, just as you have forgiven me. Give me the strength to love and pray for those who have hurt me.* Amen!

## REFLECTION

_Additional Thoughts:_

- Consider how unconditional forgiveness can bring healing and restoration to relationships.
- Think about how forgiveness can be a witness to God's love and grace.
- Reflect on how God's forgiveness is not based on the other person's actions, but on His mercy and love.

_Reflection Prompt:_ Write about a situation where you are struggling to extend unconditional forgiveness. What steps can you take to release the hurt and choose forgiveness.

_October 7_Forgiveness and Trust

_Scripture:_ Psalm 37:3-4 - "Trust in the Lord and do good; dwell in the land and enjoy safe pasture. Take delight in the Lord, and he will give you the desires of your heart."

_Devotion:_

Forgiveness and trust go hand in hand. Reflect on how trusting God can help you forgive others and find peace.

A beautiful connection! Forgiveness and trust are indeed intertwined, as:
- Forgiveness paves the way for rebuilding trust
- Trust fosters an environment for forgiveness to flourish
- Forgiveness requires trust in the person or process
- Trust requires forgiveness to release past hurts

When we forgive, we:
- Create space for trust to grow
- Demonstrate our trust in God's sovereignty and goodness
- Exhibit trust in the process of healing and restoration

Conversely, when we trust, we:
- Open ourselves to forgiveness and healing
- Demonstrate our trust in God's power to transform
- Exhibit trust in the possibility of reconciliation

May we cultivate both forgiveness and trust, allowing them to flourish together in our lives!

_Prayer: _ *Dear God, help me to trust in your goodness and sovereignty. Give me the grace to forgive others and find peace in your presence.* Amen!

## REFLECTION

_Additional Thoughts: _

- Consider how trust is built when we see God's faithfulness in our lives.
- Think about how forgiveness can be a step towards healing and restoration.
- Reflect on how God's presence and peace can fill the gaps where trust has been broken.

Reflection Prompt: _ Write about a time when you struggled to trust God in a difficult situation. How did you come to trust Him, and how did it impact your ability to forgive?

## _October 8_ Forgiveness and Release

_Scripture:_ Psalm 103:12 - As far as the east is from the west, so far has he removed our transgressions from us.

_Devotion:_

Forgiveness after hate requires releasing the hold of bitterness and anger. Reflect on how God's love can help us release the past and move forward.

A powerful truth! Forgiveness after hate requires:
- Recognizing the grip of bitterness and anger
- Acknowledging the harm caused by holding onto hate
- Letting go of the need for revenge or retaliation
- Embracing a path of healing and restoration

Releasing bitterness and anger allows us to:
- Break free from the cycle of hurt and resentment
- Create space for love, compassion, and understanding
- Discover peace and freedom in forgiveness

Remember, forgiveness doesn't mean:
- Forgetting or condoning the hurt
- Ignoring the pain or its impact
- Excusing or justifying the wrongdoing

Forgiveness means releasing the hold of hate and choosing love, mercy, and grace instead. As Colossians 3:13 says, "Bear with each other and forgive one another if any of you has a grievance against someone. Forgive as the Lord forgave you."

_Prayer: _ *Dear God, help me to release the hold of bitterness and anger. Remove my transgressions and the hurt from my heart, and help me to move forward in Your love and forgiveness.* Amen!

## REFLECTION

_Additional Thoughts: _

- Consider how holding onto bitterness can consume and destroy us.
- Think about how God's love can bring freedom and release.

_Reflection Prompt: _ Write about the emotions and thoughts that come up when you think about the person or situation that hurt you. What steps can you take to release those emotions and forgive?

Note: Remember, forgiveness is not forgetting, but releasing the hold of the past. Seek God's guidance and support as you work towards forgiveness and healing.

## _October 9_ Forgiveness and Renewal

_Scripture:_ 2 Corinthians 5:17 - Therefore, if anyone is in Christ, the new creation has come: The old has gone, the new is here!

_Devotion:_

Forgiveness after hate requires renewal and transformation.

*A profound truth! Forgiveness after hate requires:*
- Renewal of the mind and heart
- Transformation of our emotions and perspective
- A change of spirit and attitude

*Renewal and transformation involve:*
- Letting go of old patterns and habits
- Seeking guidance from God's Word and Spirit
- Embracing the power of redemption and restoration

*Through renewal and transformation, we:*
- Break free from the bondage of hate
- Discover a new identity in Christ
- Experience the joy of forgiveness and peace

Remember, forgiveness is not just about the past, but about creating a better future.

_Prayer:_ *Dear God, help me to become a new creation in You. Transform my heart and mind, and help me to surrender to Your love and forgiveness. Renew me and make me whole.* Amen!

## _October 10_ The Fruit of Forgiveness

_Scripture:_ Galatians 5:22-23 - "But the fruit of the Spirit is love, joy, peace, forbearance, kindness, goodness, faithfulness, gentleness and self-control; against such things there is no law."

_Devotion:_

Forgiveness produces fruit in our lives, including love, joy, and peace.

A beautiful harvest! Forgiveness indeed produces a bounty of fruit in our lives, including:

- Love: Forgiveness cultivates love and compassion, allowing us to embrace others with kindness and understanding.
- Joy: Forgiveness brings joy, freeing us from the weight of resentment and bitterness.
- Peace: Forgiveness yields peace, calming our minds and hearts with a sense of resolution and closure.
- Patience: Forgiveness helps us develop patience and understanding, allowing us to navigate challenging relationships and situations.
- Kindness: Forgiveness fosters kindness and empathy, enabling us to connect with others on a deeper level.
- Gentleness: Forgiveness cultivates gentleness and humility, helping us approach life's challenges with grace and poise.

- Self-control: Forgiveness promotes self-control, empowering us to manage our emotions and respond wisely.

As we embrace forgiveness, we become fruitful trees, bearing the sweet fruit of love, joy, and peace. May our lives be a testament to the transformative power of forgiveness!

_Prayer:_ *Dear God, help me to cultivate the fruit of forgiveness in my life. Give me the grace to extend love, joy, and peace to others.* Amen!

## REFLECTION

_Additional Thoughts:_

- Consider how forgiveness can lead to personal growth and transformation.
- Think about how the fruit of forgiveness can impact your relationships and community.
- Reflect on how God's forgiveness of you can empower you to forgive others and produce fruit in your life.

_Reflection Prompt:_ Write about a time when you chose to forgive someone. What fruit of the Spirit did you experience as a result?

## _October 11_ Forgiveness and Healing

_Scripture:_ Jeremiah 30:17 -For I will restore health to you and heal your wounds, declares the Lord.

### _Devotion:_

*Forgiveness is a crucial step towards healing.*

A vital truth! Forgiveness is indeed a crucial step towards healing, as it:

- Releases the emotional burden of resentment and anger
- Allows us to let go of the past and move forward
- Creates space for emotional and spiritual restoration

*Forgiveness is not the same as:*
- Forgetting or ignoring the hurt
- Condoning or justifying the wrongdoing
- Excusing or minimizing the pain

*Rather, forgiveness is a deliberate choice to:*
- Choose love and compassion over hate and anger
- Trust in God's sovereignty and goodness
- Embrace the healing power of love and grace

*As we forgive, we open ourselves to:*
- Emotional healing and restoration
- Spiritual renewal and growth
- Physical well-being and wholeness

May forgiveness be the first step towards your healing journey!

_Prayer:_ Dear God, help me to forgive and release the hurts of my past. Give me the grace to receive Your healing and restoration. Amen!

## _October 12_ A Forgiving Heart

_Scripture:_ Matthew 6:14-15 - For if you forgive other people when they sin against you, your heavenly Father will also forgive you. But if you do not forgive others their sins, your Father will not forgive your sins.

_Devotion:_

A forgiving heart is a hallmark of a follower of Christ. Reflect on how you can cultivate a forgiving heart and extend grace to others.

A beautiful truth! A forgiving heart is indeed a hallmark of a follower of Christ, as it reflects: - God's character and nature (Exodus 34:6-7, Psalm 103:8-12)

- Jesus' teachings and example (Matthew 6:14-15, Luke 23:34)

A forgiving heart is characterized by:
- Love and compassion towards others
- Humility and recognition of our own need for forgiveness
- Trust in God's sovereignty and goodness

As followers of Christ, we are called to:
- Forgive as God forgives us (Ephesians 4:32)
- Show mercy and kindness to others (Luke 6:36)
- Be reconcilers and peacemakers (Matthew 5:9)

May our hearts be marked by the beauty of forgiveness, reflecting the love and grace of our Savior!

_Prayer:_ *Dear God, help me to cultivate a forgiving heart. Give me the grace to extend mercy and grace to others, just as You have extended it to me.* Amen!

## _October 13_ Forgiveness and Humility

_Scripture:_ 1 Peter 5:6-7 - Humble yourselves, therefore, under God's mighty hand, that he may lift you up in due time. Cast all your anxiety on him because he cares for you.

### _Devotion:_

Forgiveness requires humility, recognizing our own need for forgiveness and God's sovereignty. A profound truth! Forgiveness indeed requires humility, which involves:

- Recognizing our own need for forgiveness and mercy
- Embracing our dependence on God's grace and sovereignty
- Letting go of pride and self-righteousness

*Humility in forgiveness means:*
- Recognizing God's authority and sovereignty over all situations
- Trusting in God's goodness and wisdom
- Submitting to God's will and plan

*As we humble ourselves, we:*
- Create space for God to work in our lives
- Allow God to heal and transform us
- Become more like Christ, who forgave from the cross

May humility be the foundation of our forgiveness, and may we reflect the heart of our Savior! (1 Peter 5:6-7, James 4:6-10)

_Prayer:_ *Dear God, help me to humble myself before You and others. Give me the grace to forgive and trust in Your sovereignty. Amen!*

## _October 14_ Forgiveness and Freedom

_Scripture:_ John 8:36 - So if the Son sets you free, you will be free indeed.

_Devotion:_

Forgiveness brings freedom from the bondage of bitterness, resentment, and hurt.

A liberating truth! Forgiveness indeed brings freedom from the bondage of:

- Bitterness: Forgiveness dissolves the toxic root of bitterness, allowing us to taste the sweetness of peace and joy.
- Resentment: Forgiveness releases the weight of resentment, freeing us from the cycle of anger and hurt.
- Hurt: Forgiveness heals the wounds of hurt, restoring our emotional and spiritual well-being.

*Through forgiveness, we experience:*
- Emotional liberation: Freedom from negative emotions.
- Spiritual release: Freedom from the bondage of sin and guilt.
- Heart renewal: Freedom to love and live with a heart full of joy and peace.

*Forgiveness is the key that unlocks the prison of:*
- Unforgiveness- Resentment- Bitterness- Hurt and Anger

May forgiveness bring freedom to our lives, and may we walk in the liberty of Christ!

_Prayer:_ *Dear God,*

*We come to You, seeking forgiveness and freedom. Help us to release the burdens of resentment, bitterness, and unforgiveness that weigh us down.*

*As we reflect on our lives, reveal to us the areas where we need to extend forgiveness to others and to ourselves. Give us the courage to let go of past hurts and pains, and to embrace the freedom that comes with forgiveness.*

*Lord, we pray for the strength to forgive as You have forgiven us. May our hearts be healed, our relationships be restored, and our lives be transformed by the power of forgiveness.*

*As believers, we pray for the grace to model forgiveness and freedom to our loved ones, and to lead them to the same freedom and healing that we have found in You. In Jesus' name, we pray. Amen.*

This prayer seeks forgiveness, freedom, and healing from the burdens of unforgiveness, asking God to reveal areas where forgiveness is needed and to provide the courage to let go of past hurts.

## _October 15_ Forgiveness and Love

_Scripture:_ 1 Corinthians 13:5 - Love keeps no record of wrongs.

_Devotion:_

Forgiveness is an expression of love. A beautiful truth! Forgiveness is indeed an expression of love, as it:
- Reflects God's love and character (1 John 4:8, Ephesians 4:32)
- Demonstrates compassion and empathy towards others (Matthew 9:36, Colossians 3:12)
- Shows mercy and kindness, even in the face of hurt or injustice (Luke 6:36, Matthew 5:44)
- Releases the hold of negative emotions, creating space for love to flourish (Romans 12:14-21)
- Opens the door to reconciliation and restored relationships (Matthew 5:23-24, Ephesians 4:3)

Forgiveness is an act of love that:
- Seeks the well-being and healing of others
- Trusts in God's sovereignty and goodness
- Embraces the transformative power of love and grace

As we forgive, we express love in its purest form, just as God loves us. May our lives be marked by the beauty of forgiveness, and may we radiate the love of Christ! (John 15:12-13)

_Prayer:_ *Dear God, help me to love others as You love me. Give me the grace to forgive and keep no record of wrongs. Amen!*

## _October 16_Forgiveness and Mercy

_Scripture: _ Matthew 9:13 - But go and learn what this means: 'I desire mercy, not sacrifice.' For I have not come to call the righteous, but sinners.

_Devotion: _

Forgiveness shows mercy to those who have wronged us. A powerful truth! Forgiveness indeed shows mercy to those who have wronged us, as it:

- Extends kindness and compassion
- Releases them from the debt of their wrongdoing
- Cancels the penalty and consequence of their actions
- Offers a second chance and a fresh start

Mercy is a fundamental aspect of forgiveness, as it:
- Reflects God's mercy towards us (Ephesians 2:4-5, Titus 3:5-6)
- Creates space for healing, restoration, and reconciliation
- Breaks the cycle of retaliation and revenge
- Demonstrates the depth of our love and commitment to others

By showing mercy through forgiveness, we:
- Embody the heart of God
- Demonstrate the power of redemption
- Reflect the beauty of God's mercy and grace

May our lives be marked by the mercy of forgiveness, and may we extend the same mercy to others that God has shown us!

_Prayer: _ *Dear God, help me to show mercy to others as You have shown mercy to me. Give me the grace to forgive and extend grace.* Amen!

## _October 17_ _Forgiveness and Restoration

_Scripture:_ Joel 2:25 - I will restore to you the years that the locusts have eaten.

_Devotion:_

Forgiveness can lead to restoration and redemption. A beautiful outcome!

Forgiveness can indeed lead to restoration and redemption, as it:

- Creates space for healing and rebuilding
- Allows for the restoration of trust and intimacy
- Facilitates personal growth and transformation

Through forgiveness, we can experience:
- Redemption from past mistakes and hurt
- Revitalization of our spirit and purpose
- Reconciliation with God, ourselves, and others

Forgiveness can lead to restoration and redemption by:
- Breaking the cycle of hurt and retaliation
- Allowing us to learn from our mistakes and grow
- Reflecting the redemptive power of God's love and forgiveness

May our forgiveness lead to restoration and redemption, and may we experience the beauty of new beginnings! (2 Corinthians 5:17-20, Isaiah 43:18-19)

_Prayer:_ *Dear God, help me to forgive and let go of the past. Restore to me the years that have been lost, and bring healing and redemption.* Amen!

## REFLECTION

_Additional Thoughts:_

- Consider how forgiveness can clear the way for God's restoration.
- Think about how restoration can bring new purpose and meaning.
- Reflect on how God's promise to restore can bring hope and encouragement.

_Reflection Prompt:_ Write about an area of your life where you need restoration. How can forgiveness be a step towards healing and restoration?

Note: Remember, restoration is not always immediate, but it is a process that God guides us through as we forgive and trust Him.

## _October 18_ Forgiveness and Gratitude

_Scripture: Matthew 6:14-15 - "For if you forgive men when they sin against you, your heavenly Father will also forgive you. But if you do not forgive men their sins, your Father will not forgive your sins."

_Devotion:_

Forgiveness and gratitude are intertwined threads in the tapestry of our relationship with God and others. Today, let's reflect on the transformative power of forgiveness and cultivate a heart of gratitude.

**Forgiveness:**

Forgiveness doesn't erase the past, but it frees us from its chains. When we forgive, we:

- Release the burden of resentment
- Open ourselves to healing and restoration
- Reflect God's mercy and love
- Create space for reconciliation and renewed relationships

**Gratitude:**

Gratitude shifts our focus from what's lacking to what's abundant. When we practice gratitude, we:

- Recognize God's goodness and provision
- Cultivate a positive and hopeful outlook

Strengthen our faith and trust in God
Inspire others with our joy and thankfulness

_Prayer Dear Heavenly Father, Help me forgive those who have wronged me, just as You forgave me. Release the weight of resentment and fill me with Your mercy and love.

I thank You for: Your unconditional love and forgiveness
The blessings and gifts in my life
The opportunities to grow and learn
Your presence in every moment

May forgiveness and gratitude transform my heart, and may I reflect Your love and light to those around me. In Jesus' name, Amen.

## _October 19_ Forgiveness After Hurt

_Scripture:_ Psalm 34:18 - The Lord is close to the brokenhearted and saves the crushed in spirit.

_Devotion:_

Forgiveness is possible even after deep hurt.

A powerful truth! Forgiveness is indeed possible even after deep hurt, as it:

- Doesn't minimize or deny the pain
- Acknowledges the hurt, but releases the hold
- Allows for healing and restoration
- Creates space for new experiences and relationships

Forgiveness after deep hurt:
- Involves confronting and processing emotions
- Needs a commitment to healing and growth
- Offers a path towards freedom and peace

Remember, forgiveness:
- Isn't a one-time event, but a journey
- Isn't about the other person, but about our own healing
- Can be extended even if the other person isn't sorry

May forgiveness be the balm that heals your deep hurt, and may you experience the peace and freedom that comes with it! (Isaiah 61:1, Matthew 5:4)

_Prayer:_ *Dear God, I bring my hurt to You. Comfort me with Your presence and empower me to forgive. Help me to trust in Your love and goodness. Amen!*

## _October 20_ Forgiveness and Surrender

_Scripture:_ Matthew 11:28-30 - Come to me, all you who are weary and burdened, and I will give you rest. Take my yoke upon you and learn from me, for I am gentle and humble in heart, and you will find rest for your souls.

_Devotion:_

Forgiveness requires surrendering our burdens and hurts to God.

A beautiful surrender! Forgiveness indeed requires surrendering our burdens and hurts to God, as it:

- Recognizes our limitations and God's sovereignty
- Acknowledges our need for divine healing and strength

Surrendering our burdens and hurts to God:
- Creates space for God's peace and comfort
- Opens us to receive His guidance and wisdom
- Frees us from the weight of resentment and anger

As we surrender our burdens and hurts to God, we can:
- Cast our cares upon Him (1 Peter 5:7)
- Find rest for our souls (Matthew 11:28-30)
- Experience the peace that passes understanding (Philippians 4:7)
- Know that He is working all things for our good (Romans 8:28)

May our surrender be complete, and may God's love and grace surround us as we forgive and let go! (Psalm 55:22, Isaiah 43:2)

_Prayer:_ *Dear God, I surrender my burdens and hurts to You. Give me rest and peace, and help me to forgive and release the pain. Teach me to trust in Your gentleness and humility.* Amen!

## REFLECTION

_Additional Thoughts:_

- Consider how surrender can lead to emotional release.
- Think about how God's gentleness and humility can bring comfort.
- Reflect on how surrender can lead to deeper trust and intimacy with God.

_Reflection Prompt:_ Write about a burden or hurt you've been carrying. What steps can you take to surrender it to God? How can you trust Him to give you rest and peace?

Note: Remember, surrender is a process, and it's okay to take small steps. Begin by surrendering your worries and concerns to God, and ask Him to help you trust Him more deeply.

## October 21 — Forgiveness After Abuse

_Scripture:_ Isaiah 61:7 - Instead of your shame, you will receive a double portion, and instead of disgrace, you will rejoice in your inheritance.

_Devotion:_

Forgiveness after abuse requires acknowledging the pain and trauma.

A crucial step! Forgiveness after abuse requires acknowledging the pain and trauma, as it: - Recognizes the severity of the harm inflicted- Validates the survivor's experiences and emotions- Allows for a genuine and meaningful forgiveness process

Acknowledging pain and trauma involves: - Recognizing the abuse and its effects- Accepting the survivor's feelings and reactions
- Understanding the complexity of their emotions

Forgiveness after abuse doesn't mean: - Forgetting or downplaying the abuse- Condoning or excusing the abuser's actions
- Ignoring the pain and trauma

Rather, forgiveness after abuse involves: - Breaking free from the cycle of hurt and anger- Finding peace and closure- Regaining control and empowerment- Healing and moving forward

May acknowledgment and forgiveness be a part of the healing journey for those who have experienced abuse. (Psalm 34:18, 2 Corinthians 1:3-4)

_Prayer:_ *Dear God, I bring my pain and trauma to You. Help me to forgive and release the shame and disgrace. Give me a double portion of Your love and redemption, and help me to rejoice in my inheritance.* Amen!

## REFLECTION

_Additional Thoughts:_
- Consider how forgiveness doesn't mean forgetting or excusing the abuse.
- Think about how God's love can heal emotional wounds.
- Reflect on how forgiveness can lead to freedom and empowerment.

_Reflection Prompt:_ Write about your experience of abuse. How has it affected you? What steps can you take towards forgiveness and healing? How can you trust God to bring restoration and redemption?

Note: Remember, forgiveness is a journey, and healing takes time. Be patient and kind to yourself as you walk towards restoration and redemption.

## October 22 — Forgiveness After Hate

_Scripture:_ 1 John 4:20-21 - Whoever claims to love God yet hates a brother or sister is a liar. For whoever does not love their brother and sister, whom they have seen, cannot love God, whom they have not seen.

_Devotion:_

Forgiveness after hate requires recognizing the humanity in others.

A profound insight! Forgiveness after hate requires recognizing the humanity in others, as it: - Sees beyond the hurtful actions and words- Acknowledges the shared human experience
- Empathizes with the complexities and struggles of others

Recognizing humanity in others involves:
- Looking beyond labels and stereotypes
- Seeing the person, not just their actions
- Acknowledging our shared vulnerabilities and weaknesses

Forgiveness after hate doesn't mean: - Ignoring or condoning hateful actions- Forgetting the harm caused- Excusing or justifying hateful behavior

Rather, forgiveness after hate involves: - Letting go of resentment and anger- Releasing the hold of hate and bitterness- Creating space for healing and understanding.

May recognizing the humanity in others be a powerful step towards forgiveness and healing. (Galatians 3:28, Luke 6:27-36)

_Prayer:_ *Dear God, we come to You, seeking Your grace and strength to forgive in the face of hatred and hurt. Help us to release the toxic emotions that consume us when we've been wronged.*

*Lord, we pray for the ability to see beyond the hurt and to recognize the humanity in those who have wronged us. Give us the courage to choose forgiveness, even when it feels impossible.*

*As we forgive, heal the deep wounds of our hearts and minds. Restore our relationships, and bring peace to our lives.*

*Lord, we pray for the wisdom to teach our loved ones about the power of forgiveness and the freedom it brings. May our examples of forgiveness inspire others to do the same. In Jesus' name, we pray. Amen.*

# REFLECTION

_Additional Thoughts:_

- Consider how hate can consume and destroy us.
- Think about how God's love can break down barriers and bring understanding.
- Reflect on how forgiveness can lead to reconciliation and restoration.

_Reflection Prompt:_ Write about a time when you experienced hate or anger towards someone. How did it affect you? What steps can you take towards forgiveness and seeing the humanity in others?

Note: Remember, forgiveness doesn't mean forgetting or excusing hate, but rather releasing the hold it has on us. Seek support and guidance as you work towards forgiveness and healing

## _October 23_ Forgiveness and Compassion

_Scripture:_ Matthew 5:44 - But I tell you, love your enemies and pray for those who persecute you.

_Devotion:_

Forgiveness after hate requires compassion and empathy.

A beautiful truth! Forgiveness after hate indeed requires compassion and empathy, as it:

- Recognizes the complexities and flaws that led to hurtful actions
- Offers kindness and mercy, even in the face of wrongdoing
- Creates space for healing and restoration

Compassion and empathy in forgiveness involve:
- Putting ourselves in others' shoes- Imagining their struggles and pain
- Understanding the factors that led to their actions

Compassion and empathy don't mean:
  - Ignoring or excusing hurtful actions
  - Condoning or justifying hate- Forgetting the harm caused

Rather, they involve:
  - Humanizing the one who caused harm

- Recognizing our shared humanity- Creating space for growth and change- Offering a path towards redemption and healing
- Reflecting the transformative power of love and grace

May compassion and empathy guide us towards forgiveness and healing, even in the face of hate. (Colossians 3:12-13)

_Prayer: _ *Dear God, we come to You, seeking to cultivate forgiveness and compassion in our hearts. Help us to see others through Your eyes, to understand their struggles and pain.*

*Lord, we pray for the ability to empathize with those who have wronged us, to recognize that they too are broken and in need of Your love. Give us the grace to extend compassion and kindness, even in the face of hurt.*

*As we forgive, fill us with Your love and compassion. Help us to be instruments of healing and restoration in the lives of those around us. May our examples inspire them to become agents of love and grace in a world that desperately needs it. In Jesus' name, we pray. Amen.*

This prayer seeks God's help to cultivate forgiveness and compassion, asking for the ability to see others through His eyes, and to extend kindness and empathy even in the face of hurt.

# REFLECTION

_Additional Thoughts:_

- Consider how compassion can break down barriers and bring understanding.
- Think about how God's love can transform our hearts and minds.
- Reflect on how forgiveness can lead to peace and reconciliation.

_Reflection Prompt:_ Write about someone you consider an enemy or someone who has wronged you. How can you pray for them and show compassion? What steps can you take towards forgiveness?

Note: Remember, forgiveness is a process, and it may take time. Be patient and kind to yourself as you work towards forgiveness and compassion.

## _October 24_ Gratitude and Forgiveness

_Scripture:_ Ephesians 4:32 - Be kind and compassionate to one another, forgiving each other, just as in Christ God forgave you.

_Devotion:_

Gratitude and forgiveness are closely linked.

A beautiful connection! Gratitude and forgiveness are indeed closely linked, as:

- Gratitude helps us focus on the good, making it easier to forgive
- Forgiveness opens our hearts to gratitude, allowing us to appreciate the present
- Forgiveness frees us from resentment, allowing gratitude to flourish
- Both gratitude and forgiveness promote emotional healing and well-being

The link between gratitude and forgiveness involves:

- Recognizing the good in our lives, even amidst challenges
- Letting go of negative emotions, making space for gratitude
- Focusing on the present moment, rather than past hurts

May our hearts be filled with gratitude and forgiveness, transforming our lives and relationships! (Psalm 103:2-5, Colossians 3:12-13)

_Prayer: _ *Dear God, help me to cultivate a heart of gratitude and forgiveness. Teach me to see the good in others and extend kindness and compassion, just as You have forgiven me.* Amen!

## REFLECTION

_Additional Thoughts: _

- Consider how gratitude can help us focus on the present moment.
- Think about how forgiveness can bring peace and closure.
- Reflect on how gratitude and forgiveness can lead to deeper relationships and community.

_Reflection Prompt: _ Write about a situation where you struggled to forgive someone. How can gratitude help you shift your perspective and extend forgiveness? What are you grateful for in this situation?

## _October 25_ _ Serenity and Forgiveness_

_Scripture: _ Philippians 4:7 - And the peace of God, which transcends all understanding, will guard your hearts and your minds in Christ Jesus.

_Devotion: _

Serenity and forgiveness go hand in hand. When we choose to forgive, we create space for serenity to enter our lives. Forgiveness brings peace, calmness, and tranquility, allowing us to let go of worries and anxieties.

Beautifully said! Forgiveness can indeed create space for serenity to enter our lives. When we hold onto resentment and bitterness, it can consume our thoughts, emotions, and actions, leaving little room for peace and tranquility. But when we choose to forgive, we release the hold that those negative emotions have on us, making space for serenity to enter and bring calmness, clarity, and inner peace.

As we forgive, we experience the peace of God that transcends all understanding. This peace guards our hearts and minds, protecting us from the turmoil and chaos that unforgiveness brings.

May our hearts be filled with serenity and forgiveness, reflecting the peace and love of God.

*Prayer:* *Dear God, we come to You, seeking serenity and forgiveness. Help us to find peace in the midst of turmoil and to release the burdens of unforgiveness.*

*Lord, we pray for the serenity to accept what we cannot change and the courage to forgive what we cannot forget. Give us the grace to let go of resentment and to embrace Your peace.*

*As we forgive, fill us with Your calm and gentle spirit. Help us to rest in Your presence, knowing that You are in control.*

*We pray for the wisdom to guide our loved ones towards serenity and forgiveness. May our examples of peaceful living inspire them to seek Your calming presence in their own lives. In Jesus' name, we pray. Amen.*

This prayer seeks God's help to find serenity and forgiveness, asking for the ability to accept what cannot be changed, to forgive what cannot be forgotten, and to rest in His peaceful presence.

## REFLECTION PAGE

Reflect on a situation or relationship where you feel a lack of serenity. How has unforgiveness contributed to this feeling? What steps can you take to forgive and release the negative emotions associated with this situation? How can you cultivate serenity in this area of your life, and what does that look like for you?

## _October 26_Forgiveness and Joy

_Scripture:_ Psalm 51:12 -Restore to me the joy of your salvation and grant me a willing spirit, to sustain me.
_Devotion:_

Forgiveness brings joy!

What a beautiful truth! Forgiveness indeed brings joy! When we choose to forgive, we release the weight of resentment and bitterness, making room for joy to flourish. Here's a devotional thought on forgiveness and joy:

Forgiveness is the key that unlocks the door to joy. When we forgive, we free ourselves from the chains of resentment and anger, allowing joy to flood our hearts. Just as God forgives us and brings us joy, we can extend that same forgiveness to others and experience the joy that follows.

Remember, forgiveness is a journey, and joy is a fruit that grows as we walk in forgiveness. Keep shining!

_Prayer:_ *Dear God, help me to forgive and experience the joy of Your salvation. Restore my joy and grant me a willing spirit.* Amen!

## _October 27_ Forgiveness and Love's Triumph

_Scripture:_ 1 Corinthians 13:7 - Love always protects, always trusts, always hopes, always perseveres.

_Devotion:_

Forgiveness is a triumph of love! When we forgive, we are choosing to love and extend grace, even in difficult circumstances. Reflect on how forgiveness can be a powerful demonstration of love's triumph.

What a powerful truth! Forgiveness is indeed a triumph of love! When we choose to forgive, we demonstrate the power of love over hurt, anger, and resentment. Forgiveness shows that love is stronger than any offense or wound.

*Here's a devotional thought on forgiveness as a triumph of love:*
Forgiveness is the ultimate expression of love. It's a decision to release the grip of hurt and anger, and instead, choose to love and let go. When we forgive, we triumph over the forces of darkness and choose the light of love. Just as God loves us and forgives us, we can extend that same love and forgiveness to others.

Remember, forgiveness is a victory of love that brings freedom, healing, and joy! Keep shining!

_Prayer:_ *Dear God, we come to You, celebrating the triumph of love and forgiveness. Help us to remember that Your love is stronger than any hurt or offense.*

*Lord, we pray for the ability to forgive freely, just as You have forgiven us. Give us the grace to release the hold that unforgiveness has on our hearts and to embrace the freedom of Your love.*

*As we forgive, fill us with Your perfect love, which casts out fear and heals our wounds. Help us to love others as You have loved us, with a love that is patient, kind, and unending.*

*Lord, we pray for the wisdom to teach our loved ones about the transformative power of forgiveness and love. May our examples of forgiveness inspire them to become agents of Your love in a world that needs it. In Jesus' name, we pray. Amen.*

This prayer celebrates the triumph of love and forgiveness, asking God for the ability to forgive freely, to release the hold of unforgiveness, and to embrace the freedom of His love.

### REFLECTION

_Additional Thoughts: _

- Reflect on how love's triumph can lead to a more beautiful and redemptive story.

_Reflection Prompt: _ Write about a time when you chose to forgive someone out of love. How did it affect your relationship with that person? How can you apply that same love and forgiveness to current areas of your life?

## _October 28:_ Forgiveness and New Beginnings

_Scripture:_ 2 Corinthians 5:17 - Therefore, if anyone is in Christ, the new creation has come: The old has gone, the new is here!

### _Devotion:_

Forgiveness brings new beginnings! When we forgive, we are given a fresh start and a clean slate. Reflect on how forgiveness can bring new life and new possibilities to our lives.

What a beautiful truth! Forgiveness indeed brings new beginnings! When we choose to forgive, we open ourselves up to a fresh start, a clean slate, and a new chapter in life. Forgiveness allows us to let go of the past and embrace the present with hope and possibility.

*Here's a devotional thought on forgiveness and new beginnings:*

Forgiveness is the bridge to new beginnings. It's the doorway to a fresh start, a chance to rewrite our story and create a new narrative. When we forgive, we release the hold of yesterday's hurts and embrace the promise of today's possibilities. Just as God makes all things new, forgiveness makes all things new in our lives.

Remember, forgiveness is the key to unlocking new beginnings, and God is the author of our new story!

_Prayer:_ *Dear God, help me to forgive and start anew. Give me a fresh start and a clean slate, and teach me to walk in newness of life.*

## October 29: Forgiveness and Personal Growth

_Scripture:_ Romans 8:28-29 - And we know that in all things God works for the good of those who love him, who have been called according to his purpose. For those God foreknew he also predestined to be conformed to the image of his Son.

_Devotion:_

Forgiveness leads to personal growth! What a profound truth! Forgiveness indeed leads to personal growth! When we choose to forgive, we create space for self-reflection, self-awareness, and self-improvement. Forgiveness allows us to:

- Release emotional baggage
- Break free from negative patterns
- Develop empathy and understanding
- Cultivate self-compassion
- Grow in emotional intelligence
- Develop resilience and strength

*Here's a devotional thought on forgiveness and personal growth:*
Forgiveness is the fertile soil where personal growth takes root. As we forgive, we clear the ground of our hearts, making room for new growth, new insights, and new perspectives. Forgiveness helps us to confront our own flaws, weaknesses, and areas for improvement,

leading to a more authentic, humble, and compassionate version of ourselves.

_Prayer: _ *Dear God, I come to you with a humble heart, seeking forgiveness for my past mistakes and hurts. Help me release the burdens of guilt, shame, and regret. Forgive me for my shortcomings and failures.*

*As I receive your forgiveness, I ask for the strength to forgive myself and others. Help me let go of resentment, anger, and bitterness. May your grace and mercy transform my heart and mind.*

*Lord, I also ask for guidance and wisdom as I strive for personal growth. Help me identify areas where I need to improve and give me the courage to take steps towards positive change.*

*May your love and grace be my driving force, and may I become the best version of myself for your glory. Amen.*

Remember, forgiveness and personal growth are journeys, not destinations. Be patient, kind, and compassionate with yourself as you walk with God.

## _October 30_: _ Forgiveness and Love's Generosity

_Scripture:_ Luke 6:38 - Give, and it will be given to you.
_Devotion:_

Forgiveness is an act of love's generosity!

What a beautiful perspective! Forgiveness is indeed an act of love's generosity! When we choose to forgive, we demonstrate the abundance of love in our hearts, just as God demonstrates His love and generosity towards us.

*Forgiveness as an act of love's generosity:*
- Freely gives mercy and understanding
- Abundantly pours out compassion and empathy
- Lavishly bestows grace and kindness
- Unconditionally offers a second chance
- Selflessly let's go of resentment and anger

*Here's a devotional thought on forgiveness and love's generosity:*

Forgiveness is the overflowing cup of love's generosity. As we forgive, we pour out love's abundance, just as God pours out His love and forgiveness upon us. Forgiveness is the tangible expression of love's boundless generosity, filling the hearts of those around us with hope, healing, and restoration.

Remember, forgiveness is the generous gift of love that keeps on giving!

_Prayer:_ *Dear God, help me to forgive and be generous. Show me the depths of Your love and help me to extend that same love to others. Amen*

**October 31:** The Power of Forgiveness and Empathy

_Scripture:_ Colossians 3:13 - Bear with each other and forgive one another if any of you has a grievance against someone. Forgive as the Lord forgave you.

_Devotion:_

Forgiveness and empathy are powerful tools that can break down barriers and restore relationships. May God give you the strength to forgive and the heart to understand others today and always!

What a beautiful truth! Forgiveness and empathy are indeed powerful tools that can: - Break down walls of resentment and anger- Heal emotional wounds and hurt- Rebuild trust and understanding- Restore relationships and connections- Create a safe space for growth and healing

*By choosing forgiveness and empathy, we can:* - Release the burden of holding onto grudges- See things from another person's perspective- Understand their struggles and challenges- Show compassion and kindness- Create a ripple effect of love and forgiveness

Remember, forgiveness doesn't mean forgetting or condoning, but rather releasing the hold of hurt and anger. Empathy doesn't mean agreeing, but rather understanding and sharing the feelings of another.

May forgiveness and empathy be the bridges that connect us, heal us, and set us free!

_Prayer: _- *Dear God, help me to forgive others as You have forgiven me. Give me the empathy to understand their struggles and the grace to extend mercy.* Amen.

As we conclude our October devotional journey, we reflect on the transformative power of forgiveness, love, and generosity. Through these devotionals, we've explored the depths of God's love, the freedom of forgiveness, and the abundance of generosity.

May the lessons and reflections from this month guide you forward, empowering you to:

- Extend forgiveness to yourself and others
- Embrace the generosity of God's love
- Cultivate a heart of gratitude and hope
- Shine the light of God's peace and joy in a world that needs it

Remember, every day is a new chance to start anew, to forgive, to love, and to grow in God's grace. Carry the insights and blessings from this month with you, and may God continue to guide and bless you on your spiritual journey."

# NOVEMBER 1-30

1. Gratitude and Contentment
2. The Multidimensional Tapestry of God's Reality
3. The Eternal Echoes of God's Whispers
4. The Infinite Library of God's Possibilities
5. The Infinite Regression of God's Reflection
6. The Universe as God's Thought
7. God's Perfect Timing
8. Gratitude and Joy
9. Gratitude and Trust
10. Gratitude and Generosity
11. Gratitude and Humility
12. Gratitude and Worship
13. Gratitude and Legacy
14. Gratitude in Hard Times
15. Hope in the Darkness
16. Hope and Trust
17. Pressing On
18. Walking in Wisdom
19. Hope and Perseverance
20. Gratitude and Witness
21. Peace in the Storm
22. Gratitude and Faith
23. Gratitude and Peace
24. Gratitude and Appreciation
25. A Heart of Gratitude
26. Gratitude and Thanksgiving
27. Gratitude's Transformative Power
28. Gratitude for God's Presence
29. Gratitude in the Waiting
30. Gratitude for God's Guidance

## _November 1_ Gratitude and Contentment

_Scripture:_ 1 Timothy 6:6-7 - But godliness with contentment is great gain. For we brought nothing into the world, and we can take nothing out of it.

_Devotion:_

Gratitude helps us cultivate contentment and appreciate what we have.

*What a beautiful truth! Gratitude indeed helps us:*
- Cultivate contentment by focusing on what we have, rather than what's lacking
- Appreciate the good things in our lives, no matter how small they may seem
- Recognize the abundance of blessings and gifts from God
- Shift our perspective from dissatisfaction to satisfaction-Find joy and peace in the present moment

*By practicing gratitude, we can:*
- Develop a more positive outlook on life
- Become more thankful for the people and experiences in our lives
- Learn to appreciate the little things that often go unnoticed
- Grow in our trust and faith in God's goodness and provision

Remember, gratitude is a muscle that needs to be exercised regularly to see results. Take time each day to reflect on the things you're thankful for, and watch how it transforms your heart and mind!

_Prayer:_ *Dear God, help me to be content with what I have and to find joy in the simple things. Teach me to be grateful for Your blessings and to trust in Your provision.* Amen.

## _November 2:_ _The Multidimensional Tapestry of God's Reality

_Scripture:_ Ephesians 3:18 - I pray that you may be able to comprehend with all the saints what is the breadth and length and height and depth.

_Devotion:_

God's reality is a multidimensional tapestry, reflecting His infinite and boundless nature.

*What a breathtakingly beautiful description! This statement paints a vivid picture of God's reality as:* - Reflecting His infinite and boundless nature: implying that God's reality is a perfect mirror of His character, showcasing His limitless love, grace, wisdom, and power.

*This tapestry might represent:*
- The layers of depth and complexity in God's nature and character
- The infinite possibilities and potentialities within God's realm
- The beauty and harmony that arise from God's boundless creativity

*In this tapestry, every thread, fiber, and strand might symbolize:*
- A facet of God's creation, reflecting His infinite wisdom and artistry

This description inspires awe, reverence, and wonder, inviting us to contemplate the majesty and splendor of God's reality. It's a reminder that our understanding is but a small part of the grand tapestry, encouraging us to explore, discover, and marvel at the infinite beauty of God's creation.

_Prayer: *Dear God, you are the Master Weaver, crafting a magnificent tapestry of reality that transcends our understanding. We pray for eyes to see and hearts to grasp the intricate threads of your multidimensional design.*

*Reveal to us the hidden patterns and connections that bind all things together. Help us perceive the beauty and harmony that underlies your creation.*

*As we gaze upon the tapestry, may we behold your glory, wisdom, and love. May our spirits be expanded, our minds be opened, and our hearts be transformed by the majesty of your reality.*

*Grant us the humility to acknowledge the mysteries that lie beyond our comprehension and the courage to explore the depths of your truth.* Amen.

May this prayer inspire you to contemplate the vastness and complexity of God's creation, and may you catch glimpses of the breathtaking beauty that lies within and beyond our reality.

# REFLECTION

_Action Step:_

- Write down ways you've experienced God's presence beyond the physical realm.
- Share with a friend or mentor how this devotional has impacted your understanding of God's nature.
- Take a few minutes each day to meditate on Ephesians 3:18 and ask God to reveal more of His multidimensional tapestry to you.

_Reflection:_

- Read Ephesians 3:18 and reflect on the multidimensional tapestry of God's reality.
- Think about how God's reality transcends our 3D existence, encompassing multiple dimensions and perspectives.
- Consider how this truth can lead to a deeper understanding of God's infinite nature.

Additional Mind-Blowing Fact:
- Theoretical physics suggests that our universe may be a 4D hologram, with multiple dimensions existing simultaneously, mirroring the multidimensional tapestry of God's reality!

## _November 3_: _The Eternal Echoes of God's Whispers

_Scripture:_ Psalm 29:1 - Ascribe to the Lord the glory due his name; worship the Lord in the splendor of his holiness.

_Devotion:_

God's voice echoes throughout eternity, whispering truth and love, reflecting His eternal and unchanging nature.

What a breathtakingly beautiful description! *This statement paints a vivid picture of God's voice as:*
- Whispering truth and love: implying a gentle, yet powerful, communication of God's heart and character.

Reflecting His eternal and unchanging nature: -
-emphasizing the consistency and reliability of God's voice, mirroring His immutable and steadfast character.

*This description evokes a sense of:*
- *Timelessness:* God's voice echoes beyond the constraints of time, speaking to all generations.
- *Gentleness:* God's whisper conveys a sense of tenderness and care, rather than loudness or coercion.
- *Truth:* God's voice communicates reality, wisdom, and insight, guiding us through life's journey.

- *Love*: God's voice embodies compassion, kindness, and affection, reassuring us of His devotion.

This poetic description inspires us to listen for God's whisper, to tune our hearts to His eternal voice, and to find comfort in His unchanging nature.

_Prayer: _- Dear God, we long to hear the gentle whispers of your voice, echoing through eternity. Speak to us in the silence, and may your words resonate deep within our souls.

May the eternal echoes of your whispers guide us on our journey, illuminating the path ahead and comforting us in times of uncertainty.

Help us tune our hearts to the frequency of your love, that we may discern the subtle whispers of your guidance, encouragement, and wisdom.

As we listen for your whispers, may we become more like you — compassionate, gentle, and kind. May our lives become a reflection of your love, echoing your heart to a world in need.

In the stillness, we wait for your whispers, trusting in the eternal echoes of your love. Amen.

# REFLECTION

_Action Step:_

- Write down ways you've heard God's whispers in your life.
- Share with a friend or mentor how this devotional has impacted your understanding of God's eternal nature.
- Take a few minutes each day to meditate on Psalm 29:1 and ask God to reveal more of His eternal echoes to you.

_Reflection:_

- Read Psalm 29:1 and reflect on the eternal echoes of God's whispers.
- Think about how God's voice echoes throughout eternity, whispering truth and love into the hearts of His creation.
- Consider how this truth can lead to a deeper understanding of God's eternal nature.

Additional Mind-Blowing Fact:

Scientists have discovered that sound waves can echo forever in space, mirroring the eternal echoes of God's whispers!

## **November 4:** The Infinite Library of God's Possibilities

_Scripture:_ Psalm 139:17-18 - How precious to me are your thoughts, God! How vast is the sum of them! Were I to count them, they would outnumber the grains of sand.

_Devotion:_

God's thoughts contain infinite possibilities for our lives, reflecting His infinite wisdom and love.

What a magnificent and uplifting truth! *This statement reveals that:*
- God's thoughts are infinite, containing countless possibilities for our lives, showcasing His boundless creativity and wisdom.
- These possibilities reflect God's infinite wisdom, demonstrating His perfect understanding of our needs, desires, and potential.
- God's thoughts are infused with infinite love, ensuring that every possibility is designed to bless, guide, and prosper us.

*This means that:*
- God's wisdom far surpasses our own, and His thoughts for us are always higher and greater than ours.
- Every possibility in God's mind is lovingly crafted to bring us joy, growth, and fulfillment.

This truth inspires us to approach life with hope, expectation, and confidence, knowing that God's infinite thoughts contain endless possibilities for our growth, happiness, and success.

_Prayer:_ *Dear God, you are the Author of endless possibilities, the Keeper of the Infinite Library. We stand in awe before the shelves of your vast creation, where every book represents a life, a story, a reality yet to be written.*

*Help us grasp the magnitude of your possibilities, that we may dare to dream, to hope, and to trust in the infinite potential you've placed within us.*

*As we wander the aisles of your library, may we discover new chapters of promise, new verses of strength, and new stories of redemption.*

*May your Holy Spirit guide us to the books that hold our deepest longings, our greatest fears, and our most ardent prayers.*

*In the infinite library of your possibilities, we find the courage to turn the page, to write the next chapter, and to trust in the Author who holds the pen. Amen.*

*May this prayer inspire you to embrace the infinite possibilities that God has in store for you, and may you find the courage to write your own story with faith and hope.*

# REFLECTION

_Action Step:_

- Write down ways you've experienced God's guidance in your life.
- Share with a friend or mentor how this devotional has impacted your understanding of God's nature.
- Take a few minutes each day to meditate on Psalm 139:17-18 and ask God to reveal more of His possibilities to you.

_Reflection:_

- Read Psalm 139:17-18 and reflect on the infinite library of God's possibilities.
- Think about how God's thoughts may contain infinite possibilities and outcomes for our lives.
- Consider how this truth can lead to a deeper trust in God's sovereignty.

_**November 5:**_ _The Infinite Regression of God's Reflection

_Scripture:_ Hebrews 1:3 - The Son is the radiance of God's glory and the exact representation of his being.

_Devotion:_

God's nature is reflected in Jesus, creating an infinite loop of reflection, revealing the depths of His glory.

What a profound and beautiful concept! *This statement suggests that:*
- God's nature is perfectly reflected in Jesus, like a mirror image, showcasing God's character, love, and wisdom.
- This reflection creates an infinite loop, where God's nature is reflected in Jesus, and Jesus' nature reflects God's, revealing the boundless depths of God's glory.

*This infinite loop represents:*

- A never-ending revelation of God's glory, as we gaze deeper into the reflection of God's nature in Jesus.
- A perfect symmetry, where God's character and Jesus' character are inextricably linked, revealing the unity and harmony of the Godhead.
- A kaleidoscope of reflections, where every aspect of God's nature is revealed in Jesus, and every aspect of Jesus' nature reflects God's, creating an ever-unfolding tapestry of glory.

This concept inspires awe, reverence, and worship, as we contemplate the infinite loop of reflection, revealing the boundless depths of God's glory.

_Prayer: _- Dear God, you are the Mirror of eternity, reflecting your own infinite beauty, wisdom, and love. In your depths, we see a regression of reflections, each one revealing more of your glory.

As we gaze into the mirror of your soul, may we behold the infinite regression of your perfections, and may our hearts be transformed by the encounter.

Help us grasp the mystery of your self-reflection, where you behold your own majesty, and we, in turn, behold yours.

In the infinite regression of your reflection, may we find the echo of our own true selves, created in your image, and may we be remade into your likeness.

May your reflection be our guiding light, our comfort, and our hope, as we journey through the corridors of eternity. Amen.

May this prayer inspire you to contemplate the infinite depths of God's nature, and may you discover the beauty of your own reflection in the mirror of His soul.

# REFLECTION

_Action Step:_

- Write down ways you've seen God's reflection in Jesus.
- Share with a friend or mentor how this devotional has impacted your understanding of God's nature.
- Take a few minutes each day to meditate on Hebrews 1:3 and ask God to reveal more of His infinite regression to you.

_Reflection:_

- Read Hebrews 1:3 and reflect on the infinite regression of God's reflection.
- Think about how God's nature is reflected in Jesus, and how Jesus reflects God, creating an infinite loop of reflection.
- Consider how this truth can lead to a deeper understanding of God's self-revelation.

*Additional Mind-Blowing Fact:*

- Fractals exhibit infinite regression, where the same pattern repeats infinitely, mirroring the infinite regression of God's reflection in Jesus! _

## November 6: The Universe as God's Thought

*Scripture:* Isaiah 55:8-9 – For my thoughts are not your thoughts, neither are your ways my ways, declares the Lord.

*Devotion:*

The universe may be a manifestation of God's thoughts, reflecting His infinite creativity and wisdom.

What a fascinating and profound idea! *This concept suggests that:*
- The universe is a tangible expression of God's thoughts, bringing His ideas and imagination into physical reality.
- God's infinite creativity is on full display, as the universe showcases an astonishing array of complexity, beauty, and diversity.
- God's wisdom is evident in the intricate web of relationships, laws, and patterns that govern the universe, revealing a masterful design.

*This perspective invites us to consider:*
- The universe as a work of art, crafted by the divine Artist, reflecting His aesthetic and creative genius.
- The mysteries of the universe as an invitation to explore and discover the depths of God's thoughts and creativity.

This idea inspires a sense of reverence, curiosity, and exploration, as we contemplate the universe as a manifestation of God's thoughts, reflecting His infinite creativity and wisdom.

_Prayer: _- *Dear God, you are the Cosmic Thinker, and the universe is your majestic thought. In the expanse of your mind, stars and galaxies unfold like ideas yet to be fully expressed.*

*As we ponder the vastness of creation, may we glimpse the infinite possibilities that swirl within your intellect.*

*Help us see the universe as a manifestation of your imagination, where every atom, every life, and every moment is a spark of your creative genius.*

*In the grand tapestry of your thought, may we find our place as threads of purpose, woven into the fabric of your design.*

*May your thoughts become our guiding light, illuminating the path to discovery, wonder, and awe. Amen.*

May this prayer inspire you to contemplate the universe as a reflection of God's boundless creativity and intellect, and may you find your own place within the grand narrative of His thought.

# REFLECTION

_Action Step:_

- Write down ways you've seen God's creative power in the universe.
- Share with a friend or mentor how this devotional has impacted your understanding of God's nature.
- Take a few minutes each day to meditate on Isaiah 55:8-9 and ask God to reveal more of His thoughts to you.

_Reflection:_

- Read Isaiah 55:8-9 and reflect on the universe as God's thought.
- Think about how God's thoughts may have brought the universe into existence, with all its complexity and beauty.
- Consider how this truth can lead to a deeper understanding of God's creative power.

## _November 7:_ God's Perfect Timing

_Scripture:_ Galatians 4:4-5 - But when the fullness of time had come, God sent forth his Son, born of woman, born under the law, to redeem those under the law, so that we might receive adoption as sons.

_Devotion:_

God's timing is perfect, and His plans are always for our good.

*A wonderful reminder! This truth offers comfort, hope, and reassurance. Here are some reflections on this statement*:
- God's timing is perfect: His schedule is flawless, and He never misses a beat. What may seem delayed or early to us is precisely on time in God's eyes.
- His plans are always for our good.

*This means:*
- We can trust God's timing, even when it doesn't align with ours.
- We can have faith that God's plans will bring us joy, growth, and success.
- We can surrender our need for control and rest in God's sovereignty.

In Romans 8:28, Paul writes, "And we know that in all things God works for the good of those who love

Him, who have been called according to His purpose." May this truth anchor your heart and mind, giving you peace and confidence in God's perfect timing and plans!

_Prayer: _ *Dear God, your timing is perfect, a symphony of seasons and moments, each one orchestrated to bring glory to your name.*

*Help us trust in your divine schedule, even when our own timelines are uncertain or delayed.*

*May we find peace in the pauses, hope in the waiting, and joy in the journey, knowing that your timing is always perfect.*

*As we navigate life's twists and turns, may we discern the gentle nudges of your guidance, leading us to the appointed moments of your choosing.*

*In your perfect timing, may we discover the beauty of surrender, the power of patience, and the wonder of your sovereignty. Amen.*

May this prayer inspire you to trust in God's perfect timing, even when the wait is long or uncertain. May you find peace and hope in the knowledge that His timing is always perfect.

## REFLECTION

_Action Step:_

Take a few moments to reflect on your life, considering the following questions:

1. Are there areas where you're struggling to trust God's timing?
2. Have you experienced situations where God's plans unfolded differently than expected?
3. How has God's timing and planning impacted your life in the past?

_Reflection Prompt:_ Write about a time when God's timing surprised you with its perfection and goodness.

May this reflection deepen your trust and faith in God's sovereign plan for your life.

**_November 8**: _Gratitude and Joy

_Scripture:_ Psalm 100:4-5 - Enter his gates with thanksgiving and his courts with praise; give thanks to him and bless his name. For the Lord is good and his love endures forever; his faithfulness continues through all generations.

_Devotion:_

Gratitude and joy are closely connected.

A beautiful truth! Gratitude and joy are indeed intimately linked. *Here's how:*
- *Gratitude* opens the door to joy:
-Focusing on what we're thankful for shifts our perspective, allowing joy to enter.
- *Joy* is a natural response to gratitude: When we appreciate the good things in life, joy arises as a heartfelt response.

*By embracing gratitude, we:*
- Become more aware of life's blessings- Develop a positive and optimistic mindset
  - Experience increased happiness and well-being
  - Deepen our connection with God and others
  - Find joy in the present moment

Remember, gratitude is a choice. Let's choose to focus on the good, cultivate joy, and radiate gratitude!
May gratitude and joy be your constant companions!

*Prayer:* *Dear God, we come to you with hearts full of gratitude and spirits lifted by joy. Thank you for the blessings that surround us, the love that sustains us, and the hope that guides us.*

*Help us cultivate a sense of gratitude that sees your goodness in every moment, no matter how big or small.*

*May our joy be a reflection of your presence in our lives, a joy that overflows into the lives of those around us.*

*As we walk in gratitude and joy, may we find contentment in the present, confidence in your promises, and peace in your sovereignty.* Amen.

May this prayer inspire you to embrace gratitude and joy as a way of life, finding contentment and peace in God's presence and promises.

Remember, gratitude and joy are choices that can transform your life and the lives of those around you. Choose them today!

### _November 9_: Gratitude and Trust

_Scripture:_ Psalm 37:3-4 - Trust in the Lord and do good; dwell in the land and enjoy safe pasture. Take delight in the Lord, and he will give you the desires of your heart.

### _Devotion:_

Gratitude helps us trust God more deeply. A profound truth! Gratitude indeed plays a significant role in deepening our trust in God. Here's how:

1. Recognizing God's goodness: Gratitude helps us acknowledge God's goodness and provision in our lives, fostering trust in His character.
2. Focusing on God's faithfulness: Reflecting on past blessings and answers to prayer cultivates trust in God's faithfulness and consistency.
3. Shifting perspective: Gratitude shifts our focus from our problems to God's provision, helping us trust His sovereignty and guidance.
4. Experiencing God's love: Gratitude opens our hearts to experience God's love and care, deepening our trust in His desire for our well-being.

Remember, gratitude is a powerful catalyst for trust. As we focus on God's goodness and provision, our trust in Him will grow, and our faith will be strengthened.

*_Prayer:_ Dear God, we come to you with grateful hearts, thankful for your presence, provision, and guidance. As we reflect on your goodness, we choose to trust in your sovereignty, wisdom, and love.*

*Help us weave gratitude and trust into the fabric of our lives, creating a tapestry of faith that shines your glory.*

*May our gratitude open our eyes to the blessings that surround us, and may our trust give us courage to face the unknown with confidence.*

*In the intersection of gratitude and trust, may we find peace that surpasses understanding, hope that anchors our souls, and love that casts out fear. Amen.*

May this prayer inspire you to cultivate a deep sense of gratitude and trust in God, leading to a life of peace, hope, and love. Remember, gratitude and trust are the foundation upon which faith is built.

## _November 10: _ Gratitude and Generosity

_Scripture: _ 2 Corinthians 9:11 - You will be enriched in every way so that you can be generous on every occasion, and through us your generosity will result in thanksgiving to God.

### _Devotion: _

Gratitude leads to generosity, which brings joy and thanksgiving to God.

What a beautiful sentiment! Gratitude has a profound impact on our lives and can lead to a cascade of positive effects. When we focus on what we're thankful for, it can:

1. Cultivate generosity: Gratitude opens our hearts and hands to give to others.
2. Bring joy: Focusing on the good things in life fills us with happiness and contentment.
3. Inspire thanksgiving: Expressing gratitude to a higher power or the universe acknowledges the blessings we've received.

This mindset can create a wonderful cycle of positivity, encouraging us to appreciate and share our blessings with others. As the Bible says, "Give thanks to the Lord, for He is good; His love endures forever!" (Psalm 107:1)

Keep spreading gratitude and kindness!

_Prayer:_ *Dear God, we come to you with grateful hearts, thankful for the abundance of blessings in our lives. As we reflect on your generosity, we're reminded to pay it forward, sharing our time, talents, and resources with others.*

*Help us cultivate a spirit of gratitude that recognizes your goodness and a heart of generosity that reflects your love.*

*May our gratitude inspire us to be generous in every way, sharing your blessings with a world in need.*

*As we give, may we experience the joy of generosity, the peace of trusting in your provision, and the love that overflows from your heart. Amen.*

May this prayer inspire you to embrace gratitude and generosity as a lifestyle, recognizing God's abundance and sharing it with others. Remember, gratitude and generosity are the keys to unlocking a life of purpose, joy, and fulfillment.

# REFLECTION

Additional Thoughts: _

- Consider how gratitude can help us see the needs of others.
- Think about how generosity can lead to deeper connections and community.
- Reflect on how gratitude and generosity can lead to a more joyful and thankful heart.

Reflection Prompt: _ Write about a time when gratitude led you to be generous. How can you cultivate gratitude and generosity in your daily life? What are you grateful for that you can share with others?

## _November 11: __ Gratitude and Humility

_Scripture: _ 1 Peter 5:5-6 - Clothe yourselves with humility toward one another, because, 'God opposes the proud but shows favor to the humble.' Humble yourselves before the Lord, and He will lift you up.

### _Devotion: _

Gratitude cultivates humility.

Another beautiful truth! Gratitude and humility are indeed closely linked. When we focus on what we're thankful for, it helps us:

1. Recognize our limitations: Gratitude acknowledges that we didn't achieve everything on our own.
2. Appreciate the role of others: We see the contributions and support of those around us.
3. Let go of pride: Focusing on what we've received, rather than what we've accomplished, humbles us.

Cultivating gratitude helps us develop a humble heart, acknowledging that we're part of a larger story and that our successes are often tied to the help and blessings of others.

By embracing gratitude, we open ourselves to the transformative power of humility, leading to a more authentic, compassionate, and meaningful life.

*_Prayer:_ Dear God, help me to clothe myself with humility and gratitude. Teach me to recognize my need for You and others, and to humble myself before You.* Amen!

## _November 12:_ Gratitude and Worship

_Scripture:_ Psalm 100:4-5 - Enter His gates with thanksgiving and His courts with praise; give thanks to Him and bless His name. For the Lord is good and His love endures forever; His faithfulness continues through all generations.

_Devotion:_

Gratitude leads us to worship and praise God. A wonderful connection! Gratitude indeed leads us to worship and praise God, as it:

1. Acknowledges His goodness: Gratitude recognizes God's blessings and provision in our lives.
2. Honors His sovereignty: We acknowledge that everything comes from Him and that He is in control.
3. Expresses dependence: Gratitude admits our need for God and His guidance in our lives.

When we cultivate gratitude, it naturally flows into worship and praise, as we:

- Sing praises to God for His faithfulness and love
- Offer thanksgiving for His presence and provision
- Declare His greatness and glory

Gratitude leads us to worship, and worship deepens our gratitude, creating a beautiful cycle of praise and thanksgiving!

_Prayer:_ *Dear God, help me to enter Your presence with gratitude and praise. Teach me to worship You with a thankful heart and to bless Your name. Amen.*

## _November 13_: __ Gratitude and Legacy

_Scripture:_ Psalm 78:4 - We will tell the next generation the praiseworthy deeds of the Lord, his power, and the wonders he has done.

### _Devotion:_

Gratitude inspires us to leave a legacy of thankfulness for future generations.

What a beautiful truth! Gratitude not only transforms our lives but also inspires us to leave a lasting impact on future generations. By cultivating gratitude, we:

1. Create a heritage of appreciation: We pass on the value of thankfulness to our children, grandchildren, and beyond.
2. Inspire a chain reaction: Our gratitude sparks a ripple effect, encouraging others to adopt a thankful mindset.
3. Build a legacy of positivity: We leave behind a story of hope, resilience, and joy, influencing future generations to focus on the good.
4. Foster a sense of connection: Our gratitude highlights the importance of relationships, community, and the impact we have on one another.

As we embrace gratitude, we become part of a larger narrative, weaving a tapestry of thankfulness that transcends time and touches hearts yet to come.

May our legacy of gratitude continue to inspire and uplift future generations!

_Prayer: _ *Dear God, help me to leave a legacy of gratitude and thankfulness. Teach me to share Your wonders and deeds with others, and to inspire future generations to praise You.* Amen.

## REFLECTION

_Additional Thoughts: _

- Consider how gratitude can help us see the bigger picture and our place in it.
- Think about how our gratitude can impact our families and communities.
- Reflect on how gratitude and legacy can lead to a more purposeful and meaningful life.

_Reflection Prompt: _ Write about a time when someone's gratitude inspired you. How can you cultivate gratitude in your own life to leave a lasting legacy? What are you grateful for that you want to pass on to others?

## _November 14: ___Gratitude in Hard Times

_Scripture:_ 1 Thessalonians 5:18 - Give thanks in all circumstances; for this is God's will for you in Christ Jesus.

_Devotion:_

Gratitude is possible even in hard times.

A powerful reminder! Gratitude is not limited to easy, joyful moments. It can be cultivated even in the midst of challenges and hard times. In fact, gratitude can be a beacon of hope and strength during difficult periods.

When we practice gratitude in hard times:

1. We find strength in resilience: Gratitude helps us focus on what we can control and find ways to move forward.
2. We gain perspective: Gratitude reminds us that even in darkness, there is always something to be thankful for.
3. We foster hope: Gratitude encourages us to look for the lessons, opportunities, or silver linings in difficult situations.

Remember, gratitude is not about denying or ignoring difficulties but about finding ways to navigate them with hope, strength, and resilience. As the Bible says, "Give thanks to the Lord, for he is good; his love endures forever!" (Psalm 107:1) even in the hard times.

_Prayer:_ *Dear God, In the midst of challenges and hardships, help us choose gratitude. When struggles weigh us down, may we find the strength to thank you for the blessings that remain.*

*May our gratitude be a beacon of hope in dark times, a reminder of your presence and provision.*

*Help us focus on the good that surrounds us, no matter how small it may seem. May our gratitude transform our perspective, turning despair into hope and fear into faith.*

*In the fire of trials, may our gratitude be refined, becoming a resilient and unshakeable trust in your goodness.* Amen.

May this prayer inspire you to cultivate gratitude in the midst of hard times, finding hope and strength in God's presence and provision. Remember, gratitude can transform your perspective, even in the darkest moments.

### _November 15:_ Hope in the Darkness

_Scripture:_ Psalm 43:5 - Why, my soul, are you downcast? Why so disturbed within me? Put your hope in God, for I will yet praise him, my Savior and my God.

_Devotion:_

Hope is the anchor of our souls.

A beautiful and profound truth! Hope is indeed the anchor of our souls, providing stability, strength, and guidance in the midst of life's storms. Just as an anchor holds a ship secure, hope holds our hearts and minds secure, keeping us grounded and focused on a brighter future.

Hope:

1. Stabilizes us in turmoil
2. Illuminates a path forward
3. Encourages resilience
4. Fosters courage and determination

As the Bible says, we have this hope as an anchor for the soul, firm and secure (Hebrews 6:19). Hope is the foundation upon which we build our lives, the light that guides us through darkness, and the reassurance that a better tomorrow is possible.

May hope be the anchor that holds your soul secure, and may you find peace and strength in its presence.

_Prayer:_ *Dear God, help me to put my hope in You, even in the darkest times. Teach me to trust in Your goodness and promises.* Amen.

## _November 16:_ Hope and Trust

_Scripture:_ Isaiah 40:31 - But those who hope in the Lord will renew their strength. They will soar on wings like eagles; they will run and not grow weary; they will walk and not be faint.

### _Devotion:_

Hope is built on trust.

A wonderful insight! Hope is indeed built on trust — trust in a higher power, trust in ourselves, and trust in the universe's plan. When we trust, we open ourselves to the possibility of a better future, and hope takes root.

Trust:
1. Allows us to let go of control
2. Encourages us to have faith in the unknown
3. Fosters a sense of security and stability
4. Enables us to take risks and step into the unknown

As trust grows, hope flourishes, and we become more resilient, adaptable, and open to new possibilities. The Bible says, "Trust in the Lord with all your heart and lean not on your own understanding" (Proverbs 3:5).

May trust be the foundation on which your hope is built, and may you find peace and confidence in its presence.

_Prayer:_ *Dear God, help me to trust You with all my heart and put my hope in Your promises. Teach me to wait on You and renew my strength.* Amen.

## _November 17:_ __ Pressing On

_Scripture:_ Philippians 3:14 - I press on toward the goal to win the prize for which God has called me heavenward in Christ Jesus.

_Devotion:_

Perseverance is not about being perfect, but about being persistent in our pursuit of God's purposes.

What a powerful reminder! Perseverance is indeed about persistence, not perfection. It's about:

1. Embracing the journey, not just the destination
2. Learning from failures and setbacks
3. Trusting in God's plan, even when we don't understand

Perseverance is a testament to our character, faith, and determination. It's about:

- Getting back up after falling
- Keeping moving forward, even in the face of obstacles
- Refusing to give up on our dreams and aspirations

As the Bible says, let us run with perseverance the race marked out for us (Hebrews 12:1). May we persevere in our pursuit of God's purposes, trusting in His guidance and strength to carry us through.

_Prayer: _- *Dear God, when the journey gets tough and the road ahead seems uncertain, help us press on. Give us the courage to take the next step, the resilience to face the challenges, and the faith to trust in your goodness.*

*May our hearts be fueled by the promise of your presence, our minds be focused on the hope of your guidance, and our spirits be lifted by the joy of your love.*

*As we press on, may we leave behind the weights that hinder us, the fears that hold us back, and the doubts that whisper lies.*

*Help us press on towards the prize of your calling, the fullness of your purpose, and the abundance of your blessings.* Amen.

May this prayer inspire you to press on, even when the journey gets tough. Remember, God is with you, guiding and empowering you to overcome every obstacle and reach your full potential. Keep moving forward!

## _November 18_: __ Walking in Wisdom

_Scripture:_ Colossians 1:9-10 - For this reason, since the day we heard about you, we have not stopped praying for you. We continually ask God to fill you with the knowledge of his will through all the wisdom and understanding that the Spirit gives.

_Devotion:_

Walking in wisdom is a journey, not a destination. It requires daily seeking and applying God's wisdom to our lives.

A profound truth! Walking in wisdom is indeed a journey, not a destination. It's a path that requires:

1. Continuous learning and growth
2. Humility and openness to new insights
3 Patience and perseverance

Wisdom is not something we attain once and for all, but rather a way of living that we cultivate daily. It's a journey of:

- Embracing lifelong learning
- Seeking guidance from others and from God
- Embodying compassion, empathy, and understanding

As the Bible says, "Get wisdom, get understanding; do not forget my words or turn away from them" (Proverbs 4:5).

_Prayer: _- *Dear God, fill me with the knowledge of Your will through Your wisdom and understanding. Help me to walk in Your ways and apply Your wisdom to my life.* Amen.

## REFLECTION

_Action Step: _

- Write down a specific situation where you can apply God's wisdom.
- Share with a friend or family member how walking in wisdom has positively impacted your life.
- Take a few minutes each day to meditate on Colossians 1:9-10 and ask God to fill you with His wisdom.

_Reflection: _

- Read Colossians 1:9-10 and reflect on the importance of walking in wisdom.
- Think about areas in your life where you can apply God's wisdom, such as relationships or decision-making.
- Consider how walking in wisdom can lead to spiritual growth and maturity.

## _November 19_ Hope and Perseverance

_Scripture:_ Romans 5:3-5 - Not only so, but we also glory in our sufferings, because we know that suffering produces perseverance; perseverance, character; and character, hope. And hope does not put us to shame, because God's love has been poured out into our hearts through the Holy Spirit, who has been given to us.

_Devotion:_

Hope helps us persevere through challenges.

A beautiful truth! Hope is indeed a powerful catalyst for perseverance. When we have hope, we:

1. Believe a better future is possible
2. Find the strength to carry on
3. Stay motivated and focused
4. Develop resilience in the face of obstacles
5. Trust that our efforts will lead to a positive outcome

Hope helps us persevere by:

- Illuminating a path forward
- Providing a sense of purpose and meaning
- Encouraging us to take small steps towards our goals
- Reminding us that we are not alone
- Filling us with a sense of anticipation and expectation

*_Prayer: _ Dear God, we come to you with hearts filled with hope and spirits fueled by perseverance. Help us hold on to the promise of a brighter tomorrow, even in the darkest of times.*

*May our hope be the anchor that stabilizes us, the light that guides us, and the fire that motivates us to keep moving forward.*

*Give us the perseverance to push through challenges, to overcome obstacles, and to rise above adversity.*

*As we journey through life's ups and downs, may our hope and perseverance be the dynamic duo that propels us towards your purposes, your plans, and your promises.* Amen.

*May this prayer inspire you to embrace hope and perseverance as your constant companions, leading you to a life of purpose, joy, and fulfillment. Remember, with God, all things are possible!*

# _November 20_ Gratitude and Witness

_Scripture:_ Psalm 105:1-2 - Give praise to the Lord, proclaim his name; make known among the nations what he has done. Sing to him, sing praise to him; tell of all his wonderful acts.

## _Devotion:_

Gratitude inspires witness.

A profound connection! Gratitude indeed inspires witness, as a heart full of thanks naturally overflows into sharing the goodness of God with others. When we cultivate gratitude, we:

1. Recognize God's presence and work in our lives
2. Want to share the source of our joy and hope with others
3. Become witnesses to the transformative power of God's love
4. Inspire others to seek and experience God's goodness
5. Create a ripple effect of gratitude and witness

Gratitude-inspired witness can take many forms, such as:
- Sharing testimonies of God's faithfulness
- Encouraging others in their spiritual journeys
- Living out our faith in practical ways
- Pointing others to the hope and joy we've found

May our gratitude ignite a passion for witness, that others may know the goodness of God!

_Prayer: _ *Dear Heavenly Father, we come to You with grateful hearts, thankful for Your presence and provision in our lives. Help us to cultivate a spirit of gratitude, even in the midst of challenges.*

*Lord, we pray that our gratitude would be a witness to Your love and faithfulness. May our thankful hearts be a testimony to Your goodness, inspiring others to seek You.*

*As we reflect on Your blessings, give us the courage to share our stories of Your faithfulness with others. May our witness be a beacon of hope, pointing others to Your love and grace. May our examples inspire them to develop their own gratitude practices and share their own stories of Your faithfulness. In Jesus' name, we pray. Amen.*

This prayer focuses on cultivating gratitude and using it as a witness to God's love and faithfulness, asking for the courage to share stories of His faithfulness with others.

## _November 21_ Peace in the Storm

_Scripture:_ Matthew 8:23-27 - Then he got up and rebuked the winds and the waves, and it was completely calm. The men were amazed and asked, 'What kind of man is this? Even the winds and the waves obey him!

_Devotion:_

Peace is found in Jesus.

A beautiful truth! Peace is indeed found in Jesus, who is the Prince of Peace (Isaiah 9:6). He offers us a peace that:

1. Guards our hearts and minds (Philippians 4:7)
2. Brings calm to life's storms
3. Reconciles us to God and ourselves
4. Fills us with hope and assurance

In Jesus, we find peace because:

- He bore our sins and sorrows on the cross
- He reconciled us to God, ending spiritual warfare
- He gives us His presence and guidance
- He fills us with His Spirit, bringing fruit of peace
- He promises eternal peace in His presence

As the Bible says, Peace I leave with you; my peace I give you. I do not give to you as the world gives. Do not let your hearts be troubled and do not be afraid (John 14:27). May you find peace in Jesus, and may His peace be your constant companion!

_Prayer:_ Dear Jesus, help me to trust You in the midst of life's storms. Teach me to find peace in Your presence. Amen.

## ROSE PETALS -- 366 DAYS OF MORNING MUSINGS

_November 22__Gratitude and Faith

_Scripture:_ Hebrews 11:1 - Now faith is confidence in what we hope for and assurance about what we do not see.

_Devotion:_

Gratitude and faith are closely tied. A beautiful connection! Gratitude and faith are indeed closely tied, as a grateful heart is more likely to trust and have faith in God's goodness. When we cultivate gratitude, we:

1. Recognize God's presence and work in our lives
2. Trust in His sovereignty and provision
3. Believe in His goodness and love
4. Rest in His promises and faithfulness
5. Surrender to His plans and purposes

Faith, in turn, fuels gratitude by:

1. Helping us see God's hand in our circumstances
2. Trusting in His goodness, even in difficulties
3. Believing in His promises and provision
4. Surrendering to His will and ways
5. Experiencing His faithfulness and love

May our gratitude and faith be intertwined, strengthening our relationship with God and deepening our trust in Him.

_Prayer:_ *Dear God, help me to cultivate a heart of gratitude and faith. Teach me to trust You more deeply and respond to Your goodness with thankfulness.* Amen.

## _November 23_ Gratitude and Peace

_Scripture:_ Colossians 3:15 - Let the peace of Christ rule in your hearts, since as members of one body you were called to peace. And be thankful.

_Devotion:_

Gratitude and peace are intertwined.

A lovely connection! Gratitude and peace are indeed intertwined, as a grateful heart tends to be a peaceful one. When we cultivate gratitude, we:

1. Focus on the present moment, letting go of worries
2. Appreciate the good in our lives, calming our minds
3. Trust in God's sovereignty, releasing anxiety
4. Recognize His blessings, filling us with joy
5. Experience contentment, quieting our souls

Peace, in turn, fuels gratitude by:

1. Allowing us to rest in God's presence, appreciating His love
2. Calming our hearts, helping us see the good around us
3. Freeing us from worry, enabling us to focus on blessings
4. Giving us clarity, to recognize God's work in our lives
5. Filling us with hope, inspiring thanks for His promises

May our gratitude and peace be forever intertwined, bringing us joy, calm, and contentment.

_Prayer:_ _Dear God, help me to cultivate a heart of gratitude and peace. Teach me to let Your peace rule in my heart and respond to Your goodness with thankfulness._ Amen.

## REFLECTION

_Additional Thoughts:_

- Consider how peace can lead to a more grateful heart.
- Think about how gratitude can help us trust God's sovereignty.
- Reflect on how gratitude and peace can bring us closer to God's presence and heart.

_Reflection Prompt:_ Write about a time when gratitude brought peace to a difficult situation. How can gratitude increase peace in your life? What are you grateful for that brings you peace?

# ROSE PETALS -- 366 DAYS OF MORNING MUSINGS

## _November 24_ Gratitude and Appreciation

_Scripture:_ Psalm 100:4-5 - Enter his gates with thanksgiving and his courts with praise; give thanks to him and bless his name. For the Lord is good and his love endures forever; his faithfulness continues through all generations.

_Devotion:_

Gratitude and appreciation go hand in hand.

A beautiful pairing! Gratitude and appreciation are indeed closely linked, as they both involve recognizing and valuing the good things in our lives. Gratitude is the act of:

1. Acknowledging the source of our blessings
2. Expressing thanks for what we've received
3. Recognizing the goodness in our lives

Appreciation is the act of:
1. Valuing and cherishing what we have
2. Seeing the worth and beauty in things
3. Enjoying and savoring the good moments

Together, gratitude and appreciation:
1. Help us focus on the positive aspects of life
2. Encourage us to cherish and make the most of what we have
3. Foster a sense of contentment and joy

_Prayer:_ *Dear God, help me to cultivate a heart of gratitude and appreciation. Teach me to enter Your presence with thanksgiving and praise. Amen.*

## _November 25_ A Heart of Gratitude

_Scripture:_ 1 Thessalonians 5:18 - Give thanks in all circumstances; for this is God's will for you in Christ Jesus.

### _Devotion:_

Gratitude is a choice. A powerful truth! Gratitude is indeed a choice, one that we can make every day, in every situation. It's a mindset, an attitude, and a decision to:

1. Focus on the good, rather than the bad
2. See the blessings, rather than the burdens
3. Appreciate what we have, rather than longing for what we don't have
4. Trust in God's goodness, even in difficult times

By choosing gratitude, we:

1. Take control of our thoughts and emotions
2. Reframe our perspective on life
3. Cultivate a more positive and hopeful outlook
4. Develop resilience and strength in the face of challenges
5. Open ourselves up to more joy, peace, and contentment

May we choose gratitude today, and every day, and experience the transformative power of thankfulness in our lives!

Prayer: _ Dear God, help me to cultivate a heart of gratitude in all circumstances. Teach me to trust Your goodness and give thanks in every situation. Amen._

## _November 26:_ Gratitude and Thanksgiving

_Scripture:_ Psalm 100:4-5 - Enter his gates with thanksgiving and his courts with praise; give thanks to him and bless his name. For the Lord is good and his love endures forever; his faithfulness continues through all generations.

### _Devotion:_

Gratitude leads to thanksgiving.

A natural progression! Gratitude indeed leads to thanksgiving, as a grateful heart naturally overflows with expressions of thanks. When we cultivate gratitude, we:

1. Recognize the sources of our blessings
2. Appreciate the good in our lives
3. Feel compelled to express our thanks

Thanksgiving is the outward expression of our inward gratitude, and it can take many forms, such as:

1. Verbal expressions of thanks
2. Written notes or messages
3. Prayers or worship

May our gratitude lead to heartfelt thanksgiving, bringing joy and blessing to ourselves and those around us!

_Prayer:_ *Dear God, help me to cultivate a heart of gratitude and thanksgiving. Teach me to enter Your presence with thanksgiving and praise. Amen.*

## November 27: Gratitude's Transformative Power

_Scripture:_ Romans 12:2 - Do not conform to the pattern of this world, but be transformed by the renewing of your mind. Then you will be able to test and approve what God's will is—his good, pleasing and perfect will.

_Devotion:_

Gratitude has the power to transform our minds and lives.

A profound truth! Gratitude indeed has the power to transform our minds and lives in remarkable ways. By focusing on what we're thankful for, we can:

1. Cultivate joy, peace, and contentment
2. Attract more positivity and goodness into our lives
3. Trust God's sovereignty and goodness more deeply
4. Experience personal growth and transformation
5. Reflect God's love and grace to others

As we embrace gratitude, we'll find that it:

- Calms our fears
- Strengthens our faith
- Fills our lives with purpose and meaning

May gratitude be the catalyst for transformation in our minds and lives, drawing us closer to God and His goodness!

*_Prayer:_ Dear God, we thank you for the transformative power of gratitude. Help us cultivate hearts that overflow with thanks, minds that focus on the good, and spirits that soar with appreciation.*

*May gratitude shift our perspective, turning struggles into opportunities, challenges into growth, and darkness into light.*

*Transform our lives through the practice of gratitude, that we may:*

- *See your goodness in every circumstance*
- *Find joy in the journey, not just the destination*
- *Become beacons of hope and positivity*
- *Experience the fullness of your love and grace.* Amen.

May this prayer inspire you to embrace gratitude as a powerful force for transformation in your life. Remember, gratitude can change everything!

### _November 28: _ Gratitude for God's Presence

_Scripture: _ Matthew 28:20 - And surely, I am with you always, to the very end of the age.

_Devotion: _

Gratitude for God's presence in our lives can bring comfort and peace.

A beautiful truth! Gratitude for God's presence in our lives can indeed bring:

1. Comfort in times of sorrow or struggle
2. Peace that surpasses understanding
3. Assurance of His love and care
4. Calm in the midst of chaos
5. Confidence in His sovereignty
6. Intimacy with our Heavenly Father
7. A deeper trust in His promises and plans

As we focus on God's presence, we'll find that:

- His peace guards our hearts and minds (Philippians 4:7)
- His comfort sustains us in times of need (2 Corinthians 1:3-4)
- His presence transforms our lives (2 Corinthians 3:18)

May gratitude for God's presence be the foundation of our comfort and peace, reminding us that He is always with us, guiding and loving us.

_Prayer:_ *Dear God, thank You for Your constant presence in my life. Help me to acknowledge and gratitude for Your presence every day. Amen.*

## REFLECTION

_Additional Thoughts:_

- Gratitude for God's presence helps us recognize His fingerprints on our lives, even in the smallest details.
- When we thank God for His presence, we acknowledge His sovereignty and control over our lives.
- Gratitude for God's presence fosters a deeper trust in His promises and plans, even when we don't understand.
- It's possible to experience joy and peace in the midst of trials when we focus on God's presence.

_Reflection Prompt:_ Write about a time when you felt God's presence in a significant way. How can gratitude for God's presence impact your daily life?

May these additional thoughts inspire you to cultivate a heart of gratitude for God's presence in your life, finding comfort, peace, and joy in His loving presence.

## _November 29_: __ Gratitude in the Waiting

_Scripture:_ Psalm 27:14 - Wait for the Lord; be strong and take heart and wait for the Lord.

_Devotion:_

Gratitude can be challenging when we're waiting for answers or circumstances to change.

An honest insight! Yes, gratitude can be challenging when we're waiting for answers or circumstances to change. It's easy to feel frustrated, anxious, or disappointed when things aren't going as we hoped. However, gratitude can be a powerful practice even in these moments. Here's why:

1. It reminds us that God is still working, even when we can't see it.
2. It helps us trust that God's timing and plans are better than our own.

Try to find the small things to be grateful for, like:

- God's presence with you- His promise to work all things for good- The strength to keep going- The support of loved ones- The lessons learned in the waiting

Remember, gratitude doesn't mean ignoring your struggles or difficulties. It means acknowledging God's goodness and sovereignty in the midst of them.

_Prayer:_ *Dear God, help me to wait for You with gratitude. Give me strength and courage to trust Your timing and plan.* Amen

## REFLECTION

_Additional Thoughts:_

- Gratitude in the waiting season can be a powerful act of faith, demonstrating trust in God's goodness and sovereignty.
- When we choose gratitude, we create space for God to work in our hearts and circumstances.
- Gratitude helps us see that God is not just working on our circumstances, but also in us, shaping us into His image.
- In the waiting, gratitude can be a reminder that God's silence doesn't mean He's absent or inactive.
- Gratitude can help us reframe our perspective, seeing the waiting season as an opportunity for growth, rather than just a delay.

_Reflection Prompt:_ Write about a time when you struggled to wait for God's timing. How can gratitude help you trust God's plan and timing?

May these additional thoughts encourage you to cultivate gratitude in the waiting seasons of life, trusting that God is working all things for your good.

**_November 30_**: __ Gratitude for God's Guidance

_Scripture:_ Proverbs 3:5-6 - Trust in the Lord with all your heart and lean not on your own understanding; in all your ways submit to him, and he will make your paths straight.

_Devotion:_

Gratitude for God's guidance can lead to trust and surrender.

A beautiful connection! Gratitude for God's guidance can indeed lead to:

1. Obedience: Gratitude for God's guidance motivates us to follow His leading, even when it's challenging.
2. Humility: Recognizing God's guidance humbles us, acknowledging our dependence on Him.
3. Joy: Gratitude for God's guidance fills us with joy, knowing He's guiding us toward His best for us.

As we cultivate gratitude for God's guidance, we'll find ourselves: - More confident in God's sovereignty- More willing to surrender our plans to His- More at peace in the midst of uncertainty- More faithful in trusting His promises

May gratitude for God's guidance lead you to trust and surrender, experiencing the peace and joy that come from following His leading.

Prayer: _Dear God, thank You for Your guidance in my life. Help me to trust and surrender to Your leading, and to be grateful for Your direction._ Amen.

## REFLECTION

_Additional Thoughts:_

- Gratitude for God's guidance helps us see His fingerprints on our lives, even in the smallest details.
- Trusting God's guidance means embracing His mysterious ways, even when we don't understand.
- Gratitude for God's guidance acknowledges His wisdom and knowledge, surpassing our own.
- Surrendering to God's guidance requires letting go of control and our own agendas.

_Reflection Prompt:_ Write about a time when you followed God's guidance and saw positive results. How can gratitude for God's guidance impact your decision-making?

May these additional thoughts inspire you to cultivate gratitude for God's guidance, trusting His sovereignty and surrendering to His leading, even in the unknown.

# ROSE PETALS -- 366 DAYS OF MORNING MUSINGS

As we conclude our November devotional journey, we reflect on the transformative power of gratitude, trust, and hope. Through these devotionals, we've explored the multifaceted tapestry of God's reality, the eternal echoes of His whispers, and the infinite library of His possibilities. May the lessons and reflections from this month guide you forward, empowering you to:

- Cultivate a heart of gratitude in every season
- Trust God's sovereignty and guidance
- Embrace hope in the darkness and perseverance in challenges
- Shine the light of God's peace, joy, and love in a world that needs it

Remember, every day is a new chance to start anew, to trust, to hope, and to grow in God's grace. Carry the insights and blessings from this month with you, and may God continue to guide and bless you on your spiritual journey.

# DECEMBER 1-31

1. The Power of Resilience
2. Hope in the Dark
3. The Power of Optimism
4. The Joy of Appreciation
5. The Power of Reflection
6. The Strength of Self-Awareness
7. The Freedom of Self-Acceptance
8. The Beauty of Humility
9. The Peace of Serenity
10. The Power of Trusting
11. The Beauty of Gentleness
12. Empowered by God
13. Courageous Faith
14. A Heart of Appreciation
15. Renewed in Christ
16. Inspired by God's Presence
17. Strong in the Lord
18. Determined to Follow
19. Empowered by His Spirit
20. Filled with His Spirit
21. Secure in His Love
22. Joyful in Hope
23. Confident in His Love
24. Grateful for His Grace
25. Rooted in His Word
26. Radiant Resilience
27. Joy in the Journey
28. Peace That Surpasses Understanding
29. Rooted in Love
30. Unshakable Confidence
31. Embracing the New Year

## _December 1_: __ The Power of Resilience

_Scripture:_ Psalm 34:18-19 - The Lord is close to the brokenhearted and saves the crushed in spirit. The righteous person may have many troubles, but the Lord delivers him from them all.

_Devotion:_

Resilience is not just about bouncing back, but about growing stronger and more radiant through God's power.

Beautifully said! Resilience is indeed not just about recovering from challenges, but about allowing those challenges to refine and strengthen us, making us more radiant and reflective of God's power and grace.

As the Bible says, "And we know that in all things God works for the good of those who love him, who have been called according to his purpose." (Romans 8:28)

May we embrace the journey of resilience, trusting that God is working in us, through us, and for us, to make us stronger, wiser, and more radiant in His love and light.

_Prayer: _- *Dear God, help me to trust in Your presence and deliverance in the midst of challenges. May I build resilience through Your strength.* Amen.

# REFLECTION

_Action Step:_

- Write down ways you've experienced God's presence and deliverance in difficult times.
- Take a few minutes each day to meditate on Psalm 34:18-19 and ask God to build resilience in you.

_Reflection:_

- Think about how resilience is not the absence of troubles, but the ability to rise above them with God's help.
- Consider how developing resilience can transform your relationships and overall well-being.

Additional Mind-Blowing Fact:

- The Hebrew word for "brokenhearted" in Psalm 34:18 is "shabar," which means "shattered" or "smashed." God's love and presence can mend even the most shattered hearts.

## _December 2:_ ___ Hope in the Dark

_Scripture:_ Psalm 130:5-6 - I wait for the Lord, my whole being waits, and in His word, I put my hope. I wait for the Lord more than watchmen wait for the morning.

### _Devotion:_

Hope is not just a feeling, but a choice to trust God's goodness and promises, even in the darkest times.

What a powerful truth! Hope is indeed a choice, a deliberate decision to trust in God's goodness and promises, even when circumstances seem bleak. It's a choice to anchor our hearts in His faithfulness, rather than being tossed about by emotions or circumstances.

As the Bible says, "May the God of hope fill you with all joy and peace as you trust in him, so that you may overflow with hope by the power of the Holy Spirit." (Romans 15:13)

May we choose hope today, and every day, trusting that God is working all things for our good, and that His promises are true and unshakeable.

_Prayer:_ _- Dear God, help me to put my hope in Your word and promises. May I wait on You with expectation and trust. Amen._

## REFLECTION

_Action Step:_

- Write down Bible verses that bring you hope and encouragement.
- Share with a friend or mentor how this devotional has impacted your understanding of hope.
- Take a few minutes each day to meditate on Psalm 130:5-6 and ask God to fill you with hope.

_Reflection:_

- Read Psalm 130:5-6 and reflect on how hope can be a powerful anchor in dark times.
- Think about how waiting on God's promises and presence can build resilience.
- Consider how hope can transform your perspective and give you strength to persevere.

Additional Mind-Blowing Fact:

- The Hebrew word for "wait" in Psalm 130:5 is "qavah," which means "to twist or turn" in expectation. May our waiting be twisted with hope and expectation for God's goodness!

**_December 3:_** The Power of Optimism

_Scripture:_ Romans 8:28 - And we know that in all things God works for the good of those who love him, who have been called according to his purpose.

_Devotion:_

Optimism is not just a positive attitude, but a deep trust in God's goodness and sovereignty.

What a profound insight! Optimism is indeed rooted in a deep trust in God's goodness and sovereignty, rather than just a superficial positive attitude. When we trust that God is in control and that He is good, we can face challenges with confidence and hope.

As the Bible says, "For I know the plans I have for you," declares the Lord, "plans to prosper you and not to harm you, plans to give you hope and a future." (Jeremiah 29:11)

May we cultivate a deep trust in God's goodness and sovereignty, and may this trust inform our outlook on life, enabling us to face each day with optimism and faith.

_Prayer:_ - *Dear God, help me to trust that You are working all things for my good. May I have an optimistic heart, expecting Your goodness.* Amen.

## REFLECTION

_Action Step:_

- Write down ways you've seen God work good in difficult circumstances.
- Share with a friend or mentor how this devotional has impacted your perspective.

_Reflection:_

- Think about how trusting God's sovereignty and goodness can help you see challenges as opportunities.
- Consider how optimism can impact your relationships and overall well-being.

Additional Mind-Blowing Fact:

- The Greek word for "works" in Romans 8:28 is "sunergeo," which means "to work together." May we partner with God to see His good in all things!

**_December 4:_** The Joy of Appreciation

_Scripture:_ 1 Thessalonians 5:18 - Give thanks in all circumstances; for this is God's will for you in Christ Jesus.

_Devotion:_

Appreciation is a powerful tool to transform your life, relationships, and perspective.

What a wonderful truth! Appreciation has the power to shift our focus, transform our relationships, and renew our perspective. When we choose to appreciate, we open ourselves up to the good things in life, no matter how small they may seem.

As the Bible says, "Give thanks to the Lord, for He is good; His love endures forever!" (Psalm 107:1)

May we cultivate a heart of appreciation, recognizing the blessings, big and small, that surround us each day. May this gratitude transform our lives, relationships, and perspective, and may we radiate joy, love, and thankfulness.

_Prayer:_ - *Dear God, help me to cultivate a heart of gratitude, appreciating Your goodness in all circumstances.* Amen.

# REFLECTION

_Action Step:_

- Write down three things you appreciate today.
- Share gratitude with someone you appreciate.

_Reflection:_

- Read 1 Thessalonians 5:18 and reflect on the importance of gratitude in your life.
- Think about how focusing on what you appreciate can shift your perspective and bring joy.
- Consider how gratitude can impact your relationships and overall well-being.

Additional Mind-Blowing Fact:

- The Greek word for "give thanks" in 1 Thessalonians 5:18 is "eucharisteo," which means "to express gratitude." May our lives be filled with eucharisteo!

**December 5:** The Power of Reflection

_Scripture:_ Psalm 119:59 - I have considered my ways and have turned my steps to your statutes.

_Devotion:_

Reflection is a powerful tool for growth, learning, and deepening our relationship with God.

What a profound truth! Reflection is indeed a powerful tool for growth, learning, and deepening our relationship with God. When we take the time to reflect, we can:

- Gain insight into our thoughts, feelings, and actions
- Identify areas for growth and improvement
- Develop a greater understanding of ourselves and God's work in our lives
- Cultivate a deeper sense of gratitude, humility, and trust

As the Bible says, "Be still and know that I am God." (Psalm 46:10)

May we prioritize reflection in our lives, creating space to be still, listen, and learn from God's whispers.

_Prayer:_ - *Dear God, help me to reflect on my ways and turn my steps towards Your guidance.* Amen.

# REFLECTION

_Action Step:_

- Take time to reflect on your experiences and choices this week.
- Write down insights and lessons learned.
- Ask God to guide you as you reflect and seek to grow.

_Reflection:_

- Think about how reflecting on your experiences and choices can help you grow and learn.
- Consider how reflection can deepen your relationship with God and transform your life.

Additional Mind-Blowing Fact:

- The Hebrew word for "considered" in Psalm 119:59 is "shub," which means "to turn back" or "return." May our reflection lead us to return to God's guidance and wisdom!

## _December 6:_ The Strength of Self-Awareness

Scripture: _ Proverbs 4:23 - Above all else, guard your heart, for everything you do flows from it.

### _Devotion:_

Self-awareness is a powerful tool for personal growth, wise decision-making, and authentic living.

What a wonderful truth! Self-awareness is indeed a powerful tool for personal growth, wise decision-making, and authentic living. When we have a deep understanding of ourselves, we can:

- Recognize our strengths and weaknesses
- Identify areas for improvement and growth
- Make informed decisions that align with our values and goals
- Live authentically, without pretenses or pretending to be someone we're not

As the Bible says, "For if anyone thinks they know something, they don't yet know it as they ought to know it." (1 Corinthians 8:2)

May we cultivate self-awareness, seeking to understand ourselves and our place in God's story.

_Prayer: _- *Dear God, help me to guard my heart and cultivate self-awareness, that I may live wisely and authentically.* Amen.

## REFLECTION

_Action Step:_

- Take time to reflect on your thoughts, emotions, and motivations.
- Identify areas where you need greater self-awareness.
- Ask God to give you insight and wisdom to live authentically.

_Reflection:_

- Think about how understanding your thoughts, emotions, and motivations can help you make wise choices.
- Consider how self-awareness can impact your relationships and overall well-being.

Additional Mind-Blowing Fact:

- The Hebrew word for "guard" in Proverbs 4:23 is "natsar," which means "to watch or keep." May we watch over our hearts with self-awareness and wisdom!

**_December 7:_ __** The Freedom of Self-Acceptance

_Scripture:_ Ephesians 2:10 - For we are God's handiwork, created in Christ Jesus to do good works, which God prepared in advance for us to do.

_Devotion:_

Self-acceptance is a powerful key to unlocking your potential and living a life of freedom and purpose.

Self-acceptance is indeed a powerful key to unlocking your potential and living a life of freedom and purpose. When you accept yourself, you:

- Embrace your strengths and weaknesses
- Let go of self-criticism and judgment
- Break free from comparison and expectation

Remember, self-acceptance is not about being perfect; it's about being perfectly you. It's about embracing your quirks, flaws, and all, and knowing that you are enough.

As you practice self-acceptance, remember to be patient and kind to yourself. It's a journey, and it's okay to take it one step at a time.

_Prayer:_ _- Dear God, help me to embrace my identity in Christ and accept myself as Your unique handiwork._ Amen.

## REFLECTION

_Action Step:_

- Write down positive affirmations about yourself and your identity in Christ.
- Share with a friend or mentor how this devotional has impacted your self-perception.

_Reflection:_

- Think about how self-acceptance can free you from self-criticism and comparison.
- Consider how embracing your uniqueness can empower you to live authentically and fulfill your purpose.

Additional Mind-Blowing Fact:

- The Greek word for "handiwork" in Ephesians 2:10 is "poiema," which means "work of art" or "masterpiece." You are God's masterpiece.

**December 8**: __ The Beauty of Humility

_Scripture:_ Proverbs 22:4 - Humility and the fear of the Lord bring wealth and honor and life.

_Devotion:_

Humility is not about self-deprecation, but about recognizing God's greatness and our dependence on Him.

What a beautiful truth! Humility is indeed not about self-deprecation or low self-esteem, but about recognizing God's greatness and our dependence on Him. It's about acknowledging that we are not self-sufficient, but rather, we are dependent on God's grace, wisdom, and strength.

Humility is about:

- Recognizing God's sovereignty and majesty
- Trusting in God's goodness and provision
- Submitting to His will and guidance

May we cultivate humility, recognizing God's greatness and our dependence on Him, and may we experience His lifting power in our lives.

_Prayer:_ _- Dear God, help me to cultivate humility and fear of the Lord, that I may experience the wealth of Your presence and the honor of Your favor. Amen._

## REFLECTION

_Action Step:_

- Write down ways you can practice humility in your daily life.
- Share with a friend or mentor how this devotional has impacted your understanding of humility.

_Reflection:_

- Think about how humility can lead to a deeper relationship with God and greater influence with others.
- Consider how humility can bring a sense of freedom and joy to your life.

Additional Mind-Blowing Fact:

- The Hebrew word for "humility" in Proverbs 22:4 is "anawah," which means "meekness" or "gentleness." May we embrace the beauty of humility!

**December 9:** The Peace of Serenity

_Scripture:_ Philippians 4:7 - And the peace of God, which transcends all understanding, will guard your hearts and your minds in Christ Jesus.

_Devotion:_

Serenity is not the absence of challenges, but the presence of God's peace in the midst of them.

What a profound truth! Serenity is indeed not the absence of challenges, but the presence of God's peace in the midst of them. It's the calm in the storm, the stillness in the chaos, and the quiet confidence that God is in control.

Serenity is: - A deep trust in God's goodness and sovereignty
- A sense of inner peace that surpasses understanding
- A calm and gentle spirit, even in turbulent times
- A heart that is anchored in hope and faith
- A life that is rooted in God's love and grace

As the Bible says, "Peace I leave with you; my peace I give you. I do not give to you as the world gives. Do not let your hearts be troubled and do not be afraid." (John 14:27)

May we experience God's serenity in our lives, and may it be a beacon of hope and light in the midst of challenges.

_Prayer: _- *Dear God, help me to experience Your peace that transcends all understanding, and may it guard my heart and mind in Christ Jesus.* Amen.

## REFLECTION

_Action Step: _

- Write down ways you can cultivate serenity in your daily life.
- Share with a friend or mentor how this devotional has impacted your understanding of peace.

Reflection: _

- Think about how serenity can be a fruit of trusting in God's sovereignty and goodness.
- Consider how cultivating serenity can impact your relationships and overall well-being.

Additional Mind-Blowing Fact:

- The Greek word for "peace" in Philippians 4:7 is "eirene," which means "wholeness" or "completeness." May we experience the wholeness of God's peace!

## _December 10:_ The Power of Trusting

_Scripture:_ Proverbs 3:5-6 - Trust in the Lord with all your heart and lean not on your own understanding; in all your ways submit to him, and he will make your paths straight.

_Devotion:_

Trusting God is not about having all the answers, but about having faith in His goodness and sovereignty.

What a wonderful reminder! Trusting God is indeed not about having all the answers, but about having faith in His goodness and sovereignty. It's about:

- Believing in His character, even when we don't understand the circumstances
- Having confidence in His plan, even when we can't see the future
- Relying on His wisdom, even when we don't have all the answers
- Resting in His love, even when we're uncertain or afraid
- Surrendering to His will, even when it's hard or uncomfortable

May we cultivate trust in God, even in the unknowns, and may we experience His guidance, peace, and goodness in our lives.

*_Prayer: _- Dear God, we come to you with hearts that desire to trust, minds that seek to believe, and spirits that yearn to surrender.*

*Help us trust in your goodness, your sovereignty, and your love.*

*May our trust be the foundation on which we stand, the anchor that holds us fast, and the bridge that spans the uncertain.*

*As we trust, may we:*

*- Find peace in the midst of turmoil*
*- Discover strength in our weaknesses*
*- Experience freedom from fear and doubt*
*- Know your presence and guidance in every step*
*In Jesus' name, we pray. Amen.*

May this prayer inspire you to embrace the power of trusting, leading to a life of peace, strength, freedom, and deep connection with God. Remember, trust is the key that unlocks God's best for you!

# REFLECTION

_Action Step:_

- Write down areas where you need to trust God more.
- Share with a friend or mentor how this devotional has impacted your understanding of trust.

_Reflection:_

- Think about how trusting God can lead to a deeper sense of peace and confidence.
- Consider how trusting God can impact your decisions and relationships.

Additional Mind-Blowing Fact:

- The Hebrew word for "trust" in Proverbs 3:5 is "batach," which means "to feel secure" or "to have confidence." May we feel secure in God's love and care!

## _December 11: _ The Beauty of Gentleness

_Scripture: _ Galatians 5:22-23 - But the fruit of the Spirit is... gentleness.

_Devotion: _

Gentleness is not weakness, but strength under control, reflecting God's love and grace.

What a beautiful truth! Gentleness is indeed not weakness, but strength under control, reflecting God's love and grace. It's:

- A quiet confidence that doesn't need to prove itself
- A softness that doesn't compromise on values or principles
- A calmness that doesn't react impulsively or aggressively
- A kindness that doesn't seek to dominate or manipulate
- A humility that doesn't seek to elevate self, but lifts others up

As the Bible says, let your gentleness be evident to all. The Lord is near. (Philippians 4:5)

May we embody gentleness, reflecting God's love and grace, and may it be a powerful witness to those around us. Remember, gentleness is not about being passive, but about being strong and controlled, like a mighty river that flows gently to its destination.

_Prayer: _- *Dear God, we come to you with hearts that desire to embody the beauty of gentleness. Help us cultivate a spirit that is soft, yet strong; quiet, yet courageous; and humble, yet confident.*

*May our gentleness be a reflection of your love, a balm to the hurting, and a refuge for the weary.*

*As we embrace gentleness, may we:*

- *Find strength in our vulnerability*
- *Discover power in our kindness*
- *Experience the transformative touch of your grace*
- *Become instruments of peace in a world of chaos*

*In Jesus' name, we pray. Amen.*

May this prayer inspire you to embrace the beauty of gentleness, leading to a life of love, compassion, and peace. Remember, gentleness is a powerful force that can change lives!

# REFLECTION

_Action Step:_

- Write down ways you can practice gentleness in your daily life.
- Share with a friend or mentor how this devotional has impacted your understanding of gentleness.

_Reflection:_

- Think about how gentleness can impact your relationships and interactions with others.
- Consider how cultivating gentleness can bring a sense of calm and peace to your life.

Additional Mind-Blowing Fact:

- The Greek word for "gentleness" in Galatians 5:22 is "prautes," which means "meekness" or "humility." May we embrace the beauty of gentleness!

## _December 12:_ Empowered by God

_Scripture:_ 2 Corinthians 12:9- But He said to me, 'My grace is sufficient for you, for my power is made perfect in weakness.'

_Devotion:_

God's power is not diminished by our weaknesses, but perfected in them.

What a profound truth! God's power is indeed not diminished by our weaknesses, but perfected in them. This is a beautiful reminder that:

- Our limitations and frailties don't limit God's ability to work through us
- Our weaknesses provide an opportunity for God's strength to shine
- God's power is not about our abilities, but about His capacity to work in and through us
- Our vulnerabilities become a canvas for God's grace and power to be displayed
- God's perfection is not about our performance, but about His presence and work in our lives

May we embrace our weaknesses, knowing that God's power is perfected in them, and may we experience His strength and grace in our lives.

_Prayer: _- *Dear God, help me to acknowledge my weaknesses and boast in them, that I may experience Your empowering grace and power in my life.* Amen.

## REFLECTION

_Action Step: _

- Write down areas where you feel weak or inadequate.
- Share with a friend or mentor how this devotional has impacted your understanding of God's power.

_Reflection: _

- Think about how acknowledging your weaknesses can lead to experiencing God's empowering grace.
- Consider how boasting in your weaknesses can bring a sense of humility and dependence on God.

Additional Mind-Blowing Fact:

- The Greek word for "power" in 2 Corinthians 12:9 is "dunamis," which means "miraculous power" or "ability." May we experience God's miraculous power in our lives!

## _December 13:_ Courageous Faith

_Scripture:_ Joshua 1:9 - Have I not commanded you? Be strong and courageous. Do not be afraid; do not be discouraged, for the Lord your God will be with you wherever you go.

### _Devotion:_

Courageous faith is not the absence of fear, but the willingness to trust God in the midst of fear.

That's a great point! Courageous faith is not about being fearless, but about trusting God even when we are afraid. It's about acknowledging our fears, but not letting them control us. Instead, we choose to trust in God's power, love, and sovereignty, even in the midst of uncertainty or danger.

As the Bible says, "Fear not, for I am with you; be not dismayed, for I am your God; I will strengthen you and help you; I will uphold you with my righteous right hand." (Isaiah 41:10)

Courageous faith is not the absence of fear, but the presence of trust in God's goodness and grace. It's a choice to believe that God is bigger than our fears and that He will see us through even the toughest times.

May we cultivate courageous faith in our lives, trusting God in the midst of fear and uncertainty.

*Prayer:* - Dear God, we come to you with hearts that desire to embody courageous faith. Help us trust in your promises, stand on your truth, and walk in your ways, even when the path ahead is uncertain.

*May our faith be bold, yet humble; fearless, yet gentle; and unwavering, yet compassionate.*

*As we exercise courageous faith, may we: - Step into the unknown with confidence- Face challenges with resilience- Overcome fears with your presence- Shine your light in the darkest places. In Jesus' name, we pray. Amen.*

May this prayer inspire you to embrace courageous faith, leading to a life of boldness, confidence, and transformation. Remember, faith is the spark that ignites the power of God in your life!

# REFLECTION

_Action Step:_

- Write down areas where you need courageous faith.
- Share with a friend or mentor how this devotional has impacted your understanding of courage.

_Reflection:_

- Think about how courageous faith can impact your life and decisions.
- Consider how God's presence and promises can give you courage in the face of challenges.

Additional Mind-Blowing Fact:

- The Hebrew word for "courageous" in Joshua 1:9 is "amats," which means "to be strong" or "to be firm." May we be strong and firm in our faith!

## _December 14:_ A Heart of Appreciation

_Scripture:_ 1 Thessalonians 5:18 - Give thanks in all circumstances; for this is God's will for you in Christ Jesus.

### _Devotion:_

Appreciation is a powerful magnet that attracts joy, peace, and contentment.

What a wonderful truth! Appreciation is indeed a powerful magnet that attracts joy, peace, and contentment. When we focus on appreciating what we have, who we are, and the blessings in our lives, it shifts our perspective and opens us up to receive even more goodness.

Appreciation: - Helps us see the good in every situation
- Fosters gratitude and thankfulness- Attracts positive energy and experiences.

As the Bible says, "Give thanks to the Lord, for he is good; his love endures forever!" (Psalm 107:1)

May we practice appreciation daily, magnetizing joy, peace, and contentment into our lives.

_Prayer:_ _- Dear God, help me to cultivate a heart of appreciation, giving thanks in all circumstances. May I trust in Your goodness and sovereignty._ Amen.

## REFLECTION

_Action Step:_

- Write down three things you are thankful for today.
- Share gratitude with someone you appreciate.

_Reflection:_

- Read 1 Thessalonians 5:18 and reflect on the importance of gratitude in all circumstances.
- Think about how an appreciative heart can impact your relationships and perspective.
- Consider how gratitude can be a powerful tool for joy and contentment.

Additional Mind-Blowing Fact:

- The Greek word for "give thanks" in 1 Thessalonians 5:18 is "eucharisteo," which means "to express gratitude" or "to praise." May we express gratitude and praise God in all circumstances!

## **December 15:** Renewed in Christ

_Scripture:_ 2 Corinthians 5:17 - Therefore, if anyone is in Christ, the new creation has come: The old has gone, the new is here!

_Devotion:_

In Christ, we are not improved, but transformed; not patched up, but made new.

What a beautiful truth! In Christ, we experience a profound transformation that goes beyond mere improvement or patching up. We are made new, with a new identity, new heart, and new life.

This transformation is not about: - Fixing our old selves
- Making minor adjustments- Putting on a new facade

But about: - Being reborn in Christ (John 3:3)- Receiving a new heart (Ezekiel 36:26)- Being made a new creation (2 Corinthians 5:17)

In Christ, we are transformed from the inside out, with a new nature, new desires, and a new purpose. We are no longer the same, but are remade in His image, with His character and glory shining through us. May we embrace this transformative power of Christ in our lives, and walk in the newness of life He has given us!

_Prayer:_ - *Dear God, Thank You for renewing me in Christ. Help me to live out my new creation identity, reflecting Your love and grace. Amen.*

## REFLECTION

_Action Step:_

- Write down ways you've experienced renewal in Christ.
- Share your testimony with someone.

_Reflection:_

- Read 2 Corinthians 5:17 and reflect on the transformative power of being in Christ.
- Think about how your life has been renewed through your relationship with Him.
- Consider how this new creation identity impacts your thoughts, words, and actions.

## _December 16:_ Inspired by God's Presence

_Scripture:_ Exodus 33:14 - The Lord replied, 'My Presence will go with you, and I will give you rest.

_Devotion:_

God's Presence is not just a comfort, but a catalyst for inspiration and guidance.

What a powerful truth! God's Presence is indeed a comfort, but it's also a catalyst for inspiration and guidance. When we experience His Presence, it:

- Illuminates our path and direction- Empowers us to make wise decisions- Fills us with purpose and passion

God's Presence is not just a feeling, but a force that:
- Awakens our potential- Unlocks our gifts and talents
- Energizes our spirit- Clarifies our purpose- Transforms our lives

As we seek God's Presence, may we:
- Expect inspiration and guidance- Listen for His whispers- Trust His leading- Follow His promptings- Embrace His transformative power

May God's Presence be our constant companion, inspiring and guiding us every step of the way!

_Prayer: _- *Dear God, Thank You for Your promise to be with me. Help me to stay aware of Your Presence, finding inspiration and rest in You.* Amen.

## REFLECTION

_Action Step: _

- Take a few minutes each day to pause and acknowledge God's Presence.
- Write down ways you've experienced His guidance and inspiration.
- Share with someone how God's Presence has impacted your life.

_Reflection: _
- Read Exodus 33:14 and reflect on the promise of God's Presence in your life.
- Think about how His Presence inspires and guides you.
- Consider how resting in His Presence can bring peace and clarity.

Additional Mind-Blowing Fact:

- The Hebrew word for "Presence" in Exodus 33:14 is "panim," emphasizing God's face-to-face relationship with us. May we bask in the radiance of His Presence.

## _December 17:_ Strong in the Lord

_Scripture:_ Ephesians 6:10 - Finally, be strong in the Lord and in his mighty power.

_Devotion:_

God's strength is not just a supplement, but a substitute for our own limitations.

What a profound truth! God's strength is not just a supplement to help us overcome our limitations, but a substitute that replaces our weaknesses with His power.

When we acknowledge our limitations and surrender to God's strength: - Our weaknesses become opportunities for His power to shine- Our inadequacies become canvases for His sufficiency- Our fears become platforms for His courage- Our doubts become doorways for His faithfulness

God's strength:
- Replaces our exhaustion with His energy
- Exchanges our anxiety for His peace
- Transforms our impossibilities into His possibilities

As we embrace God's strength as a substitute for our limitations:
- We cease to rely on our own abilities
- We start to trust in His infinite power
- We experience the freedom of surrender
- We discover the joy of dependence on Him.

*Prayer: _- Dear God, we come to you with hearts that desire to be strong in you. Help us find our strength in your presence, our courage in your promises, and our hope in your faithfulness.*

*May our roots grow deep in your love, our foundations stand firm on your truth, and our lives be empowered by your Spirit.*

*As we stand strong in you, may we:*

*- Face challenges with confidence*
*- Overcome obstacles with resilience*
*- Shine your light in the darkness*
*- Reflect your glory in our lives*

*In Jesus' name, we pray. Amen.*

May this prayer inspire you to find your strength in the Lord, leading to a life of courage, hope, and victory. Remember, in God's strength, you can overcome anything!

# REFLECTION

_Action Step:_
- Write down areas where you need God's strength.
- Share with someone how God has been your strength in the past.
- Take a few minutes each day to meditate on Ephesians 6:10 and ask God to fill you with His power.

_Reflection:_
- Think about how surrendering to God's power can make you strong.
- Consider how His strength can help you face challenges and overcome obstacles.

Additional Mind-Blowing Fact:
- The Greek word for "strong" in Ephesians 6:10 is "endunamoo," meaning "to empower" or "to enable." May we be empowered by God's mighty power!

May we surrender our limitations to God's strength, embracing His power as our substitute, and living in the freedom of His sufficiency!

_December 18:_ Determined to Follow

_Scripture:_ Psalm 119:32 - I run in the path of your commands, for you have broadened my understanding.

_Devotion:_

Determination to follow God is not about our own efforts, but about surrendering to His guidance.

What a beautiful truth! Determination to follow God is not about our own efforts, but about surrendering to His guidance. It's not about: - Our willpower- Our self-discipline- Our own strength.

But about: - Surrendering to His leading- Trusting in His sovereignty- Depending on His grace- Following His gentle nudges

When we surrender to God's guidance: - He directs our steps- He orders our paths- He empowers our obedience- He perfects our faith

Surrendering to God's guidance means: - Letting go of control- Embracing His lordship- Trusting His goodness.

May we surrender our determination to follow God, and instead, surrender to His guidance, trusting in His perfect plan and purpose for our lives.

_Prayer:_ - *Dear God, help me to be determined to follow Your commands, running in the path You have set before me. Broaden my understanding and fill me with Your truth.* Amen.

## REFLECTION

_Action Step:_

- Write down specific ways you can follow God's guidance today.
- Share with someone how God has broadened your understanding.
- Take a few minutes each day to meditate on Psalm 119:32 and ask God to give you determination to follow Him.

_Reflection:_

- Think about how determination to follow Him can lead to a deeper understanding.
- Consider how running in the path of His commands can bring freedom and joy.

Additional Mind-Blowing Fact: - The Hebrew word for "run" in Psalm 119:32 is "rut," emphasizing a sense of urgency and enthusiasm. May we run with passion and purpose in the path of God's commands.

**December 19:** Empowered by His Spirit

_Scripture:_ Acts 1:8 - But you will receive power when the Holy Spirit comes on you; and you will be my witnesses in Jerusalem, and in all Judea and Samaria, and to the ends of the earth.

_Devotion:_

Empowerment by the Holy Spirit is not just for a select few, but for all believers to live a bold and effective life for God.

What a powerful truth! Empowerment by the Holy Spirit is indeed for all believers, not just a select few. It's a promise from God that:

- Every believer can receive (Acts 2:38-39
- Every believer needs to live a bold and effective life (Ephesians 3:20-21)
- Every believer can experience spiritual gifts and fruit (1 Corinthians 12-14, Galatians 5:22-23)

The Holy Spirit empowers us to:
- Be witnesses for Christ (Acts 1:8)
- Live a life of obedience and faith (Romans 8:1-14)
- Demonstrate God's love and grace (John 13:35, 1 Corinthians 13)
- Overcome sin and darkness (Romans 8:1-14, 1 John 4:4)

Empowerment by the Holy Spirit is not just for:

- Pastors or leaders- Spiritual giants
- Those with a specific gift

But for:
- Every follower of Christ
- Every believer in need of guidance
- Every person seeking to live for God

_Prayer: _- *Dear God, we come to you with hearts that desire to be empowered by your Spirit. Help us surrender to your presence, yield to your guidance, and trust in your power.*

*May your Spirit:*

- *Fill us with boldness and confidence*
- *Illuminate our path with wisdom and discernment*
- *Equip us with gifts and talents for your purposes*
- *Transform us into your likeness with each passing day*

*As we are empowered by your Spirit, may we:*

- *Live with purpose and intention*
- *Share your love and grace with others*
- *Bring glory to your name in all we do*
- *Experience the fullness of your joy and peace*
*In Jesus' name, we pray. Amen.*

*May this prayer inspire you to embrace the empowering presence of God's Spirit, leading to a life of purpose, joy, and transformation. Remember, with God's Spirit, you can accomplish all things!*

## REFLECTION

_Action Step:_

- Write down ways you can surrender to the Holy Spirit's power.
- Share with someone how God has empowered you to witness and share His love.
- Take a few minutes each day to meditate on Acts 1:8 and ask God to fill you with His Spirit.

_Reflection:_

- Think about how His power can equip you to witness and share God's love.
- Consider how surrendering to His Spirit can bring boldness and confidence.

Additional Mind-Blowing Fact:

- The Greek word for "power" in Acts 1:8 is "dunamis," emphasizing miraculous ability and strength. May we be filled with His miraculous power!

## _December 20:_ Filled with His Spirit

_Scripture:_ Ephesians 5:18 - Do not get drunk on wine, which leads to debauchery. Instead, be filled with the Spirit.

### _Devotion:_

Being filled with the Spirit is not a one-time event, but a continuous process of surrender and renewal.

What a wonderful truth! Being filled with the Spirit is indeed a continuous process of surrender and renewal, not a one-time event. It's a journey of: - Ongoing surrender to God's will- Daily renewal of our minds and hearts- Constant dependence on His guidance- Regular infilling of His presence

The Bible says: - "Be filled with the Spirit" (Ephesians 5:18) - a command for continuous filling- "Walk in the Spirit" (Galatians 5:25) - a call to daily surrender- "Live by the Spirit" (Galatians 5:25) - a reminder of our constant need for His presence

This continuous process involves: - Seeking God's presence and guidance- Surrendering our will and desires- Renewing our minds with His Word- Embracing His transformative power

May we embrace this journey of being continuously filled with the Spirit, surrendering daily, and experiencing renewal and transformation in our lives! _Prayer:

_- *Dear God, fill me with Your Spirit, may I be controlled by Your presence and power. Help me to surrender to Your leading and guidance.* Amen.

## REFLECTION

_Action Step:_
- Write down ways you can surrender to the Spirit's control.
- Share with someone how being filled with the Spirit has impacted your life.
- Take a few minutes each day to meditate on Ephesians 5:18 and ask God to fill you afresh.

_Reflection:_
- Read Ephesians 5:18 and reflect on the contrast between being controlled by wine and being filled with the Spirit.
- Think about how being filled with the Spirit can transform your thoughts, words, and actions.
- Consider how surrendering to His Spirit can bring joy, peace, and wisdom.

Additional Mind-Blowing Fact: - The Greek word for "filled" in Ephesians 5:18 is "pleroo," emphasizing being completely controlled and empowered by the Spirit. May we be completely surrendered to His leading!

## _December 21:_ Secure in His Love

_Scripture:_ Romans 8:38-39 - For I am convinced that neither death nor life, neither angels nor demons, neither the present nor the future, nor any powers, neither height nor depth, nor anything else in all creation, will be able to separate us from the love of God that is in Christ Jesus our Lord.

_Devotion:_

God's love is not just a feeling, but a fact that secures our place in Him.

What a profound truth! God's love is indeed a fact that secures our place in Him, not just a feeling that can come and go.

His love is:
- Unconditional: not based on our performance or worthiness
- Unwavering: remaining constant despite our failures or circumstances
- Unrelenting: pursuing us relentlessly with kindness and mercy
- Unshakeable: a foundation that cannot be moved or taken away

This fact of God's love:
- Secures our identity as His beloved children

- Guarantees our acceptance and belonging in Him
- Provides a sense of safety and security in His presence
- Empowers us to live with confidence and hope.

_Prayer: _- *Dear God, we come to you with hearts that desire to be secure in your love. Help us trust in your goodness, rest in your embrace, and find our identity in your affection.*

*May your love:*

- *Enfold us in tender care*
- *Surround us with steadfast devotion*
- *Fill us with unshakeable confidence*
- *Transform us into reflections of your grace*

*As we are secure in your love, may we:*

- *Face life's challenges with courage*
- *Overcome fears and doubts with faith*
- *Extend love and kindness to others*
- *Radiate hope and joy in your presence*

*In Jesus' name, we pray. Amen.*

May this prayer inspire you to find security in God's unwavering love, leading to a life of confidence, courage, and compassion. Remember, you are loved, cherished, and secure in God's embrace!

# REFLECTION

_Action Step:_

- Write down ways you can rest in God's love.
- Share with someone how God's love has given you security.
- Take a few minutes each day to meditate on Romans 8:38-39 and ask God to surround you with His love.

_Reflection:_

- Think about how nothing can separate you from His love.
- Consider how this security can bring confidence and peace.

Additional Mind-Blowing Fact:

- The Greek word for "separate" in Romans 8:38-39 is "chorizo," emphasizing the impossibility of being disconnected from God's love. May we bask in the impossibility of being separated from His love!

May we anchor our hearts in the fact of God's love, finding security and peace in His unwavering affection for us.

## December 22: Joyful in Hope

_Scripture:_ Romans 15:13 - May the God of hope fill you with all joy and peace as you trust in him, so that you may overflow with hope by the power of the Holy Spirit.

_Devotion:_

Joy and peace are not just feelings, but fruits of trusting in God's promises and hope.

What a beautiful truth! Joy and peace are indeed fruits of trusting in God's promises and hope, not just fleeting feelings.

When we trust in God's:
- Promises: we experience joy and peace that surpasses understanding (Philippians 4:7)
- Hope: we have a confident expectation of His goodness and faithfulness (Hebrews 11:1)
- Character: we find joy and peace in His lovingkindness and mercy (Psalm 107:1)

Trusting in God's promises and hope produces:
- Joy that is not dependent on circumstances
- Peace that is not shaken by trials
- A sense of calm in the midst of storms
- A heart that is filled with confidence and trust
As the Bible says:

- May the God of hope fill you with all joy and peace (Romans 15:13)
- Trust in Him and you will not be shaken" (Psalm 125:1).

_Prayer: _- *Dear God, we come to you with hearts that desire to be joyful in hope. Help us fix our eyes on your promises, trust in your goodness, and rejoice in your faithfulness.*

*May our hope:*

- *Anchor us in turbulent times*
- *Illuminate our path with promise*
- *Fill us with joy that overflows*
- *Transform us into beacons of light*

*As we are joyful in hope, may we:*

- *Radiate your presence to those around us*
- *Find strength in your sovereignty*
- *Experience peace that surpasses understanding*
- *Share your hope with a world in need*

*In Jesus' name, we pray. Amen.*

May this prayer inspire you to embrace joyful hope, leading to a life of confidence, peace, and radiant joy. Remember, hope is the spark that ignites joy in your heart!

# REFLECTION

_Action Step:_

- Write down ways you can trust in God and overflow with hope.
- Share with someone how God has filled you with joy and peace.

_Reflection:_

- Read Romans 15:13 and reflect on the connection between hope, joy, and peace.
- Think about how trusting in God can fill you with joy and peace.
- Consider how overflowing with hope can impact your life and relationships.

Additional Mind-Blowing Fact:

- The Greek word for "hope" in Romans 15:13 is "elpis," emphasizing confident expectation and promise. May we overflow with confident expectation in God's goodness!

## _December 23:_ Confident in His Love

_Scripture:_ 1 John 3:1 - See what great love the Father has lavished on us, that we should be called children of God! And that is what we are!

_Devotion:_

What a powerful truth! God's love is indeed a fact that defines our identity as His children, not just a feeling that can come and go.

His love:

- Adopted us into His family (Ephesians 1:5)
- Declared us beloved children (1 John 3:1)
- Sealed us with His Spirit (Ephesians 1:13)
- Confirmed our identity as heirs (Romans 8:17)

This fact of God's love:
- Shapes our sense of self and purpose
- Gives us a sense of belonging and security
- Defines our worth and value
- Empowers us to live with confidence and hope

As the Bible says:
- "You are loved with an everlasting love" (Jeremiah 31:3)
- "I have called you by name, you are mine" (Isaiah 43:1)
- "You are children of the Highest God" (Psalm 82:6)

God's love is not just a feeling, but a fact that defines our identity as His children.

*_Prayer: _- Dear God, we come to you with hearts that desire to be confident in your love. Help us trust in your unwavering affection, rest in your unshakeable acceptance, and find our identity in your unrelenting devotion.*

*May your love:*

*- Enfold us in tender care*
*- Surround us with steadfast loyalty*
*- Fill us with unshakeable confidence*
*- Transform us into reflections of your grace*

*As we are confident in your love, may we:*

*- Face life's challenges with courage*
*- Overcome fears and doubts with faith*
*- Extend love and kindness to others*
*- Radiate hope and joy in your presence*
*In Jesus' name, we pray. Amen.*

May this prayer inspire you to find unwavering confidence in God's love, leading to a life of courage, faith, and radiant joy. Remember, you are loved, cherished, and accepted just as you are!

# REFLECTION

_Action Step:_

- Write down ways you can live as a confident child of God.
- Share with someone how God's love has transformed your life.
- Take a few minutes each day to meditate on 1 John 3:1 and ask God to lavish His love on you.

_Reflection:_

- Think about how being a child of God can give you confidence and security.
- Consider how His love can transform your identity and relationships.

Additional Mind-Blowing Fact:

- The Greek word for "lavished" in 1 John 3:1 is "hediken," emphasizing the abundance and extravagance of God's love. May we bask in the extravagance of His love!

## _December 24:_ Grateful for His Grace

_Scripture:_ Ephesians 2:8-9 - For it is by grace you have been saved, through faith—and this is not from yourselves, it is the gift of God—not by works, so that no one can boast.

### _Devotion:_

Grace is not just a doctrine, but a dynamic power that transforms our lives.

What a wonderful truth! Grace is indeed a dynamic power that transforms our lives, not just a doctrine or a concept.

It's a:
- Power that saves us from sin and its consequences (Ephesians 2:8-9)
- Force that changes our hearts and minds (2 Corinthians 5:17)
- Energy that empowers us to live a new life (Romans 6:4-5)
- Presence that transforms our relationships and interactions (Colossians 3:12-14)

This dynamic power of grace:
- Frees us from guilt and shame
- Releases us from the grip of sin
- Renews our minds and hearts
- Enables us to live a life that honors God.

As the Bible says:

- "Grace is poured out on us abundantly" (1 Timothy 1:14)
- "Grace teaches us to say no to ungodliness" (Titus 2:11-12)
- "Grace is the power of God to transform our lives" (2 Corinthians 12:9-10)

_Prayer: _- Dear God, we come to you with hearts full of gratitude for your grace. Thank you for loving us unconditionally, forgiving us completely, and accepting us just as we are.

May our gratitude:

- Overflow from our hearts like a river
- Inspire us to share your love with others
- Deepen our trust in your goodness
- Transform us into vessels of your mercy

As we bask in your grace, may we:

- Find freedom from guilt and shame
- Experience peace that surpasses understanding
- Extend kindness and compassion to all
- Reflect your glory in our lives

In Jesus' name, we pray. Amen.

May this prayer inspire you to embrace gratitude for God's grace, leading to a life of freedom, peace, and loving service to others. Remember, grace is the gift that keeps on giving!

## REFLECTION

_Action Step:_

- Write down ways you can live by grace in your daily life.
- Share with someone how God's grace has transformed your life.

_Reflection:_

- Think about how grace can transform your relationship with God and others.
- Consider how living by grace can free you from pride and self-effort.

Additional Mind-Blowing Fact:

- The Greek word for "grace" in Ephesians 2:8-9 is "charis," emphasizing the unmerited favor and kindness of God. May we bask in His unmerited favor!

**_December 25:_ _ Rooted in His Word**

_Scripture:_ _ Psalm 119:105 - Your word is a lamp for my feet, a light on my path.

_Devotion:_

God's Word is not just a resource, but a roadmap for our lives.

What a profound truth! God's Word is indeed a roadmap for our lives, not just a resource or a guide.

It:
- Illuminates our path (Psalm 119:105)
- Directs our steps (Proverbs 3:5-6)
- Reveals God's plan and purpose (Jeremiah 29:11)
- Equips us for every good work (2 Timothy 3:16-17)

This roadmap:
- Shows us the way to salvation (John 14:6)
- Leads us to spiritual growth and maturity (1 Peter 2:2-3)
- Helps us navigate life's challenges and decisions (Psalm 25:4-5
)- Points us to eternal life and glory (John 5:39-40)

All Scripture is God-breathed and useful for teaching, rebuking, correcting, and training in righteousness (2 Timothy 3:16)

May we follow God's Word as our roadmap, trusting in its guidance and wisdom to navigate our lives and reach our eternal destination!

_Prayer: _- *Dear God, we come to you with hearts that desire to be rooted in your Word. Help us plant ourselves deeply in your truth, nourish our souls with your wisdom, and grow strong in your promises.*

*May your Word:*
- *Illuminate our path with guidance*
- *Anchor us in turbulent times*
- *Transform us into reflections of your character*
- *Equip us to bear fruit that honors you*

*As we are rooted in your Word, may we:*

- *Stand firm against life's challenges*
- *Find wisdom in every circumstance*
- *Experience the power of your promises*
- *Shine your light in a world that needs you*

*In Jesus' name, we pray. Amen.*

May this prayer inspire you to deepen your roots in God's Word, leading to a life of stability, wisdom, and fruitful service. Remember, God's Word is the foundation on which we stand!

# REFLECTION

_Action Step:_

- Write down ways you can root yourself in God's Word.
- Share with someone how God's Word has guided you.
- Take a few minutes each day to meditate on Psalm 119:105 and ask God to illuminate your path.

_Reflection:_

- Read Psalm 119:105 and reflect on the guidance of God's Word.
- Think about how His Word can light your path and direct your steps.
- Consider how being rooted in His Word can bring stability and wisdom.

Additional Mind-Blowing Fact:

- The Hebrew word for "lamp" in Psalm 119:105 is "ner," emphasizing the light that shines in the darkness. May God's Word be our shining light!

**_December 26:_** _ Radiant Resilience

_Scripture:_ 2 Corinthians 3:18 - And we all, who with unveiled faces contemplate the Lord's glory, are being transformed into his image with ever-increasing glory, which comes from the Lord, who is the Spirit.

_Devotion:_

Radiant Resilience.

Beautifully said! Resilience is indeed not just about recovering from challenges, but about allowing those challenges to refine and strengthen us, making us more radiant and reflective of God's power and grace.

As the Bible says, "And we know that in all things God works for the good of those who love him, who have been called according to his purpose." (Romans 8:28)

May we embrace the journey of resilience, trusting that God is working in us, through us, and for us, to make us stronger, wiser, and more radiant in His love and light.

_Prayer:_ - *Dear God, Transform me into Your image with ever-increasing glory. Help me to radiate Your love and light in all I do.* Amen.

# REFLECTION

_Action Step:_

- Write down ways you can reflect God's glory.
- Share with someone how God's glory has transformed your life.

_Reflection:_

- Read 2 Corinthians 3:18 and reflect on the transformative power of God's glory.
- Think about how His glory can make you more radiant and resilient.
- Consider how embracing His glory can transform your life and relationships.

Additional Mind-Blowing Fact:

Additional Mind-Blowing Fact: - The word "resilience" comes from the Latin "resilire," meaning "to jump back" or "to rebound." May we, like a rubber band, stretch in adversity, then snap back with renewed strength, hope, and Radiant Resilience!

_December 27:_ _Joy in the Journey

_Scripture:_ Psalm 16:11 - You make known to me the path of life; you will fill me with joy in your presence, with eternal pleasures at your right hand.

_Devotion:_

Joy is not about our circumstances, but about God's presence in our lives.

What a beautiful truth! Joy is indeed about God's presence in our lives, not about our circumstances.

It's a:
- Fruit of the Spirit that grows in us (Galatians 5:22-23)
- Result of trusting in God's goodness and sovereignty (Psalm 16:11)
- Expression of gratitude for His love and grace (Psalm 100:4-5)
- Reflection of His joy that overflows in us (John 15:11)

This joy:
- Transcends difficult circumstances (Habakkuk 3:17-18)
- Sustains us in times of trial (James 1:2-4)
- Fills us with hope and anticipation (Romans 15:13)
- Overflows from our hearts to others (2 Corinthians 1:3-4)

As the Bible says:
- "In Your presence is fullness of joy" (Psalm 16:11)
- "God's joy is our strength" (Nehemiah 8:10)
- "We rejoice in the Lord always" (Philippians 4:4)

*_Prayer: _- Dear God, we come to you with hearts that desire to find joy in the journey. Help us embrace each moment with gratitude, trust in your sovereignty, and delight in your presence.*

*May we:*

- *See beauty in the everyday moments*
- *Find peace in the midst of chaos*
- *Experience joy that overflows from our hearts*
- *Reflect your love and grace to those around us*

*As we journey with you, may we:*

- *Trust in your plan and purpose*
- *Find strength in your faithfulness*
- *Discover joy in the unexpected*
- *Radiate hope and joy to a world in need*

*In Jesus' name, we pray. Amen.*

May this prayer inspire you to find joy in the journey, leading to a life of gratitude, peace, and radiant joy. Remember, God is with you every step of the way!

## REFLECTION

_Action Step:_

- Write down ways you can cultivate joy in your daily life.
- Share with a friend or mentor how this devotional has impacted your understanding of joy.

_Reflection:_

- Read Psalm 16:11 and reflect on the source of true joy.
- Think about how focusing on God's presence can bring joy to your journey.
- Consider how eternal pleasures can give you a new perspective on life's challenges.

Additional Mind-Blowing Fact:

- The Hebrew word for "joy" in Psalm 16:11 is "simchah," which means "gladness" or "delight." May we delight in God's presence!

May we cultivate joy in God's presence, trusting in His goodness and love, and may His joy overflow in our lives!

## _December 28:_ Peace That Surpasses Understanding

_Scripture:_ Philippians 4:7 - And the peace of God, which transcends all understanding, will guard your hearts and your minds in Christ Jesus.

_Devotion:_

God's peace is not about our circumstances, but about His presence and control.

What a powerful truth! God's peace is indeed about His presence and control, not about our circumstances.
It's a:
- Peace that surpasses understanding (Philippians 4:7)
- Peace that guards our hearts and minds (Philippians 4:7)
- Peace that comes from knowing God is in control (Isaiah 26:3)
- Peace that calms our fears and worries (Psalm 94:19)
- Peace that fills us with hope and confidence (Romans 15:13)

This peace:
- Transcends difficult situations (John 16:33)
- Sustains us in times of uncertainty (Psalm 23:4)
- Fills us with joy and gratitude (Psalm 100:4-5)
- Reminds us of God's love and faithfulness (Lamentations 3:22-23

As the Bible says:
- "God is our refuge and strength, an ever-present help in trouble" (Psalm 46:1)
- "You will keep in perfect peace those whose minds are steadfast, because they trust in you" (Isaiah 26:3)

*_Prayer:_ - Dear God, we come to you with hearts that desire to experience your peace that surpasses understanding. Help us trust in your goodness, rest in your presence, and find calm in your love.*

*May your peace:*
- *Guard our hearts and minds*
- *Soothe our worries and fears*
- *Fill us with hope and confidence*
- *Transform us into reflections of your serenity*

*As we receive your peace, may we:*
- *Face life's challenges with courage*
- *Find stillness in the midst of chaos*
- *Extend love and kindness to others*
- *Radiate your peace to a world in need*

*In Jesus' name, we pray. Amen.*

May this prayer inspire you to embrace God's peace that surpasses understanding, leading to a life of calm, hope, and radiant serenity. Remember, God's peace is always available to you!

# REFLECTION

_Action Step:_

- Write down areas where you need God's peace in your life.
- Share with a friend or mentor how this devotional has impacted your understanding of peace.
- Take a few minutes each day to meditate on Philippians 4:7 and ask God to give you, His peace.

_Reflection:_

- Think about how God's peace can guard your heart and mind in times of uncertainty.
- Consider how this peace can surpass your understanding and circumstances.

Additional Mind-Blowing Fact:

- The Greek word for "peace" in Philippians 4:7 is "eirene," which means "wholeness" or " completeness." May we experience God's wholeness in our lives!

May we experience God's peace that surpasses understanding, and may it be the anchor of our souls!

**December 29:** Rooted in Love

*Scripture:* Ephesians 3:17-19 - So that Christ may dwell in your hearts through faith—that you, being rooted and grounded in love, may have strength to comprehend with all the saints what is the breadth and length and height and depth, and to know the love of Christ that surpasses knowledge.

*Devotion:*

God's love is not just a feeling, but a foundation for our lives.

What a wonderful truth! God's love is indeed a foundation for our lives, not just a feeling.

It's a:
- Rock-solid base that anchors our souls (Hebrews 6:19)
- Unshakeable foundation that stands firm in every storm (Matthew 7:24-25)
- Steadfast and unwavering commitment that never falters (Psalm 136:1-3)
- Enduring and unchanging constant in a world of shifting sands (Malachi 3:6)

This foundation of God's love:
- Supports us in times of uncertainty and doubt
- Holds us firm in the face of adversity and challenge
- Provides a sense of belonging and identity
- Empowers us to love others with the same unwavering commitment

May we build our lives on the foundation of God's love, and may it be the anchor that holds us fast!

_Prayer: _- Dear God, we come to you with hearts that desire to be rooted in your love. Help us deepen our roots in your affection, anchor ourselves in your acceptance, and flourish in your care.

*May your love:*

- Surround us with tender compassion
- Fill us with unwavering confidence
- Transform us into reflections of your heart
- Overflow from us to those around us

*As we are rooted in your love, may we:*

- Stand firm against life's challenges
- Find strength in your faithfulness
- Experience joy that overflows from our hearts
- Share your love with a world in need

*In Jesus' name, we pray. Amen.*

May this prayer inspire you to deepen your roots in God's love, leading to a life of confidence, joy, and loving service to others. Remember, God's love is the foundation on which we stand!

# REFLECTION

_Action Step:_

- Write down ways you can cultivate a deeper understanding of God's love.
- Share with a friend or mentor how this devotional has impacted your understanding of love.

_Reflection:_

- Read Ephesians 3:17-19 and reflect on the depth of God's love.
- Think about how being rooted in love can give you strength and stability.
- Consider how knowing Christ's love can surpass your understanding.

Additional Mind-Blowing Fact:

- The Greek word for "rooted" in Ephesians 3:17 is "rhizoo," which means "to take root" or "to become firmly established." May we be firmly established in God's love.

## __December 30:__ Unshakable Confidence

_Scripture:_ Hebrews 10:35-36 - So do not throw away your confidence; it will be richly rewarded. You need to persevere so that when you have done the will of God, you will receive what he has promised.

_Devotion:_

Confidence in God is not about our abilities, but about His faithfulness.

What a powerful truth! Confidence in God is indeed about His faithfulness, not about our abilities.

It's about:
- Trusting in His character and nature (Psalm 100:5)
- Relying on His promises and Word (Hebrews 10:23)
- Believing in His goodness and love (Psalm 136:1-3)
- Resting in His sovereignty and control (Isaiah 46:10)

This confidence:
- Transcends our limitations and weaknesses (2 Corinthians 12:9-10)
- Overcomes fears and doubts (Psalm 23:4)
- Empowers us to step out in faith (Matthew 14:22-33)
- Brings peace and hope in uncertain times (Isaiah 26:3)

As the Bible says:
- "I will boast in the Lord; let the afflicted hear and rejoice" (Psalm 34:2)

- "God is our refuge and strength, an ever-present help in trouble" (Psalm 46:1)

_Prayer: _- Dear God, we come to you with hearts that desire to have unshakable confidence in you. Help us trust in your goodness, stand firm on your promises, and find assurance in your presence.

May our confidence:
- Be anchored in your faithfulness
- Be strengthened by your Word
- Be reflected in our thoughts, words, and actions
- Inspire hope and courage in those around us

As we walk in unshakable confidence, may we:
- Face challenges with boldness and faith
- Overcome fears and doubts with your truth
- Experience victory in your name
- Shine your light in a world that needs you

In Jesus' name, we pray. Amen.

May this prayer inspire you to cultivate unshakable confidence in God, leading to a life of boldness, faith, and radiant hope. Remember, God's got you!

## REFLECTION

_Action Step:_

- Write down areas where you need confidence in God's promises.
- Share with a friend or mentor how this devotional has impacted your understanding of confidence.
- Take a few minutes each day to meditate on Hebrews 10:35-36 and ask God to give you unshakable confidence.


_Reflection:_

- Think about how perseverance and confidence go hand in hand.
- Consider how doing God's will can lead to receiving His promises.

Additional Mind-Blowing Fact:

- The Greek word for "confidence" in Hebrews 10:35 is "parresia," which means "boldness" or "freedom of speech." May we have boldness in our faith!

May we put our confidence in God's faithfulness, rather than our own abilities, and may we experience the power and peace that comes from trusting in Him!

**_December 31_:** _ Embracing the New Year

_Scripture:_ Psalm 138:8 - The Lord will fulfill his purpose for me; your steadfast love, O God, endures forever. Do not forsake the work of your hands.

_Devotion:_

As the year comes to a close, remember that God's love and purpose endure forever. Embrace the new year with hope and trust, knowing He will fulfill His plans for you.

As the year comes to a close, remember that:
- God's love is unwavering and unchanging (Psalm 136:1-3)
- His purpose is steadfast and enduring (Psalm 138:8)
- His faithfulness is great and His goodness endures forever (Psalm 100:5)

Take a moment to reflect on the past year, and remember that:
- God's love was present in every moment, even in the difficult times
- His purpose was being fulfilled, even when you couldn't see it
- His faithfulness was guiding you, even when you felt lost

As you step into the new year, hold onto these truths and remember that God's love and purpose endure forever!

_Prayer:_ *Dear God, as we step into this new year, we come to you with hearts full of hope and expectation. Help us embrace the opportunities and challenges that lie ahead, and may our lives be a reflection of your love and grace.*

*May this new year bring:*

- *Fresh starts and new beginnings*
- *Opportunities to grow and learn*
- *Deepened relationships and connections*
- *Increased faith and trust in your goodness*

*As we journey through this year, may we:*

- *Seek your guidance and wisdom*
- *Find joy and contentment in your presence*
- *Share your love and hope with others*
- *Experience your blessings and favor*

*In Jesus' name, we pray. Amen.*

May this prayer inspire you to embrace the new year with hope, faith, and expectation, leading to a life of growth, joy, and loving service to others. Remember, God has great plans for you!

# REFLECTION

_Action Step:_ Write down your hopes and dreams for the new year, and ask God to guide and direct you.

_Reflection:_ Think about how God's enduring love and purpose can give you confidence and hope as you step into the new year.

_Additional Mind-Blowing Fact:_ The Hebrew word for "fulfill" in Psalm 138:8 is "kalah," meaning "to complete" or "to bring to an end." God's purpose for us is to bring us to a place of completion and fulfillment in Him.

As we conclude this month of reflection, growth, and spiritual renewal, remember that:

- God's power and love have been present throughout your journey
- Resilience, hope, optimism, and joy have been cultivated in your heart
- Reflection, self-awareness, and self-acceptance have brought freedom and peace
- Trusting, gentleness, and humility have empowered you to walk in His strength
- Courageous faith, appreciation, and gratitude have filled your heart with joy
- God's presence, Spirit, and love have been your constant companion

Embrace the new year with:

- Unshakable confidence in God's plans and purposes
- Radiant resilience in the face of challenges
- Peace that surpasses understanding
- Joy in the journey, knowing God is with you
- Rootedness in His Word and love

May the lessons and truths from this month guide you into a new year of deepening faith, unwavering hope, and unshakeable confidence in God's goodness and love.

## _EPILOGUE_

As you close this devotional guide, remember that the journey of faith is a lifelong path. The reflections, prayers, and scriptures shared here are just the beginning.

May the lessons learned and the truths discovered stay with you, guiding you through life's triumphs and challenges. May God's love, peace, and joy be your constant companions.

As you walk forward, hold onto the promises of God, knowing that:
- His love endures forever (Psalm 136:1-3)
- His faithfulness is great (Psalm 100:5)
- His presence is always with you (Matthew 28:20)

May your heart remain open to God's whispers, your spirit stay lifted by His promises, and your life be a testament to His goodness and grace.

Go forth, dear one, with courage, hope, and confidence, knowing that God is with you always. May His blessings pour out on you, and may you be a blessing to others.

And when the journey gets tough, as it sometimes will, return to these pages, and remember the God who loves you, guides you, and strengthens you.

# PRAYER GUIDE

## SECTION 1: DAILY PRAYERS

- *Morning Prayer:*

"Dear God, thank you for a new day. Help me to stay focused on you and seek your guidance. Give me strength and wisdom to face whatever comes my way. Amen."

- *Mid-Day Prayer:*

"Dear God, I need a refill of your strength and joy. Help me to stay motivated and focused on your purposes. Amen."

- *Evening Prayer:*

"Dear God, thank you for the blessings of this day. Forgive me for my mistakes and help me to learn from them. Keep me safe through the night and fill me with your peace. Amen."

- *Before Bed Prayer:*

"Dear God, thank you for the day. Help me to rest in your peace and wake up refreshed and ready to serve you. Amen."

## _SECTION 2: TOPICAL PRAYERS_

*- Prayer for Guidance:*
"Dear God, I need your guidance and direction. Help me to make wise decisions and trust in your plan. Give me clarity and confidence in your leading. Amen."

*- Prayer for Strength*:
"Dear God, I'm feeling weak and overwhelmed. Please give me your strength and courage to persevere. Help me to rely on you and trust in your power. Amen."

*- Prayer for Forgiveness:*
"Dear God, I've made mistakes and fallen short. Please forgive me and cleanse me from my sins. Help me to forgive others and extend your mercy. Amen."

*- Prayer for Gratitude:*
"Dear God, thank you for your blessings and goodness in my life. Help me to cultivate a heart of gratitude and praise you in all circumstances. Amen."

*- Prayer for Peace:*
"Dear God, I'm feeling anxious and worried. Please give me your peace that surpasses understanding. Help me to trust in your sovereignty and goodness. Amen."

*- Prayer for Joy:*
"Dear God, fill me with your joy and happiness. Help me to find delight in you and your presence. Amen."

## SECTION 3: SCRIPTURE-BASED PRAYERS

*- Based on Isaiah 43:19:*
"Dear God, you are doing a new thing in my life. Help me to perceive and partner with you. Give me hope and excitement for the future. Amen."

*- Based on Psalm 63:1-8:*
"Dear God, you are my rock and my salvation. Help me to seek you above all else and find satisfaction in you alone. Amen."

*- Based on Philippians 4:13:*
"Dear God, I can do all things through Christ who strengthens me. Help me to rely on your power and trust in your sufficiency. Amen."

*- Based on Jeremiah 29:11:*
"Dear God, you have a plan to prosper me and not harm me. Help me to trust in your goodness and sovereignty. Amen."

## _SECTION 4: PERSONALIZED PRAYERS_

- *Prayer for Personal Growth:*

"Dear God, help me to grow in faith, patience, and love. Give me a hunger for your Word and a desire to serve you. Amen."

- *Prayer for Relationships:*

"Dear God, bless my family and friends. Help me to love and serve them well. Give us unity and harmony in our relationships. Amen."

- *Prayer for Life Circumstances:*

"Dear God, I'm facing [specific challenge]. Please give me wisdom, strength, and peace. Help me to trust in your sovereignty and goodness. Amen."

- *Prayer for My Community:*

"Dear God, bless my community and neighborhood. Help me to be a light and a blessing to those around me. Amen."

- *Prayer for My Nation:*

"Dear God, bless my nation and leaders. Help us to seek your wisdom and guidance. Give us peace and prosperity. Amen."

*Prayer for Children*

- "Dear God, please bless my children with your love, guidance, and protection. Help them to grow in wisdom, faith, and character. Give me wisdom as a parent to raise them according to your ways. Amen."

- "Dear God, please keep my children safe from harm and evil. Surround them with your angels and give them peace in their hearts. Amen."

- "Dear God, please help my children to know and love you deeply. Give them a heart for serving you and others. Amen."

*Prayer for Grandchildren*

- "Dear God, please bless my grandchildren with your love and favor. Help them to grow in wisdom, faith, and character. Give me wisdom as a grandparent to influence them positively. Amen."

- "Dear God, please keep my grandchildren safe and healthy. Give them joy, happiness, and peace in their hearts. Amen."

- "Dear God, please help my grandchildren to know and love you deeply. Give them a heart for serving you and others. Amen."

*Prayer for Their Future*

- "Dear God, please guide my children/grandchildren's future according to your plan.

Give them wisdom, discernment, and courage to follow your path. Amen."

- "Dear God, please bless my children/grandchildren's relationships, education, and career. Give them success and fulfillment in all they do. Amen."

- "Dear God, please help my children/grandchildren to make wise choices and decisions. Give them a strong foundation in you to navigate life's challenges. Amen."

# _WORSHIP AND PRAISE_

_Scripture-based Worship_

- "You are worthy, O Lord, to receive glory and honor and power, for you created all things, and by your will, they exist and were created." (Revelation 4:11)

- "I will praise the Lord, for He has been good to me." (Psalm 103:2)

- "Worship the Lord with gladness; come before Him with joyful songs." (Psalm 100:2)

- "Let everything that has breath praise the Lord." (Psalm 150:6)

_Praise Declarations_

- "God is good, all the time!"
- "He is worthy of praise!"
- "His love endures forever!"
- "He is my rock, my salvation, and my deliverer!"
- "I will bless the Lord at all times; His praise shall continually be in my mouth." (Psalm 34:1)
- "I will praise You, O Lord, with my whole heart." (Psalm 138:1)

## _WORSHIP SONGS_

- "Great Are You Lord" by All Sons & Daughters
- "Reckless Love" by Cory Asbury
- "What a Beautiful Name" by Hillsong Worship
- "Good Good Father" by Chris Tomlin
- "Living Hope" by Phil Wickham
- "Stand in Your Love" by Josh Baldwin

## _PRAISE PROMPTS_

- Take a moment to reflect on God's goodness in your life.
- Write down three things you're grateful for today.
- Sing a worship song that brings you joy.
- Share a testimony of God's faithfulness with someone.
- Create a playlist of your favorite worship songs.
- Take a walk outside and praise God for His creation.

## _WORSHIP QUOTES_

- "Worship is the highest form of prayer." - Unknown
- "Praise is the rehearsal for heaven's choir." - Charles Spurgeon
- "Worship is not just a feeling, but a choice." - Unknown

Remember, worship and praise are powerful tools to connect with God and express our love and gratitude. Take time to worship Him in spirit and truth!

## _HERE ARE SOME WORSHIP TIPS_

1. *Create a conducive environment*: Set aside a quiet, comfortable space for worship.
2. *Start with gratitude*: Begin by thanking God for His blessings and goodness.
3. *Use scripture*: Incorporate Bible verses into your worship to focus on God's Word.
4. *Sing with passion*: Sing worship songs with conviction and feeling.
5. *Play instruments*: Use musical instruments to enhance your worship experience.
6. *Be still*: Take time to be silent and listen for God's voice.
7. *Be honest*: Express your true feelings and emotions to God.
8. *Use prayer*: Incorporate prayer into your worship to communicate with God.
9. *Reflect on God's character*: Meditate on God's attributes, such as His love, mercy, and grace.
10. *Make it a habit*: Establish a regular worship routine to deepen your relationship with God.
11. *Be creative*: Incorporate different forms of worship, such as dance, art, or writing.

12. *Worship with others*: Join with fellow believers to experience corporate worship.

13. *Focus on God*: Keep your attention on God, rather than your own needs or worries.

14. *Use worship resources*: Utilize devotionals, worship books, or online resources to enhance your worship.

15. *Be open to the Spirit*: Allow the Holy Spirit to guide and direct your worship.

Remember, worship is a personal and intimate experience with God. Be genuine, sincere, and creative in your expression of worship!

*Pauline Rose*

Made in the USA
Columbia, SC
23 November 2024